Six
Middle English
Romances

Edited, with an introduction by

Maldwyn Mills

Senior Lecturer in English,
University College of Wales,
Aberystwyth

Dent, London
Rowman and Littlefield, Totowa, N.J.

© Introduction and notes, J. M. Dent & Sons Ltd, 1973
All rights reserved
Made in Great Britain
at the
Aldine Press · Letchworth · Herts
for
J. M. DENT AND SONS LTD
Aldine House · Albemarle Street · London
First published in this edition in 1973
First published in the United States 1973
by ROWMAN AND LITTLEFIELD, Totowa, New Jersey

Dent edition
Hardback ISBN 0 460 10090 4
Paperback ISBN 0 460 11090 x

Rowman and Littlefield edition
Hardback ISBN 0 87471 403 6
Paperback ISBN 0 87471 396 x

Contents

Acknowledgments

I should like to express my gratitude to the staffs of the libraries named on pp. xxx–xxxi for all help given during the preparation of the texts of these romances. Otherwise, my chief debt has been to previous editors, who have supplied me with some additional readings, and have suggested many of my emendations. I also thank Mrs D. R. Sutherland, of Lady Margaret Hall, Oxford, and Dr D. G. Hoggan, of the University College of Wales, Aberystwyth, for help with points of detail.

Introduction

Medieval romance is one of the most comprehensive of literary forms, and its range of subject-matter and of metrical styles is even wider in English than in French. In twelfth- and thirteenth-century France, it was dominated by stories in rhyming couplets that told, at considerable length, of the interaction of love and chivalry. Their plots were tortuous and could be extended at will, by incorporating fresh episodes of combats or of chivalrous encounters; they were usually worked out against a variety of exotic locations. This kind of romance, which may be labelled 'chivalrous', quite often made its way into Middle English literature, and there too, it was often told in short rhyming couplets, and at considerable length (even if the English redactors were always likely to trim down the lengthier passages of description). But although this type of romance was reasonably popular, it was very far from being ubiquitous. Other types of subject-matter and other metrical forms were also much in evidence, and these in combination were to produce some distinctively English modes of romance-writing.

A useful pointer to the other types of subject-matter that were available is supplied by L. H. Loomis in her survey of those Middle English romances that lie outside the major story-cycles.[1] She groups these under three heads: one of them implies the kind of story defined above ('Romances of Love and Adventure'); another is 'Romances of Legendary English Heroes'; a third, 'Romances of Trial and Faith'. If we represent each of these by a single adjective—the first (as before), by 'chivalrous'; the second, by 'heroic'; the third, by 'edifying'—then we will have provided ourselves with a useful basic vocabulary for discussing the romances. In a 'heroic' romance, the dominant ethos will be masculine, with the stress placed upon communal battle rather than individual combats, and upon the need for supporting (and, if necessary, avenging) one's sworn companions. In an 'edifying' romance, the mood will be primarily one of suffering and endurance, which comes about either as a just punishment for past sin, or because of quite gratuitous human malice; at the end of the story the hero or heroine may even achieve a measure of sanctity. This said, it should also be pointed out that our three terms will often prove more useful to describe parts of romances—and especially the longer romances—than wholes. The attitude of a romance-author to his material was more likely to be comprehensive than rigorously selective, and the ideals informing his story might be quite different at the end of it from at the beginning. We have a remarkably full example of this in *Guy of Warwick*, which begins as a chivalrous romance (with the hero's

[1] *Medieval Romance in England*, New York, 1924.

every action being controlled by his love for his lady), continues as a heroic one (in that he becomes progressively closer to his companions in arms than to her), and concludes in an edifying manner (since he rejects all the comforts of his secular life, his lady included, to devote himself to the service of God). This is a very long romance and a very extreme case, but even works on a very modest scale may change their preoccupations drastically from time to time.

When we come to consider the metrical forms used in the Middle English romance, we find a remarkable diversity: various kinds of couplet, various types of alliterative line, various stanza-patterns. But through all this diversity, some broad potentialities can be discerned. The couplet is the most economical and perspicuous; the alliterative line, most impressionistic and powerful in impact; the stanza, most lyrical and best suited to express emotion. In other words, there is a theoretical correspondence between these three main types of poetic form, and the three main types of romance subject-matter. And very often such a correspondence is worked out in practice: leisurely and detailed stories of love and adventure are told in the couplet form; accounts of large-scale fighting, in the alliterative line; tales of suffering and piety, in stanzas of one kind or another. There are some notable exceptions, it is true, which arise from the fact that the choice of form was determined by the geographical situation of the poet as well as by the nature of the story he was telling (the West Midlands had a special fondness for the alliterative line, the East Midlands for the tail-rhyme stanza),[1] but they remain in the minority.

All of the romances contained in the present selection are composed in a single one of these metrical forms: the twelve-line tail-rhyme stanza, which was, after the short rhyming-couplet, the most popular of all romance measures in English in the fourteenth and early fifteenth centuries. To give an idea of the structure of this stanza and of the stylistic effects to which it most readily lent itself, we may quote from the *Ipomedon* A, recently noted as a work of considerable length (it runs to close on nine thousand lines), and one unusual in its full-scale treatment of the refinements of chivalrous love. We shall not find sentiments like the following expressed with the same precision in the other tail-rhyme romances:

> Love is so mekyll off myghte,   *extremely powerful*
> That it will daunte bothe kyng and knyght,   *vanquish*
>   Erle and bold barowne;
> They, that wyseste is of witte,
> Fro tyme they be takyne wyth it,
>   Hit takythe fro them there reasowne.

---

[1] Two very sizeable romances of chivalry are told in forms other than the rhyming couplet: *William of Palerne* (in alliterative long lines) and the *Ipomedon* A (in tail-rhyme stanzas).

Love may save, love may spille,   *destroy*
Love may do, what that he will,
 And turne all up and downe.
After, when they suppud had
And they were all blythe and glad,
 To bedde they made them boune. (7346-57) *got ready for*

But if the sentiments are extraordinary, the metrical pattern and the rhyme-structure are thoroughly typical. It will be seen that the limits of the stanza are defined by the rhyme-value common to its third, sixth, ninth and twelfth lines; this will, of course, be different in the stanzas which immediately precede and follow the one quoted. These crucial lines are the tail-lines; between them, the lines are grouped in rhyming couplets, which are clearly set off by having four main stresses against the three of the tail-lines. This is the most common pattern of the stanza, but we shall occasionally find minor variants of both the rhyme-pattern and the metre: the first two couplets of the stanza may rhyme together (giving aabaabccbddb), or the couplets, no less than the tail-lines, may have three stresses.

The classic study of the potentialities and achievements of the tail-rhyme style is that of A. McI. Trounce,[1] and especially relevant is his summary characterization of these works as 'popular and religious in subject-matter and outlook, and lively in tone',[2] since these qualities are very much in evidence in the romances of the present selection. The heroic and the edifying, if we like, prevail over the chivalrous, but they are all vital works. They are also remarkably closely linked one to the other, and mutually illuminating: themes that are merely sketched in—and can even seem redundant—in one of them, will acquire real significance in another. For this reason, I have tried to arrange them in a sequence that will make us alert to their full narrative potentialities, beginning with two relatively 'pure' works—the first in the heroic, the second in the edifying mode—and following these with others in which these two impulses are variously combined.

The work in the heroic manner is *The Sege of Melayne*, which, although in date of composition one of the later tail-rhyme romances,[3] in its subject-matter looks back to an earlier mode of heroic literature. But before we say anything about this text, some notice must be taken of *Horn Childe*, which is, in its first part at least, as starkly masculine in temper as *Melayne*, but

---

[1] See the Bibliography.   [2] *Medium Ævum* I (1932), 102.
[3] We can date the manuscripts in which these works occur with some precision, but it is much more difficult to fix the time of their original composition. Trounce placed *Octavian*, *Isumbras* and *Amadace* between 1325 and 1350; *Gowther*, just before 1375, and *Emaré* and *Melayne* just after 1400; the recent revision of Wells's *Manual*, however, places *Isumbras* before *Octavian* (in the early fourteenth century) and brings forward *Amadace* to the late part of the century, and *Gowther* to about 1400.

which looks back to a different literary tradition; it is also interesting as being probably the earliest in date of all these romances, belonging to the early years of the fourteenth century.

Its most distinctive part is its first quarter (1–252), since this is unlike anything to be found in the two other major versions of the story that have survived, the ME. *King Horn* and the Anglo-Norman *Horn et Rimenild*; it evokes the imaginative world of Old English battle poetry, and does so so powerfully that it used to be suggested that oral traditions of some antiquity lay behind it. This section falls into two main parts, each of which tells of fighting between the English and pagan invaders. In the first, the invaders are Vikings, and are successfully repelled; in the second, they are Irish, and are not. Each contains some unusually graphic scenes; in the first, the description of how the invaders came to land:

> Out of Danmark com an here,   *(raiding) army*
> Opon Inglond forto were   *make war*
>   With stout ost and unride;   *army, numerous*
> With yren hattes, scheld and spere: *helmets*
> Alle her pray to schip thai bere   *booty, carried*
>   In Clifland bi Teseside.
> Schepe and nete to schip thai brought,
> And al that thai have mought,   *cattle*
>   In herd is nought to hide.   *might*
> When Hatheolf it herd say,   *among men*
> He busked bothe night and day,
>   Oyain hem forto ride. (49–60)   *made preparation*

In the second is described the English king's reaction to the news that the army from Ireland has landed. Trounce quoted this as an example of the heroic manner at its best:[1]

> He bad the harpour leven his lay: *stop his playing*
> 'For ous bihoveth another play,   *we must begin*
>   Buske armour and stede.'   *horse*
> He sent his sond night and day   *messenger(s)*
> Also fast as he may,   *as*
>   His folk to batayl bede: *summoned*
> 'Bid hem that thai com to me,
> Al that hold her lond fre,   *as freemen*
>   Help now at this nede;

---

[1] He commented on 'the energy here expressed by the sudden change to direct speech, the lines beginning with a strong stress, the clanging appeals in the tail-line, [and] the clinching of the whole in the climax of the sentiment of the last three lines' (I.92).

Better manly to be slayn
Than long to live in sorwe and pain,
   Oyain outlondis thede.'   (157–68)   *foreigners*

From one point of view, the ideals expressed in this last passage are not
far removed from those voiced in *Melayne*, in the speeches of the archbishop
Turpin. One of these, in particular, stands out:

'The more powere that thay be,
The more honour wyn sall we,
   We dowte noghte tham to dynge!'   (1508–10)   *are not afraid*

Not only Hatheolf, but Byrhtnoth, the hero of the Old English *Battle of
Maldon*, would have felt very much at home with this sentiment. But in some
other, equally important respects, the differences between *Horn Childe* and
Melayne are very striking indeed. The heroism displayed in the second is
altogether less stark, more in the service of the Christian faith. As a
Charlemagne romance, *Melayne* reflects the ideals, not of the older Teutonic
battle poetry, but of the French *chansons de geste* of the late eleventh century
onwards—heroic poems in which the enemy was the heathen, from whose
control lands and shrines that were once Christian must now be wrested. In
these works, miracles are not infrequent, and any Christians that are killed
fighting with Saracens will achieve a martyr's crown. Within the tail-rhyme
romances there are four which present this type of story. Two of these
(*Roland and Vernagu* and the Fillingham *Otuel and Roland*), although now
surviving in different manuscript collections, seem once to have belonged
together, making up a heroic poem of unusually wide range; the other two
(*Melayne* and *Roland and Otuel*), although set down in the same collection,
do not seem very closely related,[1] and *Melayne* may be taken in itself and on
its own terms, as the most interesting of the English Charlemagne romances.

It is also, with the exception of the fragmentary *Song of Roland*, the most
genuinely heroic of them; the lines quoted above are typical both of the
speaker and of the general tone of the work. Its basic pattern is one of large
contrasts. An overwhelming defeat of the Christian forces who come to
relieve Milan (217–384) is succeeded, first by a limited act of revenge (the
miraculous blinding of the Saracen captors of the few Christian survivors,
and the killing of the Sultan (470–90)), and then by a larger and more decisive
one (the assault that is so vigorously being made on Milan when the text
breaks off abruptly (1523–600)). This pattern turns up elsewhere in the
chansons de geste relating to Charlemagne, most notably in the composite
formed by the *Destruction de Rome* and *Fierabras*, that lies behind the English
Charlemagne romance of *The Sowdon of Babylon*, while an approximation to
it is also found in the great *Chanson de Roland* itself. And within this heroic

---

[1] See the note to 1600.

framework there are a number of equally heroic motifs. The men of the story have it all their own way, since the women are excluded from any significant part in the action, at most appearing very briefly to lament the fates of the Christian warriors at the appropriate moments (198, 216). These warriors respond to the heroic exhortations of Turpin by performing super-human feats of courage and endurance (1415–26), and, when dying, are very conscious that the heavens are opening to receive them (313–24). What is more, we have specific parallels with the *Chanson de Roland* in the part played by the treacherous Ganelon, since he malevolently nominates Roland for a dangerous mission (181–92), and later tries to dissuade Charles from taking the field to avenge the disastrous defeat of his army (650–61).

The consistency with which the heroic actions and ideals are presented in *Melayne* is reinforced by the use of a stylistic device that is rarely found in the other Charlemagne romances. For the author consistently identifies both himself and his audience with the fortunes of the heroes by alluding to them in the first person instead of the third: they become *oure knyghtis, oure folke, oure worthy men*, etc. These are presumably taken over directly from phrases such as *nos Crestiens* or *nos gens* in the lost French source of *Melayne*; in the Middle English *Song of Roland* we find a few scattered examples (*our kinge* (77), *our men* (248), *our knyght* (677)), but these could well have been the result of carelessness. In *Melayne*, the density of examples is so great that they seem bound to be deliberate:[1] an attempt to naturalize a foreign mode of poetry so that its new audience might be totally involved in it.

But perhaps the most distinctive feature of the romance is the characteriza-tion of the archbishop Turpin. Trounce praised this in no uncertain manner as

> the finest piece of characterization in Middle English literature, with the exception of Chaucer's best, and, possibly, of Gawayne in *Gawayne and the Grene Knyght*. He is primarily the vigorous ecclesiastic, champion of the church; but the poet delights in him as a personality, paints him with individual touches ... and shows us his power of unflinching endurance ... his stern integrity. (I.100–1)

Turpin is certainly the mainspring of the action to a degree not found in any other romance (or *chanson de geste*, for that matter), but the impression that he is likely to make upon the modern reader is one more comic than serious. When Charles shows himself ready to follow Ganelon's comfortable advice to stay quietly at home and let Turpin—who likes that sort of thing—go off and do the actual fighting, the archbishop excommunicates him and shows himself prepared to destroy the city of Paris in his anger (650–769). Even more peculiar is the later scene, in which he rashly charges at troops coming to the help of the French, under the impression that they are Saracens, and so appears as a kind of ecclesiastical Quixote, tilting at sheep (1448–62).

---

[1] See particularly lines 253–76, 494–505, 1235–306 and 1511–46.

But strangest of all is an earlier one in which, as soon as he has learned of the French defeat, he reviles a statue of the Virgin in a manner hardly fitting to an archbishop (548–65). And here it is very difficult to avoid the feeling that he is being presented as pagan rather than Christian. A stock scene in the *chansons de geste* and the heroic romances was that in which a sultan, after hearing of the rout of his forces, did physical violence to the images of his gods,[1] and while Turpin does not quite go as far as laying hands on the statue, it seems an uncomfortably near thing.

To say all this is not to deny that at other points in the story Turpin is presented as an unquestionably heroic figure, while the example of the romance of *Richard Cœur de Lion* (of which a copy is found in the same manuscript collection as *Melayne*) shows that energy of an almost diabolical kind would be applauded as long as it was directed against the Saracen; but in two of the three scenes considered above, Turpin's energy is not so directed. The only way of explaining away these two moments would be to suppose that the author never forgot that Turpin was in the last resort French, and therefore always a little unreliable. A comparison with *Richard* is again illuminating at this point, since in that romance the French crusading king, Philip Augustus, is on several occasions represented in an unfavourable light. The author of *Melayne* can never consistently do the same for Turpin since there are no Englishmen in the story to serve as its real heroes: Turpin, Charles and Roland are the only champions of Christendom that he has. But he might still have felt free to let the archbishop act with total lack of commonsense when to do so would not affect the general conduct of his story. The end-product of it all is certainly a figure that stands out from most pieces of characterization in these romances, even if in a rather different way from that defined by Trounce.

If the heroic romances are often closely bound up with the *chansons de geste*, the edifying romances are equally closely linked with the pious legends (or saints' lives) of the Middle Ages. But when the principal character in one of these is male, it is likely that a good deal of the action will still have a heroic colour; however penitent or self-condemning its hero may be, it is still permissible for him to give vent to his masculine instinct for aggression by turning it against the hosts of the Saracen, who, as the enemies of God, can be slaughtered without hindering his chances of salvation. But if the chief figure is a woman, the heroic element, though never quite eliminated, will probably be more effaced. This is especially true of *Emaré*, the second romance of our selection;[2] in this the Saracens dwindle to an off-stage menace, and affect the fortunes of the heroine only indirectly.

At the same time, however, *Emaré* has a basic structure that is curiously like that of *Horn Childe*, which is unusually symmetrical for a romance plot.

---

[1] See the note to 548–65 in the Commentary.
[2] And of its more pious first cousin, Chaucer's *Man of Law's Tale*.

Horn Childe begins in the country of the hero's father (A¹); when this is overrun by the heathen, Horn takes refuge at the court of another king (B¹); when a false accusation sends him once more into exile, he is welcomed by a third (C). Subsequently, he retraces his steps, first avenging himself on his calumniator (B²), and then winning back his father's kingdom (A²).¹ This pattern is modified in *Emaré* to suit the different sex of the central figure. Since Emaré herself is a defenceless heroine, not an aggressive hero, she cannot seek out her former persecutors in their own lands; instead, they must be impelled by penitence to seek her out. Because of this, the symmetry of the plot has more to do with personal relationships than with any geography. It begins in her father's land (A¹); when she rejects his incestuous proposals, she is exiled and comes to the land of a king who courts and marries her (B¹); from this, she is exiled by the contrivings of her mother-in-law and at last finds shelter (with her new-born baby) at Rome (C). To this city there comes first her husband (B²), and then her father (A¹). The patterning here is much more clear-cut than that of the *Man of Law's Tale*, in which it has been complicated by the invention of new trials for the lady.² And the symmetry is worked out on the smallest scale as well as the largest. As Rickert pointed out in her edition of the text:

> *Emaré* is peculiar, even among romances of its class, for the large proportion of repetitions that it contains. Whenever the idea recurs the phrase, line, sentence, stanza, or even group of stanzas, is repeated, with only slight necessary changes. (p. xxvi)

And the small-scale parallels do much to reinforce the impact of the larger ones. The two voyages of exile, for example, become still more alike by containing what is essentially the same stanza (325–36, 673–84). But sometimes the effect of such insistent repetition is to emphasize a similarity of function at the expense of individuality. This comes out very clearly when we compare the author's treatment of the actions of the heroine's father and of her husband. We might have expected a very sharp differentiation here: the father is one of the monsters of the story—an ageing lecher, who treats Emaré quite ruthlessly when she will have nothing to do with him; the husband, on the other hand, is its Prince Charming. But by applying very similar motifs to each, the author makes them seem curiously alike. Each of the two men, whether intentionally or not, is responsible for putting the life of the heroine in danger (265–76, 586–97), bitterly regrets what has happened when it is too late (280–300, 769–83), sets out on a pilgrimage of atonement to Rome (817–40, 949–60) and is there reunited with the lady and the son (913–36, 985–1020). But at the deepest level of significance, the

---

¹ In fact, this symmetry emerges still more clearly in the two other romance versions of the story, which present A and C with less duplication of material.
² *Canterbury Tales*, B 536–686, 911–45.

careful patterning of the events of the tale is curiously reassuring. In a dangerous world of unjust sentences and alarming sea-voyages it provides a reassuring sense of orderliness. Everything that goes wrong for the heroine in the first half of the story is bound to find its benevolent mirror-image in the second.

The author's remarkable lack of concern with fighting as a romance-theme has already been noted; it is this, indeed, which makes *Emaré* such a perfect complement to *Melayne*. But it is more usual, even in stories of suffering heroines, for a good deal of space to be allotted to this theme, by dividing the reader's attention between the lady and the man or men who champion her cause against the evilly-disposed. An example of a story of this kind is the tail-rhyme *King of Tars*, in which the heroine is responsible for the battles that dominate the first part, in that her beauty has caused the Sultan of Damascus to fall in love with her, and when his offer of marriage is rejected, he makes war against her father. This 'heroic' part of the story comes to an end when the lady decides that she will marry the sultan after all, in order to avoid further bloodshed, and from this point on the romance is dominated by the marital difficulties of the ill-assorted pair. The sultan, who is loathsome to the heroine, forces her to pay lip-service to his religion, and when she finally does produce a child, it is monstrous, not by false report as in *Emaré*, but in actual fact; inert and shapeless. But this time no exile by sea follows the sinister birth; instead, the lady, by her prayers, brings about the miraculous restoration of the child to human shape, and this persuades her husband of the truth of the Christian religion. He accepts baptism (and at once turns white), and subsequently makes vigorous war against those of the heathen who resent his conversion. In the tail-rhyme romance of *Le Bone Florence of Rome*, the initial situation is very similar (except that the unwanted suitor here is not a Saracen, but the hideously senile emperor of Constantinople), but this time the war fought in the lady's defence is successful, and the persecution which she afterwards suffers is at the hands of a largely fresh group of characters.

In the romance of *Octavian*, the third of our selection, the drift of the story is in the opposite direction from that of *Florence*; that is, it moves from the edifying to the heroic. This time no rejected suitor harasses the lady or drives her into exile, but serious trouble is made for her by a spiteful mother-in-law, who accuses her of adultery. Her first attempt at convincing her son of his wife's guilt is unsuccessful (she tells him that since the lady has had twins, more than one man must have slept with her), but she later gains her ends by persuading a serving boy to lie naked in bed with the lady, while the latter is asleep. The emperor is fetched, the boy beheaded, and the lady sent into exile with her children. Her sufferings are increased when both of these are carried off by animals, but she recovers one of them in the course of her wanderings, first by land and then by sea. She comes at length to

Jerusalem, where she lives quietly with this one son under the protection of the king of the land. She is not reunited with the other son and with her husband until very much later in the story, when she returns to France.

All this could be seen as a telescoped version of the story told in *Emaré*, with the absence of the incestuous father counterbalanced by the presence of the kidnapping animals. In the same way, the later phases of *Octavian* could be represented as a condensation of *Melayne*. The same balance is achieved between the major scenes of battle: the fighting between the French and the heathen, at first indecisive (1369–416) finally turns out disastrously for the former (1573–620), but this catastrophe is later avenged by a great victory for the Christians (1651–80). But at the same time, the general texture of the writing is very different. The author will remark, traditionally enough, upon the scale of the carnage (1402–4) or emphasize the sufferings of the Christian captives (1618–20); what he never does is to sound the genuine heroic note, and the catastrophe itself is hurried over so very rapidly that little sense of either heroic suffering or pious exaltation is communicated. Most important of all, there is no feeling for the wars against the heathen as an essentially communal enterprise; they exist much more as proving-grounds for the valour of the twin brothers, after they have grown to manhood. For most of the time, these battles could just as well have been tournaments.

But there is a third part to the romance, lying between the story of the mother and the final battles, and this is altogether more interesting. For this tells a story of a kind not encountered in either *Melayne* or *Emaré*: that of the upbringing of Florent, the twin who grows up away from his mother, and the real hero of *Octavian*. In its fullness and vivacity this is very far removed from the sketchy account that is given of the other child's upbringing at his mother's side (511–16), or, for that matter, the fuller but still rather colourless description of the young Segramowre's education in *Emaré* 727–41. A central issue here is the conflict between Florent's inborn nobility of nature, and the essentially bourgeois ethos of the butcher Clement, who has brought the boy up. Clement, obsessed with merchandise, is the great comic character of the romance, and he fights a long and losing battle against the boy's inability to extract the smallest financial advantage from any commercial transaction entrusted to him. And so the butcher finds it something of a relief when the wars against the heathen begin, and the boy finds for himself a profession at which he is undeniably very good; he never learns the value of money, but he does know how to cope with Saracen giants. What is more, the early stages of these wars allow Clement, likewise, to distinguish himself: he undertakes a daring visit to the Sultan's camp to steal a valuable horse (1501–48). If the author had wished it, Clement could have been developed into a Christian champion who, in his own rough-and-ready way, would have been hardly less impressive than Florent; a comic figure still, but a formidable one, like the kitchen boy Rainouart in the

Chanson de Guillaume, or Ascopart of *Bevis of Hamtoun*. But this is not done; the main actions of the story remain throughout in the hands of the members of Octavian's family, and Clement, memorable as he is, is made to know, and keep, his narrative place.

Sir Isumbras, the next of our romances, is also the story of a family separated by a series of misfortunes, but there are some important differences of emphasis here. The hero's children are again carried off by animals, but the part which they subsequently play in the action is very much more limited than in *Octavian* or, for that matter, than in the nearest French equivalent of *Isumbras*, the romance of *Guillaume d'Angleterre*. Nothing is heard about their upbringing away from their parents, and they do not reappear until the very end of the story, when they turn up unexpectedly to help Isumbras and his wife in battle against the Saracens; at this point, they seem more like supernatural agencies than characters of flesh and blood, and it is not surprising that the Thornton text should state that they had the look of angels (at 757). The hero's wife is a rather more solid figure than they, and since she is forcibly separated from Isumbras by a heathen king who has fallen in love with her, it might seem that our attention is to be diverted to a story-development of the kind found in *Tars*. But it is not; having got possession of the lady, the king at once sends her off to his own country, where she is to rule in his place (301–6), and she passes out of the story until such time as her husband is able to find her once again. Once he has done this, and each has recognized the other, she is able to restore him to a state of material prosperity (715–20).

This relatively sketchy treatment of the fortunes of the wife and the children means that Isumbras dominates his story as much as Emaré had done hers. Nothing is allowed to distract our attention from him for long, and it is he and he alone who truly suffers and endures. It is stressed that these sufferings are deserved, since in the days of his prosperity he had been guilty of the sin of pride, and neglected his God. His story brings us very close to the territory of the pious legend; at some essential points it closely resembles the life of Saint Eustace, another important motif suggests the the legend of Pope Gregory, while the initial series of disasters which befall the hero quite strikingly resemble those at the beginning of the *Book of Job*. But, as a popular romance, *Isumbras* is not concerned to argue the rights and wrongs of its hero's afflictions in any detail; it works itself out through scenes of action, not meditation, and, as in *Octavian*, his opponents, whether in battle (409–56, 727–62) or tournament (604–12), are always the Saracens.[1] And since their leader had been directly responsible for separating Isumbras from his wife, the knight has this time a double personal motive for fighting them. In doing so, he will at once help to expiate his past sins, and obtain

[1] In the spiritual context of this romance, he could hardly have fought again in tournament against other Christians.

revenge for past injuries. It is interesting that, at the moment of their separation, his wife had stressed the importance of killing the sultan and taking
over his kingdom; only thus, she pointed out, would he be able to recover
his former prosperity (331-6). At moments such as this, Isumbras appears
quite as much a man who suffers undeservedly at the hands of human male-
factors as one who does so deservedly at the hands of God; less as a figure
of saintly endurance than as a very human one, who can be driven by the
same impulses against his old enemies as Horn Childe had been.

Our fifth romance, *Sir Gowther*, likewise works out the related themes of
the private expiation of sin and the public warring against the heathen, but
the desire for personal revenge is never a living issue here. Gowther has no
personal grudge against the sultan who makes war on the German emperor
(because the latter will not give him his daughter in marriage), nor is he
sentimentally involved with the daughter herself. The more human instincts
which are given expression from time to time in *Isumbras* are here suppressed
because of the single-mindedness of Gowther's search for divine forgiveness.
Nor is this surprising when we consider the extraordinary sinfulness of his
past life. He represents, in the flesh, the kind of monstrous offspring that had
existed only as a malicious fiction in *Emaré* 536-40; the son of a devil, he
shows his inherited nature in a series of actions so dreadful that only the
most degrading penance will serve to atone for them, and the Pope decrees that
he must feign dumbness and eat only what food is brought to him in the mouths
of dogs. In other words, he must adopt a way of life that will keep him as
apart from other human beings as the ferocious sinning of his old days had done.

In all this, the contrast with the penitential life of Isumbras is very striking.
The latter had humbled his pride by working as an ironsmith (385-408), but
this activity did not completely isolate him from his fellow men, and had its
practical relevance to his later fighting against the heathen (since it allowed
him to provide himself with armour). What is more, he had not faded
discreetly into the background immediately after his military successes; he
was praised by the emperor and treated with great respect by the nuns who
nursed him back to health (481-6). But the horse and armour used by
Gowther are provided (and subsequently taken away) by miracle, and to
the emperor and his court he appears throughout as no one more distinguished
than Hob the fool, who is dumb and feeds with the dogs under the table.
The only person who knows the truth of the matter is the emperor's daughter,
but she, being genuinely unable to speak, cannot pass on her knowledge to
others. Each day's fighting, moreover, not only brings Gowther no public
glory, but increases his suffering by inflicting upon him wounds and bruises
which cannot be taken to anyone for healing.

So that although *Gowther* keeps many of the trappings of the romance-
manner, we seem, in reading it, to penetrate further and further into the
no-man's-land that lies between the edifying romance and the saint's life. By

the end of the story he has been given a sign from heaven that his sins have been forgiven; he is now recognized as the saviour of the Christians; he marries the princess, who is miraculously cured of her affliction (655–66). But he cannot settle down quite happily to the secular way of life; he is still tormented by the memory of his past sins, and especially by the thought of the nuns he had once burned to death in their convent. And so he founds an abbey in their honour, and miracles are worked at his tomb after his death. It is hardly surprising that the scribe of the British Museum text of *Gowther* should have written at the end of it *Explicit Vita Sancti*.

Sir Amadace takes us back to the secular world, even though the hero is made to suffer a good deal of mental and physical torment. The sin of Amadace—if, indeed, it is one at all—is that of prodigality, and this of its own nature brings disaster in its wake, without any need of divine contriving. Amadace is greatly cast down by the change in his fortunes, and laments his past folly at length in 373–420. But at the same time he is not burdened with any weight of unforgiven sin, and has at this stage in the story no lost wife or children to seek out painfully. He becomes a knight wandering at hazard in search of his fortune, and it is not long before he finds it. The discovery of a rich shipwreck (505–22) provides him with clothes and equipment, and once equipped with these he takes part in a tournament and wins a rich wife for himself as a result (577–624). But this is not the end of the story. The hero is subsequently afflicted with fresh sorrows which, paradoxically, spring from his virtues rather than his vices. The real agent of his newly-found prosperity had been a mysterious White Knight, who had made him promise to share with him whatever goods he might later acquire. This knight re-appears to claim as his due half of the hero's wife and child; Amadace, although intensely distressed, does not flinch, and is on the point of sacrificing his wife when the White Knight stops him and releases him from his bond.

This story has more radical ambiguities than the two which precede it in this collection. The first relates to the hero's 'sin', which is, after all, a quality much more often extolled than condemned in the romances (praise was often optimistically given to lords who were generous to those who entertained them). In the tail-rhyme romance of *Sir Cleges*, liberality seems very far from being reprehensible, even if it does bring financial ruin upon the man who practises it. The hero, though saddened by such ruin, can still pray to God in these terms:

> 'Lord Jesu,' he seyd, 'Hevyn kynge,
> Of nowght Thou madyst all thynge:
>   I thanke The of Thy sond.   *gifts*
> The myrth that I was wonte to make,
> At thys tyme for thy sake,
>   I fede both fre and bond.   *freeman, serf*

> All that ever cam in Thy name
> Wantyd neythyr wyld nere tame   *any kind of meat*
>   That was in my lond;
> Of rech metis and drynkkys good
> That myght be gott, be the rode,
>   For coste I wolde not lend.'   (109–20)   *hesitate*

The ambivalence of the idea first appears in the scene in which the hero
comes upon the decaying body of the prodigal who has been refused burial
by his chief creditor. He recognizes the essential similarity between them
(209), and from one point of view this corpse is plainly a last warning to him;
if he persists in his ways, he can expect no better end. But from another, it
provides the opportunity for a vitally necessary act of generosity; if Amadace
parts with the last of his remaining money, he can have the dead man buried
and masses sung for his soul. The hero remains true to his noble nature; he
ignores the warning and takes the opportunity.

Complications of a different kind appear in the second half of the romance.
Both Amadace and the author of the story refer to the White Knight as the
'companion' of the hero (*felau*, *fere*), and the two knights seem therefore to
stand in the same relationship to each other as the joint heroes of *Amis and
Amiloun*, the supreme tail-rhyme celebration of friendship and brotherhood.
In this romance, the relationship is of long standing and provides the real
backbone of the story; each man in his turn helps the other and suffers for
his sake. Thus Amiloun takes the place of Amis in a judicial duel, even
though he knows that God will afflict him with leprosy if he does this, while
Amis later sacrifices his own children to restore his brother to health by
bathing him in their blood. These actions, which could easily alienate the
audience's sympathy, are made at least temporarily acceptable by the author's
care to underline at all points the excellence of the two heroes and of the
bond which unites them. This care is particularly in evidence in the vital
scene of the sacrifice:

> Alon himself, withouten mo,
> Into the chaumber he gan to go,
>   Ther that his childer were;
> And biheld hem bothe to,
> Hou fair thai lay togider tho,
>   And slepe bothe y-fere.   *together*
> Than seyd himselve, 'Bi Seyn Jon,
> It were gret rewethe you to slon,   *pity*
>   That God hath bought so dere!'
> His kniif he had drawen that tide,
> For sorwe he sleynt oway biside   *threw*
>   And wepe with reweful chere.

Than he hadde wopen ther he stode,   *where*
Anon he turned oyain his mode   *changed*
  And sayd withouten delay:
'Mi brother was so kinde and gode,
With grimly wounde he schad his blod
  For mi love opon a day;
Whi schuld Y than mi childer spare,
To bring mi brother out of care?   *distress*
  O, certes,' he seyd, 'nay!   *indeed*
To help mi brother now at this nede,
God graunt me therto wele to spede   *prosper*
  And Mari, that best may!' (2281–304)

No such human warmth is generated in *Amadace*; what is more, the burden of suffering there seems too one-sided for us to accept the bond that unites the two men as genuinely meaningful (and therefore capable of excusing— even for a moment—the sacrifice that is called for). The behaviour of the White Knight becomes more than ever curious when he identifies himself as the corpse in the chapel,[1] and thus deeply in the hero's debt. It is not surprising that some critics have found his behaviour little short of despicable.[2]

But this very lack of flesh-and-blood reality makes it easier to accept him as a supernatural agent of God's providence, who is thus testing Amadace in a quite impersonal way. What we are told about him on his two appearances supports this view. The first of these is so sudden as to terrify the hero (424–6); on the second he is described as being like an angel in his appearance (637–9). These suggestions of the supernatural also allow the latent resemblances to the Biblical account of the sacrifice of Isaac to come through clearly (in *Amis* the emphasis placed on human feelings of love and compassion on both sides prevents this from happening). And the White Knight's cry of '*Now is tyme of pees*' after he has intervened to save the lady's life, sounds almost divine in its total authority.

These brief surveys have been chiefly concerned with the ways in which heroic and edifying impulses might work themselves out in our romances; it is now time to say something about their more chivalrous aspects. Often, these will prove to be more negative than positive, softening the harsher impulses of the basic stories, but never truly contradicting them. *Melayne* can speak of knights, ladies, and chivalry, and *Isumbras* describe a tournament as well as battles, but without really weakening their dominant ethos. But in *Octavian* and *Amadace* we are conscious of a genuinely fresh impulse

---

[1] A retrospective identification as surprising as that made by the Green Knight in *Sir Gawain and the Green Knight*, 2345 ff.
[2] See, for example, G. Kane, *Middle English Literature*, p. 19.

at some points. In the first, Florent's deeds against the heathen are inextricably bound up with his courtship of Marsabelle, the sultan's daughter, and this proves a rather mixed blessing as far as his military efficiency is concerned. It makes him very dashing, but also rather unreliable, in that he arrives late for the vital battle against the Saracens; when he at last gets there, it has already been lost (1579–96). In *Amadace*, love and duty do not come into collision in this way, but the colour of chivalry is even more apparent at some points. This time, the hero's lady is to be won by the knight who proves supreme in tournament (528), but the claims of romance are also subsequently met, since the two of them fall helplessly in love with each other once they have met (610–12). But the very modest limits of the romance make it impossible for these features to be much elaborated upon. Just how laconic the author's treatment has been comes out very clearly when we set against these scenes the corresponding parts of the French romance of *Richars li Biaus*, in which the tournament is spread over three successive days, each of which is described at progressively greater length, and in the middle of which there is an elaborate scene of courtship (4975–5045).

This laconic presentation is typical of virtually all the tail-rhyme romances with the exception of *Ipomedon*, and there is simply no room in them for the kind of lengthy description of individual combats in tournament, or of the mental torments of hero and heroine after they have fallen in love, which had been the stock-in-trade of the French chivalrous romance. But the same brevity that compels the exclusion of scenes of this kind can also produce literary effects of its own, that may seem to the modern reader both more endearing and more truly romantic than anything in the more developed romances. For whereas in these romances we find a general concern to leave nothing to chance, and no loose ends (events must be provided with causes, actions with motives, scenes with elaborate settings), in the much shorter tail-rhyme examples everything seems more arbitrary and surprising. The elements of a scene stand more often isolated than in a mutual relationship; characters will appear without warning (like the White Knight in *Amadace*); individual properties (like Gowther's sword) acquire an importance beyond that which the author's explanation of them would suggest, by force of bare repetition. Sometimes this repetition is of a very deliberate kind, and the effect produced strangely ballad-like:

And whenne that the bysschop the sothe hade	*truth*
That that traytour that lesyng made,	*lie*
He callyd a messangere,	
Bad hym to Dovere that he scholde founde,	*go*
Forto fette that eerl Wymounde:	
(That traytour has no pere!)	*equal*

'Sere Egelane and hys sones be slawe,   *killed*
Bothe i-hangyd and to-drawe.
    (Doo as I the lere!)   *tell*
The countasse is in presoun done;   *put*
Schal sche nevere out off presoun come,
    But yiff it be on bere.'   *bier*

Now with the messanger was no badde;   *delay*
He took his hors, as the bysschop radde,   *commanded*
    To Dovere tyl that he come.
The eerl in hys halle he fand: *found*
He took hym the lettre in his hand   *gave*
    On hygh, wolde he nought wone: *haste, delay*
'Sere Egelane and his sones be slawe,
Bothe i-hangyd and to-drawe.
    Thou getyst that eerldome.
The countasse is in presoun done;
Schal sche nevere more out come,
    Ne see neyther sunne ne mone.'
    (*Athelston*, 699–722)

More elaborate still is the scene at the chapel in *Amadace* (especially in its first part, before everything is explained by the widow (61–126)), although here the impact is blunted by a good deal of textual corruption. Nothing, certainly, could be further from the treatment of what is essentially the same episode in *Richars li Biaus*, where the setting is very much less evocative (the body is kept on the beams of a hall in the creditor's own house (4341–6)), and there is nothing like the careful repetitions of *Amadace*.

Emaré, as we have seen, is also much given to repetition, although in the past this has generally been dismissed as a sign of enfeebled literary imagination, rather than acknowledged as any kind of stylistic virtue. But it sometimes makes its effect, notably in the oddly haunting instructions which the lady gives her son in 907–9 and 982–4 (which are repeated by him when he performs his mission in 922–4 and 1006–8). However accidentally, and on however unassuming a level, the author seems here to create something of the sense of strangeness and of the opening up of long perspectives of time that we find so compellingly produced in the great recognition scene in *Pericles*. And there is a certain aptness to this. *Pericles* is based upon *Apollonius of Tyre*, which was in the Middle Ages the best-known representative of the late Greek romances, and these works were frequently stories telling of the separation of the members of a family by storm, shipwreck, and other reversals of fortune. Their fundamental similarity to *Emaré* and *Octavian* needs no pointing; even *Amadace*, which is not a 'family' story like the others, is quite close to *Apollonius* in its middle section. After meeting with the White Knight, the hero comes upon the shipwreck, and then makes his way to the king's court; in *Apollonius* the hero, after losing all his possessions in a shipwreck, comes to the city of Pentapolim, where he distinguishes himself in the games held there, and finally marries the daughter of the king of the country.[1] In other words, the motifs are very much the same as in *Amadace*, but more clearly and logically brought into focus.

One other literary mode of a 'romantic' kind needs mentioning as of special relevance to *Emaré* (and, this time, to *Gowther* as well). This is the Breton lay, a short narrative poem, of which the range of possible subject-matter was very nearly as wide as that of the romances themselves, but which—partly because of its brevity—had a special aptitude for dealing with tales of the supernatural. Some of its most memorable examples, in both French and English, tell how a man or woman from the Otherworld of fairy might cross into the world of men and there become the lover or mistress of a mortal; notable examples are the French *Lanval* and *Yonec*, and the English *Sir Degaré* and (with some blurring of the lover's rôle) *Sir Orfeo*. The liaison was generally broken off abruptly, and the mortal (or the mortal's son) would later set off in search of the lost partner (or parent). The stock-in-trade of this kind of Breton lay appears most obviously in the opening scenes of *Gowther* (which, like *Emaré*, actually describes itself as such a lay, in spite of the strength of its pious elements). In such 'fairy' lays as *Tydorel* and *Sir Degaré* the lady is seduced by a supernatural knight of handsome appearance, and this motif, absent from other versions of the story of Robert the Devil, is unmistakable here (64–9); a further parallel with *Tydorel* is the later accusation of the young man by a stranger, that serves to arouse his suspicions as to his real nature (*Gowther* 202–9).[2] More interesting, however, are the parallels which the second half of the story offers with the lay of *Lanval*, especially in its elaborated form as the Middle English *Sir Launfal*. This story began by telling of a knight who, like Cleges and Amadace, was reduced to poverty by his liberality. This time, however, his fortunes are restored by a meeting with a fairy; she becomes his mistress and provides him with all necessary money and equipment to live handsomely, as long as he keeps their love a secret. When he ill-advisedly breaks this taboo, the lady vanishes, and with her all his prosperity:

The knyghtes softe hym anoon,	*looked for*
But Launfal was to hys chaumber gon	
To han hadde solas and plawe;	*(sexual) sport*
He softe hys leef, but sche was lore,	*beloved, lost*
As sche hadde warnede hym before—	
Tho was Launfal unfawe!	*miserable*

[1] See Gower's *Confessio Amantis*, VIII, 597–974.
[2] See *PMLA* 20 (1905), 153–5.

> He lokede yn hys alner   *purse*
> That fond hym spendyng, all plener,   *all he wanted*
>   Whan that he hadde nede,
> And ther nas noon, forsoth to say,
> And Gyfre was y-ryde away   *ridden off*
>   Up Blaunchard hys stede.   *upon*
> All that he hadde before y-wonne,
> Hyt malt as snow ayens the sunne   *melted, in*
>   (In romaunce as we rede);
> Hys armur, that was whyt as flour,
> Hyt becom of blak colour,
>   And thus than Launfal seyde ...   (727–44)

The way in which Gowther is miraculously supplied with a horse and armour could be seen as a christianized version of the same basic situation but the transformation has not been quite absolute. There still remains, as a vital element in the scene, the lady who will later become the hero's wife, and she is set in a strangely commanding position in it. The emperor's daughter sees and knows everything that is going on; she is remote but mutely sympathetic, and a passage such as 434–5 conveys a sort of complicity between them. And this (as yet) platonic liaison is broken off as abruptly as the fully sexual one of Launfal and Tryamour. In the course of the last day's fighting, the hero is seriously hurt; the lady, when she sees this, falls from the window in the castle from which she has been watching the battle, and is to all appearances killed. When Gowther returns, he is very conscious that she is no longer in the place where he has been accustomed to seeing her (*Then myssyd he that meydon schene* (642)). The Christian bases of the story are now, of course, too important to prevent these hints of a relationship from being developed[1]—the gifts are explicitly said to be of God's sending, not the lady's, and the answer to the hero's prayers (400–9, 460 f., 554–7)— nevertheless, these hints make their effect by creating a feeling of strangeness that could not have been generated by the fully explicit style of the chivalrous romance.

In *Emaré*, too, there are hints of the fairy supernatural, which are this time actually taken up by characters within the story. They all centre around the dazzling robe which the lady's father had had made for her, and which she takes with her in all her wanderings. In herself, Emaré is an essentially pathetic figure, meek and self-effacing, enduring hardships without complaint, and quite prepared to stay quietly in Rome until such time as her husband can find her once more. But with the robe on she appears a quite different character, who has all the seductive beauty of the fairy; dazzling, but also possibly dangerous (244–6, 394–6, 700–2). It is not surprising that

[1] See, however, the note to 375.

the first reaction that she inspires in those who find her is one of wonder mixed with fear (349–51, 697–9), or that the wicked mother-in-law, always ready to believe the worst of people, should see her as diabolical (442–7).

At this point we may seem to be in danger of overpraising the literary merits of these romances; the effects we have been trying to define are in many ways intangible, and might be dismissed, by an unsympathetic reader, as the accidental by-products of a loosely-integrated narrative medium. It may therefore be an appropriate moment to consider a fact that no study of these romances can ever ignore entirely: Chaucer parodied some of the commonplaces of the tail-rhyme style in his jog-trot *Sir Thopas*, which he allows the Host to cut short brutally, and which is replaced by a long piece of moralizing in prose. Anything, it seems, is better than this *rym dogerel*. What is more, before being thus cut short, Chaucer names as two other *romances of prys*, *Horn Childe* and *Lybeaus Desconus* (both of which are composed in the tail-rhyme stanza throughout), and *Guy of Warwick* and *Bevis of Hamtoun* (both of which use the form for part of their length).[1] In spite of all that Trounce was able to say against doing so, it seems that some literary historians are still ready to use *Sir Thopas* as a stick to beat the tail-rhyme romances with, and it is therefore worth making, again, one or two points about the parody.

The first is best made by quoting L. H. Loomis, who assembled with great care all passages in the Middle English metrical romances that seemed to her to be reflected in *Sir Thopas*:

> it is in no wise a parody on any one school of romances, if the twelve-line, tail-rhyme romances are, indeed, to be so designated; it follows no previous pattern of burlesque or parody, either social or literary.[2]

The second springs inevitably from a study of the parallels which she brought together. Of these, only the merest handful involve any of the texts in our selection; we find that a few conventional phrases in *Sir Thopas* are also present in the introductory stanzas to *Octavian* and *Isumbras*, and that part of a very commonplace simile in *Isumbras* 446 is also used by Chaucer. And that is all.

But the aspect of *Sir Thopas* that most clearly sets it apart from the most representative tail-rhyme romances is, quite simply, the kind of story that it tells. Here we have a romance that is at once both 'chivalrous' and 'fairy', not by hints and suggestions, like *Gowther* and *Emaré*, but by basic plot. The two major obsessions of its hero are to secure a fairy mistress for himself, and to fight with the giant who stands guard over the lady's domain (once he has found it). Of all the romances discussed in this introduction, only *Sir*

---

[1] *Canterbury Tales* B[2] 897–900.
[2] *Sources and Analogues*, p. 486.

Launfal is truly relevant to all this,[1] and the only other that can be found anywhere is almost certainly by the same author, and stands next to *Launfal* in the
only manuscript collection in which both have survived. This romance is
Lybeaus Desconus; as we have seen, it is mentioned in Chaucer's short list,
and its special relevance to *Sir Thopas* was pointed out long ago by F. P.
Magoun,[2] who noted that one of its most important episodes brings the hero
to the land of a seductive enchantress, who is guarded by a giant with whom
Lybeaus is obliged to fight. When he has defeated him, he becomes, for a
whole year, the lady's abject slave.

The manuscript in which we find *Launfal* and *Lybeaus* together is Cotton
Caligula A.ii. Unlike the famous Auchinleck manuscript, this was put together
too late for Chaucer to have seen it, but L. H. Loomis has suggested that he
might still have known a fourteenth-century antecedent of it, which already
contained *Lybeaus* and some other romances. If we could assume, in addition,
that in this earlier collection the romances showed some of the formal
peculiarities that the Caligula texts of *Lybeaus*, *Eglamour* and *Isumbras* now
show, we might have an explanation of some of the metrical oddities of *Sir
Thopas*. For the three texts just mentioned, although basically in the twelve-
line stanza, show a marked tendency to split that up into two of six lines, by
altering the tail-rhyme; elsewhere (though more rarely) they may inflate the
basic stanza to one of fifteen or eighteen lines by similar alteration. These two
extremes might have prompted Chaucer, first, to compose his parody in
stanzas of six lines, not twelve,[3] and, second, to allow this stanza to get out
of hand for a brief period in the middle of his story, by expanding it first to
seven, and then to ten lines. Interestingly enough, the part of the romance
where this happens is that describing the hero's meeting with the giant in
the land of the *elf-queene*: the *Lybeaus*-material, in fact.

The issues raised in this last section bring us to the last major topic that
needs considering here: the state of the texts in which our romances have
survived, and the kind of treatment that they require. With the exception of
Melayne and *Emaré*, every one has come down to us in more than one copy,
each of which has a strongly-marked character of its own, but none of which
is anywhere near perfect. Three matters must be discussed in consequence:
what kind of differences exist between one copy and another? how do we
select one copy as the basis of our text? how far do we allow ourselves to
modify this text?

---

[1] Besides the fairy mistress Tryamour, we have an opponent who is described as
gigantic, even if in a very throwaway manner (512).

[2] See the Bibliography.

[3] The tail-rhyme romances of the Auchinleck manuscript hardly ever break down
like those of Caligula, but we do find a run of six-line stanzas at the head of its text
of *Bevis*.

The first question is the most difficult to answer at all concisely; but we can at least indicate a few major types of divergence, referring, wherever possible, to notes in the Commentary in which the relevant material is set out in full. One major source of divergence is the omission in one text of material that seems from all the available evidence to have formed a part of the original romance. Sometimes this was the result of copying from a damaged source-text; sometimes the product of losing one's place in the text, and skipping a number of lines inadvertently (*Octavian* 1119). But some omissions appear to have been made deliberately, perhaps because the scribe considered that a certain narrative point was being laboured (*Amadace* 85–7, 93–5, 108), or that the romance was taking a long time dying (*Amadace* 817–40). A sign of deliberation in this matter is when the scribe has taken the trouble to modify the lines which immediately precede and follow the omitted passage, in order not to leave any loose ends (*Octavian* 804, *Amadace* 301–12).

At the other extreme, we quite often find that new material has been inserted into the original romance (this will often be recognizably different in style from the more 'authentic' stanzas around it). Sometimes such new material will serve purely to heighten the emotional impact of the story (*Isumbras* 192); sometimes it will be for the sake of extra narrative clarity (*Octavian* 132, 1732–4). But it may also represent a more genuinely creative urge on the copyist's part, in that it brings out some potentiality of the basic story that was not developed by the author of the original (*Isumbras* 655–717, *Gowther* 375).

Equally striking can be differences in the handling of the tail-rhyme stanza. One scribe may leave implicit the connections between the components of his statements; another will make these connections much plainer and so produce a more logical total effect (*Octavian* 613–18). Or one may keep the three-line units of his stanza quite self-contained, while another will allow the sense to run on from one unit (or even one stanza) to the next (*Gowther* 333–6).[1] There may also be striking contrasts in the range and vividness of the vocabulary used; one scribe will be much more prone than another to substitute blandly conventional expressions for a rougher and more varied arrangement of words (*Isumbras* 1–30, *Gowther* 55–7).

Nearly all the alterations so far described are bound up with the personality of the scribes; in however fragmentary a way, they bear witness to their literary habits and prejudices. But side-by-side with such 'significant' modifications of the original text we find a number of other alterations to it that can only be called mechanical errors of copying. The scribe may produce nonsense-words by leaving out a letter (*mentrelles* in *Emaré* 867), or substitute for a word in his original another which, while meaningful in itself, is not so

---

[1] Trounce considered that apart from individual and geographical variation in the use of enjambement, it tended in any case to be used more freely in these romances as the century went on (*Athelston*, p. 55).

in its context (*worde* for *wone* in *Melayne* 168). He may obscure the rhyme-scheme of the original by inserting or omitting whole lines (*Melayne* 415–17, *Isumbras* 53) or by altering the tail-rhymes so that stanzas of more or less than twelve lines are produced (*Gowther* 352–7). Elsewhere he may make it appear that the rhyme-scheme has broken down when it has not really done so, by spelling one or two of the words in rhyme position in a way different from the others (as in the *kare: spare: sore: more* of *Emaré* 627 ff. for original **kare: spare: sare: mare*). He may also spoil the metre by inserting extraneous words or phrases into the line, especially an unwanted 'he/she said', to make it plain that there has been a change of speaker at this point (*Octavian* 1732–4). It should be noted, too, that the same mechanical errors are sometimes found in two or more of our texts, and we must then infer that these texts derive, not from the original romance, but from a lost intermediate copy that was already corrupt in some places (*Amadace* 1, 168, 463–5). Occasionally one of the texts will try, perhaps crudely, to patch up a defect in the common original that is allowed to stand in the other derivative (*Amadace* 436–8).

Every surviving copy of our texts is thus a compound of readings derived from the original, modifications deliberately introduced by the scribe, and mechanical errors perpetrated by him. This presents the editor who has to choose between two or more such texts for his own copy with a complex problem that is unlikely to be capable of being resolved in a strictly scientific way. It will rather be determined by a mixture of subjective considerations (which of the two comes closer to his idea of what a good tail-rhyme romance should be like[1]), and his notions of the kind of edition that he intends to produce of it. This second factor is of the greatest importance. If it is his wish to recreate the lost original of the romance in all its supposed purity, then he is bound to select the text that seems to him basically closest to this original, however damaged its surface may be by mechanical errors. He will then 'restore' it, in the light of his own feeling for the tail-rhyme style, and making use, wherever possible, of the 'superior' readings of the alternative surviving copies. The end-product will be a text that is consistently meaningful and smoothly-finished, even if it may never actually have existed in a state of such perfection before he created it. If, on the other hand, an editor is most concerned with producing a readable text of a copy that actually existed, his priorities will be different. He will, from the available texts, choose the one that seems to him the most enjoyable to read on its own terms; he will correct obvious mechanical errors where these affect the sense, or violently upset the rhyme, but he will not regularize the spellings of words in rhyme-position, or attempt to improve the metre by leaving out

---

[1] It may be noted that Trounce and Breul came to directly opposite conclusions about the relative value of the Auchinleck and Royal texts of *Sir Gowther*.

'unnecessary' words and phrases. The great merit of this approach—which has been followed in the present edition—is that it respects the integrity of the text; it also has the practical advantage of cutting down on the number of footnotes (these proliferate enormously in an 'edited' text). At the same time, as full a selection of variant readings as possible will be given, so that an idea of the special characteristics of the copies not printed in full may be obtained. Where these variants are short—and, in particular, where they illuminate the readings of the principal text—they will be given at the foot of the page; where they are not, they will be put in the Commentary at the end. Some of the notes will also give information of a kind helpful to the flexible reading of these texts, and made desirable by the lack of thorough-going emendation of them.

In conclusion, a few words about the detailed presentation of the text. All letters and words supplied within the line are marked off by square brackets, as are conjectural readings (mostly taken over from previous editors of these texts) of illegible or missing words and letters. But where (as, frequently, in *Melayne*) a number of words are missing, and previous editorial conjecture is either unconvincing or misguided (because of the misreading of the letters that remain), I have preferred simply to indicate the number of letters missing by dots within the square brackets. The spellings of the original have been kept throughout, except that the distribution of *u* and *v*, and *i* and *j* has been regularized according to modern usage, and that the obsolete letters *ʒ* and *þ* are replaced by their nearest modern equivalents: *w, y, gh* or *th*. Where these letters have been used in conjunction with *h, gh* or *th*, there has been some simplification of the total group. Thus *þþ* and *þh* are rendered by *th*; *ʒh* and *ʒgh*, by *gh*. Flourishes through the final consonantal groups of the individual words have not normally been expanded to *-e*, except in the text of *Amadace*, which is unusually carefully written; the horizontal mark of abbreviation has usually been taken literally, and expanded to *m* or *n* according to context, except where it is part of a final flourish. The letter *N* has been interpreted as *u* or *n* according to context; sometimes the spelling of the word with which it is linked in rhyme has determined the choice of letter. With very rare exceptions the (often inconsistent) manuscript spellings of proper names have been kept without emendation.

The various manuscript copies of our texts are represented in the notes by the following symbols:

Melayne	(British Museum, MS. Additional 31042)	M
Emaré	(British Museum, MS. Cotton Caligula A.ii)	L
Octavian	(Cambridge University Library, MS. ff.ii.38)	C
	(Lincoln Cathedral Library, MS. A.5.2)	T
Isumbras	(British Museum, MS. Cotton Caligula A.ii)	L
	(Lincoln Cathedral Library, MS. A.5.2)	T

	(National Library of Scotland, Advocates MS. 19.3.1)	E
	(Bodleian Library, MS. Ashmole 61)	A
Gowther	(National Library of Scotland, Advocates MS. 19.3.1)	A
	(British Museum, MS. Royal 17.B.43)	B
Amadace	(Ireland MS.)	I
	(National Library of Scotland, Advocates MS. 19.3.1)	A

Such symbols are only used elsewhere in the notes to *Octavian* in the Commentary, where the French source is designated by FO, the 'Northern' Middle English version by NO, and the 'Southern' by SO.

A Note on *Sir Isumbras*

As noted above, four complete MS. copies of this romance have survived, but of these, only Thornton and Caligula are possible choices for a single-text edition. The second has been preferred. It has its drawbacks: its style (like that of *Emaré* in the same collection) is often conventional, and it frequently disrupts the original division of the poem into stanzas. But it is much pleasanter reading than Thornton, and its stanzaic irregularity is in any case of interest for its possible relevance to Chaucer's *Sir Thopas* (see p. xxvii). The more authentic stanza-division of Thornton is indicated in the Commentary.

Select Bibliography

COLLECTIONS

French, W. H. and Hale, C. B. (ed.): *Middle English Metrical Romances.* New York, 1930.

Macaulay, G. C. (ed.): *The English Works of John Gower* (EETS, ES 81–2). London, 1900–1.

Robinson, F. N. (ed.): *The Complete Works of Geoffrey Chaucer.* 2nd edn., London, 1957.

Robson, J. (ed.): *Three Early English Metrical Romances* (Camden Society). London, 1842.

Rumble, T. C. (ed.): *The Breton Lays in Middle English.* Detroit, 1965.

Sands, D. B. (ed.): *Middle English Verse Romances.* New York, 1966.

SEPARATE EDITIONS

Amis and Amiloun. Ed. E. Kölbing (Altenglische Bibliothek 2). Heilbronn, 1884.

Athelston. Ed. A. McI. Trounce (EETS 224). London, 1951.

Le Bone Florence of Rome. Ed. W. Viëtor. Marburg, 1893.

Emaré. Ed. E. Rickert (EETS, ES 99). London, 1908.

Guy of Warwick. Ed. J. Zupitza (EETS, ES 42, 49, 59). London, 1883–91.

Horn Childe. Ed. J. Caro. *Englische Studien* 12 (1889), 323–66.

Ipomedon. Ed. E. Kölbing. Breslau, 1889.

The King of Tars. Ed. F. Krause. *Englische Studien* 11 (1888), 1–62.

Lybeaus Desconus. Ed. M. Mills (EETS 261). London, 1969.

Octavian. Ed. G. Sarrazin (Altenglische Bibliothek 3). Heilbronn, 1885.

The Sege off Melayne. Ed. S. J. Herrtage (EETS, ES 35). London, 1880.

Sir Amadace. Ed. C. Brookhouse (Anglistica 15). Copenhagen, 1968.

Sir Eglamour. Ed. F. E. Richardson (EETS 256). London, 1965.

Sir Gowther. Ed. K. Breul. Oppeln, 1886.

Sir Launfal. Ed. A. J. Bliss. London, 1960.

Sir Ysumbras. Ed. J. Zupitza and G. Schleich (Palaestra 15). Berlin, 1901.

Torrent of Portyngale. Ed. E. Adam (EETS, ES 51). London, 1887.

STUDIES AND WORKS OF REFERENCE

Baugh, A. C. 'The Authorship of the Middle English Romances'. *Annual Bulletin of the Modern Humanities Research Association,* 22 (1950), 13–28.

Bordman, G. *Motif-Index of the English Metrical Romances.* FF Communications 79, No. 190. Helsinki, 1963.

Bryan, W. F. and Dempster, G. (ed.): *Sources and Analogues of Chaucer's Canterbury Tales.* Chicago, 1941.

Burrow, J. *Ricardian Poetry.* London, 1971.

Donovan, M. J. *The Breton Lay: A Guide to Varieties.* University of Notre Dame Press, 1969.

Everett, D. *Essays on Middle English Literature.* Oxford, 1955.

Hill, D. M. 'Romance as Epic'. *English Studies*, 44 (1963), 95–107.

Kane, G. *Middle English Literature.* London, 1951.

Ker, W. P. *Epic and Romance.* Dover Edition, New York, 1957.

Loomis, L. H. *Mediaeval Romance in England.* New York, 1924. *Adventures in the Middle Ages.* New York, 1962.

Magoun, F. P. 'The Source of Chaucer's Rime of Sir Thopas'. *PMLA*, 42 (1927), 833–44.

Mehl, D. *The Middle English Romances of the Thirteenth and Fourteenth Centuries.* London, 1969.

Ravenel, F. L. '*Tydorel* and *Sir Gowther*'. *PMLA*, 20 (1905), 152–78.

Schelp, H. *Exemplarische Romanzen im Mittelenglischen* (Palaestra 246). Göttingen, 1967.

Severs, J. B. (ed). *A Manual of the Writings in Middle English 1050–1500.* Fasc. 1, New Haven, 1967.

Smithers, G. V. 'Story-Patterns in some Breton Lays'. *Medium Ævum* 22 (1953), 61–92.

Speirs, J. *Medieval English Poetry: the Non-Chaucerian Tradition.* London, 1957.

Trounce, A. McI. 'The English Tail-Rhyme Romances'. *Medium Ævum* 1 (1932), 87–108, 168–82; 2 (1933) 34–57, 189–98; 3 (1934), 30–50.

The Sege of Melayne

All werthy men that luffes to here
Off chevallry that byfore us were,   *knights*
 That doughty weren of dede;   *valiant*
Off Charlles of Fraunce, the heghe kynge of alle, *supreme*
5 That ofte sythes made hethyn men forto falle, *often, defeated*
 That styffely satte one stede: *boldly*
This geste es sothe, wittnes the buke,
The ryghte lele trouthe whoso will luke,
 In cronekill forto rede.
10 Alle Lumbardy thay made thaire mone *lamentation*
And saide thair gammunes weren alle gone,
 Owttrayede with hethen thede.

The sowdane Arabas the stronge
Werreyde appon Crystyndome with wronge *made war*
15 And ceties brake he downn;
Robbyde the Romaynes of theire rent, *revenues*
The popys pousty hase he schente, *power, destroyed*
 And many kynges with crownn.
In Tuskayne townnes gon he wyn *Tuscany, conquer*
20 And stuffede tham wele with hethyn kyn, *garrisoned*
 This lorde of grete renownn;   *fame*
And sythen to Lumbardy he wanne: *went*
Mighte to lett hym hade no man;   *power, stop*
 Thus wynnes he many a townn.

25 The emagery that ther solde bee, *holy statues*
Bothe the rode and the Marie free,
 Brynnede tham in a fire;   *burnt*
And than his mawmettes he sett up there *heathen idols*
In kirkes and abbayes that there were: *churches*
30 Helde tham for lordes and syre. *regarded, master(s)*
To Melayne sythen he tuke the waye *afterwards*
And wanne the cyté apon a daye;
 Gaffe his men golde till hyre.   *as wages*
Many a martyre made he there
35 Off men and childire that there were
 And ladyes swete of swyre.   *fair, neck*

7–9 This story is true—as will be seen by anyone who consults the historical account to learn the truth of the matter. 11–12 their pleasant days were over, conquered (as they were) by the heathen nation. 18 many: many a M. 26 Both of (Christ on) the cross and the noble Mary.

The lorde of Melayne, sir Alantyne,
Sawe the Crystynde putt to pyne;   *torture*
   Owte of the townn he flede,
40 To a cyté that was thereby,
Alle nyghte he thoghte therin to ly:
   He was full straytly stede.   *very hard pressed*
Thay myghte it wynn with spere and schelde;   *would be able to*
Appon the morne hym buse it yelde
45   Or laye his lyfe in wede.   *as a pledge*
Was never no knyghte putt to mare care;   *greater sorrow*
Full hertly to Criste than prayes he thare,   *devoutly*
   To knawe the lyfe he ledde.

The sawdane sent hym messangers free   *worthy*
50 And bade hym torne and hethyn bee,   *renounce his faith*
   And he solde have his awenn: *keep*
Melayne that was the riche cité
And alle the lanndis of Lumbardye,
   And to his lawe be knawenn;
55 'And if he ne will noghte to oure lawe be swornne,   *religion*
He sall be hangede or other mornne   *before, next*
   And with wylde horse be drawen;
His wyffe and his childire three,
Byfore his eghne that he myghte see,
60   Be in sondre sawenn.'   *sawn in two*

He prayede the sowdane than of grace,   *favour*
That he wolde byde a littill space
   Whils one the morne at daye,
And he sall do hym forto witt,
65 If that he wolde assent to itt,
   To leve apon his laye.   *believe, religion*
Bot than heves he up his handis to heven,   *lifts*
To Jesu Criste with mylde steven,   *humble voice*
   Full hertly gane he praye.
70 'Lorde,' he saide, 'als thou swelte appon the tree,   *died, cross*
Of thy man thou hafe peté,   *take pity on*
   And Mary mylde that maye.   *gracious, virgin*

41 He intended to lodge there that night. *44* He would have to surrender it
in the morning. *48* To make his circumstances known to him. *54* And to
acknowledge his religion. *62–3* That he should give him a brief respite until
the following dawn. *64* And he will make known to him.

If I solde Crystyndome forsake
And to hethyn lawe me take,   *devote myself*
75   The perill mon be myn;
Bot, Lorde, als thou lete me be borne,   *as*
Late never my sawle be forlorne,   *destroyed*
Ne dampnede to helle pyne.   *condemned*
Bot, Lorde, als thou swelte on the rode   *died*
80 And for mankynde schede thi blode,
Some concelle sende thou me,   *instruction*
Whethire that me es better to doo: *which*
The hethyn lawe to torne too,
Or my lyfe in lande to tyne.'   *lose*

85 Than wente that knyghte unto bedde;
For sorowe hym thoghte his hert bledde,
And appon Jesu than gan he calle.
And sone aftire that gane he falle one slepe,
Als man that was wery for-wepe;
90   Than herde by hym on a walle
Ane angelle that unto hym gane saye:
'Rysse up, sir kynge, and wende thy waye,   *go*
For faire the sall byfalle,
To Charles that beris the flour-de-lyce   *wears*
95 (Of other kynges he berys the pryce)
And he sall wreke thy wrethis alle.'   *avenge, injuries*

The angelle bade hym ryse agayne,   *told*
'And hy the faste to Charlemayne,   *hasten*
The crownnede kynge of Fraunce;
100 And say hym God byddis that he sall go   *commands, must*
To helpe to venge the of thy foo,
Bothe with spere and launce.'
The kynge was full fayne of that;   *glad*
His swerde in his hande he gatt   *took*
105   And therto graythely he grauntis.
He garte swythe sadyll hym a palfraye   *had, quickly*
And even to Fraunce he tuke the waye;   *straight*
Now herkenys of this chaunce!

---

75 I am bound to put myself in danger (of damnation).   *86* it seemed to him that.   *89* was worn out with weeping.   *93* things will (now) go well with you.   *95* He is supreme over all other kings.   *105* And readily agrees to do that.   *108* Now listen to what happened next.

The same nyghte byfore the daye,
110 Als kyng Charls in his bedde laye,
 A swevn than gan he mete;   *dream, dream*
Hym thoghte ane angele lyghte als leven *shining, lightning*
Spake to hym with mylde steven,
 That gudly hym gane grete.   *graciously*
115 That angele bytaughte hym a brande,   *gave, sword*
Gaffe hym the hiltis in his hande,
 That even was hande full mete;
And saide, 'Criste sende the this swerde,
Mase the his werryoure here in erthe,
120 He dose the wele to weite.

He biddes thou sall resceyve it tyte   *at once*
And that thou venge alle his dispyte,   *injury done him*
 For thynge that ever may bee;
And sla alle there thou sees me stryke   *kill*
125 And sythen thou birnne up house and dyke, *rampart*
 For beste he traystis in thee.'   *trusts*
The walles abowte Melayne townne
Hym thoghte the angele dange tham downn, *struck*
 That closede in that cité;   *encircled*
130 Sythen alle the lanndis of Lumbardy,
Townnes, borows and bayli: *cities, wall*
 This was selcouthe to see.   *astonishing*

When Charls wakenede of his dreme
He sawe a bryghtenes of a beme   *ray*
135 Up unto hevenwarde glyde.   *shine*
Bot when he rose the swerde he fande   *found*
That the angelle gaffe hym in his hande,
 Appon his bedde syde.
He schewede it thanne to his barouns alle,
140 And than saide his lordes bothe grete and smalle:
 'The sothe is noghte to hyde.
We wote wele that Goddis will it es
That thou sall conquere of hethennesse *heathen nation*
 Countres lange and wyde.'

117 That was well suited to (his) hand. *119–20* He tells you plainly that
he chooses you for his earthly champion. *123* Whatever the circumstances.
141 The truth cannot be hidden.

145 To mete than wente that riche kynge,   *table, noble*
    Bot sone come there newe tydynge,   *fresh news*
      Als he in sete was sette.   *in his place*
    The lorde of Melayne he sawe come in,
    That was his cosyn nere of kyn,   *closely related*
150   And hym full gudely grett.
    The grete lordis alle hailsede hee   *saluted*
    And prayede tham all sesse of theire glee,   *rejoicing*
      And sayse to Charls withowtten lett: *delay*
    'Jesu Criste hase comannde thee
155 To fare to the felde to feghte for mee,   *take*
      My landis agayne to gett.'   *recover*

    He tolde tham alle at the borde and by
    That the Sarazenes had wonn Lumbardy
      (Thay mornede and made grete mone)
160 And how the angelle bade hym goo;
    The kynge tolde his sweven alsoo,
      Thay accordede bothe in one.
    Thane sayde the beshop Turpyne:
    'Hafe done! Late semble the folke of thyne—   *call together*
165   Myn hede I undirtake   *lay as pledge*
    That Gode es grevede at the Sarazenes boste;   *made angry by*
    We salle stroye up alle theire hoste,   *destroy, army*
      Those worthely men in wo[n]e.'   *on earth*

    Bot alle that herde hym Genyenn,   *Ganelon*
170 That was a lorde of grete renownn
      And Rowlande modir hade wedde.
    Thare wery hym bothe God and sayne John:
    The falseste traytoure was he one   *one of*
      That ever with fode was fedde!
175 For landis that Rowlande solde have thare
    Dede fayne he wolde that he ware,
      The resone ryghte who redde.
    His first tresone now bygynnes here,
    That the lordis boghte sythen full dere,   *paid for, very*
180   And to ladyse grete barett bredde.   *anguish, caused*

---

150 And gave him a very gracious welcome. *157* at table and near at hand.
162 (The two accounts) agreed exactly. *168* wone: worde M. *172* May he
be cursed by both. *176* He would gladly have seen him dead. *177* Whoever gives a true account (of the facts).

'Sir,' he sayde, 'that ware a synfull chaunce:
Whatt solde worthe of us in Fraunce,   *become*
   And thou in the felde were slayne?   *if*
Thyselfe and we at home will byde,   *remain*
185 And latte Rowlande thedire ryde,   *there*
   That ever to bekyre es bayne;
With batelle and with brode banere;   *battle array*
Of his wyrchipp wolde I here,   *valour*
   Witt ye wele, full fayne.'
190 For Rowlande this resone he wroghte: *made this speech*
Everemore in his herte he thoghte   *all the time*
   He solde never come agayne.   *return*

The kynge than sent a messangere
To grette lordes bothe ferre and nere   *in all parts*
195   And bade tham make tham yare.   *ready*
Bot the peris take a concelle newe
That made alle Fraunce ful sore to rewe,   *bitterly, regret*
   And byrdis of blyse full bare.
Thay prayede the kynge on that tyde   *time*
200 That he hymselfe at home walde byde,
   To kepe that lande right thare: *protect*
'And sendis Rowlande to Lumbardy
With fourty thowsande chevalry
   Of worthy men of were.'   *war*

205 Then Rowlande thus his were than made,
Fares forthe with baners brade;   *rides*
   The kynge byleves thare still   *remains*
Within the cité of Paressche   *Paris*
Forto kepe that townn of pryce,   *excellent*
210   Als thay accordede till.   *agreed*
And if the sowdane wane the felde,
Lyghtly walde thay it noghte yelde,   *easily, would*
   To thay had foughtten thaire fill.   *until*
Bot be comen was the feftenede daye
215 Therfore myghte mornne bothe man and maye,   *for it, maiden*
   And ladyse lyke full ill.   *be very grieved*

181 that would be an evil mishap. *186* Who is always ready for a fight.
196 But the peers came to a fresh decision. *198* And ladies to lose all their
joy. *205* got ready his battle array. *211* was victorious in battle. *214*
But by the time that two weeks had gone by.

To Melayne even thay made tham bownn,   *got ready*
And batelde tham thare byfore the townn,
   Those knyghttis that were kene.   *bold*
220 And in to the sowdane thay sent a knyghte
And bade hym come owte with tham to fyghte,
   To witt withowtten wene.   *know, doubt*
The sowdane grauntis wele thertill—   *to that*
That tornede oure gud men all to gryll,
225   And many one mo to mene.
Than the Sarazens come owte of that cité,
Forty thowsandes of chevalrye,
   The beste in erthe myghte be[ne].

The forthirmaste come a Sarazene wyghte,
230 Sir Arabaunt of Perse he highte,   *was called*
   Of Gyon was he kynge:
He saide ther was na Cristyn knyghte,
Ware he never so stronge ne wyghte,
   To dede he [ne] solde hym dynge.
235 And one sir Artaymnere of Beme,
That was sir Olyvers eme,   *uncle*
   Byfore the stowre thay thrynge;   *turmoil, dash*
And even at the firste countire righte,
The Sarazen slewe oure Cristyn knyghte:
240   It was dyscomforthynge.

The lorde of Melayne to hym rade,   *rode*
Sir Alantyne, withowtten bade,   *delay*
   The Crystyn knyghte to wreke;   *avenge*
Bot he stroke oure Cristyn knyghte that stownde   *time*
245 That dede he daschede to the grounde,
   Mighte no worde after speke.
Sythen afterwarde he bare down   *bore*
Worthy lordes of grete renownn,
   Ay to his launce gane breke,   *until*
250 And sythen areste thaire nobill stedis   *took hold of*
And to the hethyn hoste tham ledis:
   Loo, thusgates fares the freke!

218 And drew up their lines of battle. 224–5 That turned to the disadvantage of our valiant men and made many others lament. 228 *bene: be* M.
229 At the head of them was a bold Saracen. 234 *ne:* omitted M; That he would not strike him down dead. 238 the very first bout. 240 a source of distress. 252 This is how that fierce warrior carries on.

Bot by that was done the grete gon mete;	
Barouns undir blonkes fete	*horses'*
255 Braythely ware borne doun.	*violently*
Thay stekede many a staleworthe knyghte,	*ran through*
The hethen folke in that fyghte,	
The moste were of renownn.	*who*
Oure knyghtis one the gronde lyse	
260 With wondes wyde one wafull wyse,	
Crakkede was many a crownn:	
Riche hawberkes were all to-rent,	*mail-shirts, torn*
And beryns thorowe thaire scheldis schent,	
That many to bery was bownn.	*ready for burial*

265 The Sarazens semblede so sarely	*attacked, hard*
That thay felde faste of oure chevalrye,	
Oure vawarde down thay dynge.	*vanguard*
Righte at the firste frusche thay felde	*attack*
Fyve thowsande knyghtis trewly telde:	*counted*
270 This is no lesynge!	
Oure knyghtis lyghtede one the bent,	*dismounted, field*
Thorowe thaire scheldis are they schent,	
Of sorowe than myghte thay synge!	*lament*
Than oure medillwarde gane tham mete;	*middle guard*
275 Thare myghte no beryns oure bales bete,	
Bot the helpe of hevens kynge.	*only*

The medillwarde sir Rowlande ledde,	
That doghty in felde was never drede	*afraid*
To do what solde a knyghte.	*ought (to do)*
280 Fyfty lordis of gret empryce,	*renown*
Of Fraunce that bare the floure-de-lyce,	
Hase loste bothe mayne and myghte.	*power*
Our medillwarde sone hade thay slayne,	
And Rowlande was in handis tane,	*captured*
285 And other seven that were knyghtes.	
But als God gaffe hym that chaunce,	*good fortune*
Thay wende he hade bene kynge of Fraunce,	*supposed*
That lyfede in thase fyghtis.	

253 the main body of soldiers joined battle. *260* Wretchedly, with gaping wounds. *263* And warriors fatally wounded through their shields. *275* reverse our disasters. *288* Who had survived that battle.

Bot of a knyghte me rewes sore,	
290 That in the felde laye wondede thore:	
The Duke of Normandy.	
He lukes up in the felde,	
His umbrere with his hande up helde,	*visor, lifted*
On Rowlande gane he cry:	
295 'Rowlande, if the tyde that chaunce	
That thou come evermore into Fraunce,	*again*
For the lufe of mylde Marie,	
Comande me till oure gentill kynge,	*commend, noble*
And to the qwene my lady yynge,	*young*
300 And to all chevalrye.	

And if thou come into Normandy,	
Grete wele my lady,	
And sir Richerd my sonne;	
And dubbe hym duke in my stede,	*create, place*
305 And bydde hym venge his fadir dede,	*tell, death*
Of myrthe if he will mone.	
Bid hym hawkes and houndes forgoo	*give up*
And to dedis of armes hym doo,	*give himself*
Thase craftes forto konn;	*skills, learn*
310 Appon the cursede Sarazens forto werre,	
Venge me with dynt of spere,	*blow*
For my lyfe es nere done.	*almost*

A, Rowlande! Byhaulde nowe whatt I see,	*see*
More joye ne myghte never bee,	
315 In youthe ne yitt in [elde].	*old age*
Loo! I see oure vawarde ledde to heven	
With angells songe and merye steven,	
Reghte as thay faughte in the felde!	
I see moo angells, loo! with myn eghe,	
320 Then there are men within Cristyanté,	
That any wapyn may welde.	
To heven thay lede oure nobill knyghtis,	
And comforthes tham with mayne and myghtis,	*all their strength*
With mekill blysse and belde.'	*much, happiness*

289 I feel great pity for. 295 if such good fortune should happen to you.
306 If he ever wishes for joy. 315 elde: age M. 317 and sound of
rejoicing. 318 Just as they were when. 321 Who are at all capable of
bearing arms.

325 Bot by Rowland gan a Sarazene stande
      That braydede owte with a bryghte brande
        When he harde hym say soo;
      And to the duke a dynt he dryvede,   *swung*
      At the erthe he smate righte of his hede: *to, cut*
330   Therfore was Rowlande woo;
      And Rowland styrte than to a brande
      And hastily hent it owte of a Sarazene hande, *snatched*
        And sone he gane hym sloo.   *kill*
      With that swerde he slewe sexty,
335 The beste of the Sarazens chevalrye,
        Off hardy men and moo.

      Than Rowlande in handis is taken agayne,
      And putt unto full harde payne,
        That sorowe it was to see;
340 And foure nobill knyghtis than have thay slayne,
      Byfore that were in handis tane,
        With sir Rowlande the free.   *noble*
      The sowdane comandis of his men
      And hundrethe knyghtis to kepe tham then,
345   Rowland and other three,
      And to oure rerewarde sythen thay rode;   *rearguard*
      Oure barouns boldely tham abode,   *awaited*
        Nowe helpe tham the Trynytee!

      The duke of Burgoyne, sir Belland,
350 The fadir of sir Gy of Nevynlande,
        The rerewarde than rewlis hee.   *commands*
      He comforthede alle oure nobyll knyghtis, *encouraged*
      Said, 'Lordis, halde your feldes and your ryghttis,
      And no Sarazene yee flee.
355 And thofe ye see thies lordis be slayne   *even though*
      Ne hope ye noghte for alle thaire payne
        That [we ne] sall solauce see;
      Bot the werkynge of oure wondis sare,   *except for, pain*
      Of the paynes of helle fele we no mare,
360   Bot hy to heven one heghe.'   *will hasten*

---

326 Who drew (and flourished). *331* rushed over to a sword. *338* And so brutally treated. *341* Whom they had earlier taken prisoner. *353* protect your lands. *356–7* And believe that we shall be given comfort in spite of all they can do. *357* we ne: ne we M.

Thay fruschede in fersely for Goddis sake;   *attacked*
Grete strokes gane thay gyffe and take,
  With wondis werkande wyde:
Bot yitt the Sarazens with thay[r] speris
365 Full ferre on bakke oure batelle berys
  And knyghtis felde undir fete.
Walde never no Crystyn knyghte thethyn flee   *from there*
Thoghe that he wyste ryghte there to dye,
  I doo yowe wele to wytt.   *give*
370 Bot alle in fere thay endide righte thare: *together, died*
That sowede the Sarazenes sythen full sare   *grieved*
  For lordis that levede the swete.   *who died*

Thus fourty thowsande hafe thay slayne
Safe foure that were in handis tane,   *except for*
375   Rowlande ande other three:
One was the gentill erle sir Olyvere,
Another was sir Gawtere,
  The kyngis cosyns nere;
The thirde was sir Gy of Burgoyne,
380 His fadir in the felde laye there slone,
  The soryare myghte he bee.   *sadder*
They ledde thies lordes into Melayne,
With that the sowdane turnes agayne   *back*
  Righte gladde of his menyee.   *army*

385 To the sowdane chambir many a man
Oure foure lordis ledd thay than
  To rekken of theire arraye.   *consider, case*
Thay ette and dranke and made tham glade,
Bot littill myrthe oure lordis hadde:
390 The sowdane gane tham saye,
'Welcome be thow, kynge of Fraunce,
The bytide a cely chaunce,
  Thi lyfe was savede this daye.
The false lawes of Fraunce sall downn,   *religion, must go*
395 The rewme sall leve one seynt Mahownn, *kingdom, believe*
  That alle the myghtyeste maye!'

---

363 With wide and painful wounds. *364 thayr: thay* M. 365 Force our divisions a long way back. 368 was quite certain that he would die there. 384 followed by *Prymus passus the first ffytt*. 392 You have been marvellously lucky. 396 Who can (perform) the most powerful (actions).

And Rowlande answerde full gentilly: *honourably*
'I ne rekke whethir I lyfe or dye,   *care*
   By God that awe this daye.
400 Kynge of Fraunce ame I none,
Bot a cosyne ame I one
   To Charlles by my faye.   *faith*
He will gyffe me golde and fee,   *goods*
Castells ryche with towris heghe,   *lofty*
405   That lorde full wele he maye.
Bot Goddis forbode and the holy Trynytee,
That ever Fraunce hethen were for mee,
   And lese oure Crysten la[y]e!   *should lose*

For sothe, thou sowdane, trowe thou moste   *truly, believe*
410 One the Fader and the Sone and the Holy Goste,
   Thire thre are alle in one;   *these*
That borne was of Marye free,
Sythen for us dyede one a tree;
   In other trowe we none.'

415 Thane loughe the sowdane withe eghne full smale,   *eyes, narrow*
And saide, 'Ane hundrethe of youre Goddis alle hale   *fully*
Have I garte byrne in a firre with bale,
   Sen ffirste I wanne this wone.   *since, place*
I sawe at none no more powstee   *in*
420 Than att another rotyn tree
   One erthe, so mote I gone!

Goo, feche one of theire goddis in,
And if he in this fire will byrne,
   Alle other sett att noghte.'   *value, nothing*
425 Than furthe ther rane a Sarazene in that tyde
To a kyrke was there byside,   *close at hand*
   A faire rode in he broghte,
Fourmede ewenn als he gane blede;
Oure Cristen knyghtis bygane thaire crede
430   And Rowland God bysoughte,   *prayed to*
And saide, 'Thou that was borne of a may,
Schewe thou, Lorde, thi meracle this day,   *demonstrate*
   That with thi blode us boghte.'   *redeemed*

---

399 who controls present events. *406* May God forbid. *408 laye: lawe*
M. *417* Have I caused to be burnt in a blazing fire. *423 byrne:* for *not
byrne?* *428* On which the wounds of Christ were exactly depicted.

They keste the rode into the fire   *threw*
435 And layde brandis with mekill ire,
    Fayne wolde thay garre hym birne.
The sowdane saide, 'Now sall ye see
What myghte es in a rotyn tree
    That youre byleve es in.   *faith*
440 I darre laye my lyfe full ryghte
That of hymselfe he hase no myghte
    Owte of this fire to wyn.   *get*
How solde he than helpe another man
That for hymselfe no gyn ne kan,
445   Nother crafte ne gyn?'

Thay caste one it full many a folde;   *time*
The rode laye still ay as it were colde;
    No fire wolde in hym too.
All if the crosse were makede of tree   *even, wood*
450 The fire yode owtt that come ther nee,   *near*
    Than wexe the sowdan woo: *became*
'And yif the devell,' he sayde, 'be hym within,
He sall be brynt or ever I blyne'—   *burnt, stop*
    Of hert he was full throo.   *angry*
455 'Thies cursede wreches that are herein
Hase wethede thaire goddis that thai may not byrn, *wetted*
    I wote wele it es soo.'

Than bromstone that wele walde birn,
And pykke and terre mengede therin,
460   Thay slange in the fire full bolde.   *threw violently*
Torches that were gude and grete
Forto helpe that mekill hete   *increase, great*
    Thay caste in many a folde.
The fire wexe owte at the laste;   *went, finally*
465 Oure knyghtis made thaire prayere faste   *hard*
    To Criste that Judas solde.
The rode braste and gaffe a crake,   *split*
That thamm thoghte that alle the byggynge brake, *building*
    That was within that holde.   *stronghold*

---

435 And angrily placed burning wood around it.   *436* They would have liked to have made it burn up.   *444–5* Who does not know of any trick or device that will help himself.   *448* would take hold of it.   *459* Mixed together with pitch and tar.

470 A fire than fro the crosse gane frusche,   *from, shot out*
      And in the Sarazene eghne it gaffe a dosche,
          Ane element als it were,
      That thay stode still als any stone,
      Hanndis nore fete myghte thay stirre none,   *move*
475   Bot drery wexe in chere;   *terrified, appearance*
      Thay wyste nother of gude ne ill;   *neither*
      Than Rowlande sais his felawes untill;   *to*
          'Sirs, hy us alle hethyn in fere.
      This meracle es schewede thorowe Goddis grace,
480 For alle the Sarazenes in this place
          May nother see nore here.'

      Sayde sir Gy of Burgoyne, 'Yitt or I goo,   *but before*
      The sowdane sall have a stroke or twoo
          That glade sall hym no glee.'
485 He ferkes owte with a fawchon   *lashes, falchion*
      And hittis the sowdane one the crownn
          Unto the girdyll welle nee.
      Thay tuke the grete lordes with ire   *angrily*
      And brynte tham in that bale fire,   *blazing*
490   Those doughty garte they dye.   *made*
      (Bot sythen the Sarazenes crouned sir Garsy,
      Tha[t] ofte sythes chaste oure chevalry;   *defeated*
          A bolde Sarazene was he).

      Alle that was than in that place
495 Thay slewe clenly thorow Goddis grace,   *entirely*
          Oure worthy men and wyghte,   *powerful*
      And sythen owte at the yates they yede;   *went*
      Ilkone of tham fande a whitte stede,   *each one*
          Sadilt and redy dighte.   *prepared*
500 Thay stirtt up on those stedis full steryn,   *mounted*
      Thay fande no man that tham wolde warne,   *hinder*
          Oure ferse men felle in fighte.   *cruel*
      And als the cronekill yitt will saye,   *still testifies*
      Even to Fraunce thay tuke the waye: *straight*
505   To Paresche thay ryde full righte.   *direct*

471–2 It struck as violently as lightning into the eyes of the Saracens. *478*
let us together hurry away from this place. *484* Which will not give him
any pleasure. *486–7* And splits the sultan from his head very nearly to his
waist. *492* That: Thay M. *504* Even: Eeven M.

Bot yitt thay wolde noghte come att Paresche
To thay had offerde to seyne Denys,
    And wendis to that abbaye;   *go*
And leves thaire stedis righte at the yate
510 And wightly in thay tuke the gate,   *without delay*
    Thaire prayers forto say.
And by thay hade thayre prayers made   *when*
Agayne thay come withowtten bade: *delay*
    Thaire horse than were away.
515 And alle the bellis that in that abbaye was
Range allone thorowe Goddis grace,   *on their own*
    Whils it was pryme of the day.

And thereby wiste those lordis of pryce
That the myghte of God and seynt Denys
520   Had broghte tham thethyn away;   *rescued*
Thaire horse that so there come to handes
Was thorowe the prayere of seynt Denys,
    Thus will the cronecle say.
Bischope Turpyne than come fro Paresche townn
525 To seynt Denys with grete processiownn,   *pomp*
    For thiese lordes forto pray
That was in Lumbardy at the were,
And when he sawe Rowlande there,
    He saide, 'Lordis, morne we may.'   *lament*

530 Thay mervelde why the bellis so range,   *marvelled*
And the clergy lefte theire sange;   *singing (mass)*
    Thoghte ferly of that fare.
Thay hade mervelle whate it myghte mene,
Als sone als the byschoppe hade Rowlande sene
535   To hym he went full yare.   *promptly*
Sayd, 'A! Rowlande, how fares Lumbardye
And all oure nobill chevallry,
    That thou hade with the thare?'
'Certis, sir bischoppe, it is noghte to layne,   *hide*
540 The Sarazenes hase oure gude men slayne,
    Thou seese of tham namare.'

---

506 But nevertheless they would not enter Paris. *517* Until it was the first
hour of the day (between 6 a.m. and 9 a.m.). *518* And those noble lords
realized from that. *532* That happening seemed strange to them. *541* You
will never see them again.

   The bischop keste his staffe hym fro,   *crozier*
   The myter of his hede also:
     'I sall never were the more,
545 Ne other habite forto bere,   *(ecclesiastical) robes*
   Bot buske me bremly to the were,
     And lerene one slyke a lore.
   A! Mary mylde, whare was thi myght,
   That thou lete thi men thus to dede be dighte,   *to be killed*
550   That wighte and worthy were?   *valiant, deserving*
   Art thou noghte halden of myghtis moste,
   Full conceyvede of the Holy Goste?   *entirely*
     Me ferlys of thy fare.

   Had thou noghte, Marye, yitt bene borne,
555 Ne had noghte oure gud men thus bene lorne: *destroyed*
     The wyte is all in the.   *blame*
   Thay faughte holly in thy ryghte,
   That thus with dole to dede es dyghte,
     A! Marie, how may this bee?'
560 The bischoppe was so woo that stownnd,   *time*
   He wolde noghte byde appon the grownnd   *wait*
     A sakerynge forto see,   *consecration*
   Bot forthe he wente, his handis he wrange,
   And flote with Marye ever amange,
565   For the losse of oure menyee.   *army*

   Then come kynge Charls appon pilgremage
   Fro Paresche town with his baronage;
     To seynt Denys he went.
   Bot when the bischoppe mett with the kynge
570 He wolde noghte say gud mornynge,
     Ne ones his browes blenke.   *raise*
   The kynge hade mervelle what that myght be,
   Bot als sone als he Rowlande see,
     Wyghtly to hym he went.   *at once*
575 Be Rowlande had his tale tolde
   The kynge myghte noghte a tere holde,   *keep back*
     For bale hym thoght he brynt.

---

546 But fiercely get myself ready for battle. *547* And become expert in such skills. *551* esteemed the most powerful of all beings. *553* Your behaviour astonishes me. *557* only to uphold your cause. *558* Who have been thus wretchedly slain. *564* And went on railing against Mary. *577* It seemed to him that he was consumed with anguish.

    'Allas,' he saide, 'cosyn [f]yne,   *noble*
    Whare are alle the nobill knyghtis of myne,
580   That ever to fighte were fayne?'   *eager*
    'Sir, bi God and by sayne John,
    The Sarazenes alle bot us hase slone,
       It is no bote to layne.
    Bot we were taken into holde,   *prison*
585 Bot als that Criste hymselfe wolde,
       That we wan owte agayne.   *escaped*
    Thorowe the grace of God omnipotent,
    In his chambir or we went   *before*
       The sowdane have we slayne.'

590 Genyonn saide, 'Lorde by my rede,
    All if the sowdane thus be dede,   *even ̗i*
       Thay will have another newe;
    A more schrewe than was the tother,   *greater villain*
    Garcy that is his awenn brothir,
595   That more barett will brewe.
    These landes of hym I rede ye halde,
    Or he will kindill cares full calde:
       Yhe trowe this tale for trewe.   *may accept*
    Or ells within thies monethes three
600 Als qwhitte of Fraunce sall yhe bee,   *deprived*
       Als yhe it never ne knewe.'

    'Now Cristis malyson,' quod the bischoppe, 'myghte he have *curse*
    That Charls firste this concell gaffe,
       And noghte bot it be righte.
605 To make homage to a Sarazene—
    Jesus kepe us fro that pyne,   *sin*
       And Marie his modir bryghte!
    Bot at home, sir kynge, thou sall keep nanne,
    Bot alle thy gud men with the tane,   *take*
610   That worthy are and wighte,
    Appon yone cursede Sarazenes forto were *make war*
    And venge the one tham with dynt of spere,
       That thus thi peris hase dyghte.

---

578 fyne: syne M. *583* It is no use hiding the fact. *595* Who will bring about greater strife. *596* I advise you to rule as his vassal. *597* bring about bitter sorrow. *604* It would be no more than just. *613* Who have treated your barons in this way.

And alle the clergy undirtake I,
615 Off alle Fraunce full sekerly,
   Thay sall wende to that were.
Of the pope I have pousté   *authority*
Att my byddynge sall thay bee,   *under, command*
   Bothe with schelde and spere.'
620 The bischoppe sendis ferre and nere   *to all parts*
To monke, chanoun, preste and frere,
   And badd tham graythe thaire gere,
And keste thaire [care] clene tham froo:
'Come helpe to feghte one Goddis foo,   *against*
625   Alle that a swerde may bere.'

The clergy grauntes alle therto,
Als doghety men of dede solde do,   *action*
   That worthy were and wyghte.
Be comen was wekes three,
630 Thare semblede a ful faire menyhé,   *assembled, army*
   In baneres burneschid bryghte.   *adorned*
A hundrethe thowsande were redy bownn
Of prestis that werede schaven crownn,   *were tonsured*
   And fresche men forto fighte.   *eager*
635 Thay lightede appon a lawnde so clere
Undir the mownte Mowmartere: *Montmartre*
   It was a ful faire syghte.

With that the bischoppe Turpyn come,
And also a cardynall of Rome,
640   With a full grete powere;
Thay semblede appon another syde,
Baners bett with mekill pryde,   *adorned, elaborately*
   The clergy that was so clere.   *virtuous*
And appon thaire knees thay knelide down;
645 The bischoppe gafe tham his benyson,   *blessing*
   Alle hollyly in fere.
And thane sent he in to the kynge
And badde hym forthe his barouns brynge,
   And saide, 'My prestis are here.'

614–16 And I indeed will see to it that all the churchmen in France will take part in that fighting. *622* And ordered them to get their equipment ready. *623 care:* omitted M; And wholly forget their sorrow. *626* agree to that completely. *629* By the end of three weeks. *635* dismounted in a clear open space. *646* All of them together.

650 Bot yitt this false **Genyonn**
     Conselde the kynge ay with treson
        That hymselfe solde duelle ther still:
     'And lette the bischoppe wende his waye,   *go*
     Doo at yone Sarazenes that he maye,
655   There sall he feghte his fill;
     And byde thiselfe in this citee: *remain*
     Slayne in the felde gife that thou bee   *if*
        Alle Fraunce may like it full ill.'
     And with his concelle and his fare   *way of acting*
660 Slyke concell he gaffe tham thare
        The kynge grauntis thertill.   *agrees to it*

     And forthe to the bischopp than sendis he,
     And for thynge that ever myghte bee
        He solde hym never beswyke,
665 Bot take his nobill chevalrye
     And wende forthe into Lumbardy:
        'For I will kepe my ryke.'   *stay in, kingdom*
     The bischopp saide, 'By Goddes tree,
     Or that Charls doo so with mee,
670   Full ill it sall hym lyke!
     I sall hym curse in myddis his face: *to*
     What! sall he nowe with sory grace   *gracelessly*
        Become ane eretyke?'   *heretic*

     The bischoppe leves his powere thare   *forces*
675 And into the cité gane he fare,
        And the cardenall with hym;
     And when he come byfore the kynge
     There was none other haylsynge   *salutation*
        Bot stowte wordes and grym.   *fierce*
680 He saide, 'Allas, sir Charllyone,
     That thou thus sone becomes a crayon: *coward*
        Me thynke thi body full dym!
     Alle the false councell that touches the crown
     Here gyffe I tham Goddis malyson,
685   Bothe in lyfe and lyme.   *limb*

651–2 Went on treacherously urging the king to stay where he was. *654*
Let him exert himself against the Saracens. *663–4* And (tell him that) he
must not let him down for any consideration. *682* You seem to me to be
feeble. *683* All those who have given the king evil advice.

    And Cristis malyson myghte he have   *may*
    That fyrste to the that concell gaffe,
      And here I curse the, thou kynge!   *excommunicate*
    Because thou lyffes in eresye
690 Thou ne dare noghte fyghte one Goddes enemy'—
      And a buke forthe gane he brynge;   *missal*
    And the sertayne sothe als I yow telle,
    He dyde all that to cursynge felle:
      This was no manere of lesynge.   *lie*
695 'Nowe arte thou werre than any Sarazene,   *worse*
    Goddes awenn wedirwyne;
      Of sorowe now may thou synge!   *complain*

    If Cristyndome loste bee,
    The wyte bese casten one the: *will be laid*
700   Allas, that thou was borne!
    Criste for the sufferde mare dere,   *injury*
    Sore wondede with a spere,
      And werede a crown of thorne.
    And now thou dare noghte in the felde
705 For hym luke undir thy schelde: *defend (yourself)*
      I tell thi saule forlorne.
    Men will deme aftir thi daye
    How falsely thou forsuke thi laye,   *renounced*
      And calle the kynge of skorne.'   *contemptible*

710 Bot then kyng Charls withowtten wene
    At the byschopp was so tene,   *with, angry*
      A fawchone hase he drawen;
    And the bischopp styrte than to a brande,   *rushed*
    Hent it owt of a sqwyers hande,   *snatched*
715   Both with myghte and mayne,
    And braydes owte the blade bare;   *draws, naked*
    By myghtfull God than he sware: *almighty*
      'If I wiste to be slayne,
    Charls, and thou touche mee,   *if*
720 Thou fares noghte forthir fete thre
      Or it be qwitt agayne.'   *repaid*

693 He went through the whole ritual of excommunication. *696* The adversary of God himself. *706* I consider your soul to be damned. *707* After you are dead it will be told. *720* You will not go more than.

Than grete lordes yede tham bytwene;   *separated*
The kynge comande his knyghtis kene
   The bischopp forto taa.   *seize*
725 And the bischopp said, 'Sirris, I will yow no scathe
And bi my faythe it es grete wathe   *peril*
   Bot if ye late me gaa.   *unless*
For certis I will noghte taken bee
With nane that I now here see,   *by*
730   Bot if yee firste me slaa.
And whilk of yow that touches me   *whichever*
Withowtten harme passes noghte hee'—
   Than with his horse com thay.

'Here,' he said, 'I avowe to mylde Marie   *swear*
735 And to hir sone God almyghttye,
   I sall noghte leve the soo.
For we are halden with the righte
Clerkes appon cursede men to fighte,   *clerics*
   I calle the Goddes foo.   *pronounce*
740 I sall gerre buske my batelle bownn
And halde the, Charls, within this townn: *keep prisoner*
   Withowt thou sall noghte goo.   *out of it*
Was never kynge that werede a crown
So foule rebuytede with relygyon:
745   Thou sall sone witt of woo.   *experience*

Goddes byddynge hase thou broken;   *commandment*
Thurghe the traytour speche spoken,   *treacherous*
   Alle Cristendom walde thou schende.   *bring to ruin*
When Criste sent the a suerde untill   *to*
750 Thou myghte wele wiete it was his will   *know*
   That thiselfe solde thedir wende;
Therefore I sall stroye the,   *destroy*
Bryne and breke downn thi cité,
   If thou be never so ten[d]e.
755 Then to yone Sarazenes wende sall I,
Fighte with tham whils I may dry,
   In Goddes servyce to ende.'   *die*

---

725 I have no wish to hurt you. *732* He will not escape without injury.
737 Because our cause is just. *740* I shall have my troops got ready.
744 So shamefully cast out by the church. *754 tende: tene* M; However
angry you may be. *756* as long as I may endure.

	The bischopp and the cardynere	*cardinal*
	Appon thaire horses gatt both in fere,	*together*
760	Owte of the townn thay rade;	
	Also faste als thay myghte dryve	*push on*
	To the grete batelle belyfe,	*quickly*
	And buskede baners full brade.	*set up*
	They romede towarde Paresche town	*made their way*
765	And thoghte to bete the cyté downe	
	With the powere that he hade.	
	(Slyke clerkes beris my benysone,	
	For trewere men of relygyonn	*the church*
	In erthe were never none made).	

	Charls over the walles bihelde	
770	And sawe the hoste come in the felde	*army*
	And drawe towardes the town.	*move*
	Bot than said duke Naymes unto the kynge:	
	'Sir, yonder comes us new tythynges	
775	With baners buskede alle bown.	
	I rede ye praye yone clergy sesse	*stop*
	And aske the bischopp forgyfnesse	
	And absolucioun.	
	And graunt hym graythely forto goo	
780	Forto feghte appon Goddis foo,	
	Or loste es thi renownn.'	*reputation*

	'In faithe,' saide the kynge, 'I graunt:	*agree*
	The bischopp es gude and evynhaunt,	*honourable*
	With baners bryghte of hewe.'	
785	Before tham a furlange and mare,	
	The kynge undid his hede alle bare:	*uncovered*
	The bischopp wele hym knewe;	*recognized*
	And appon his knees he knelid down	
	And tuke his absolucyoun:	*accepted*
790	Theire joye bygane to newe.	

The kynge says, 'Haly fader free,
This gilte I pray the forgyffe me   *sin*
  And I will wirke your will;
And with your clergye tournes agayne,   *return*
795 Riste and ryott yow by the water of Sayne,   *Seine*
  Aywhills I come yow till.'   *until, to*
The bischoppe grauntis hym in that tyde,
And pyghte pavylyons with mekill pryde,
  With wyne and welthes at will.
800 The kynge into the citee went
And aftir his baronage he sent,   *for, barons*
  Alle forwardes to fulfill.   *agreements, keep*

And by the thre wekes comen were
Charls had semblede a faire powere,
805   Hymselfe come all at hande.
Erles, dukes and the twelve duchepers,   *(douʒe) peers*
Bothe barouns and bachelers,   *young knights*
  Knyghtis full hevenhande.   *noble*
Thay offerde alle at seynt Denys,
810 And grete lordes to armes chesse,
  And Charls tuke his brande;
And thus romewes that grete powere: *moves off*
The levenynge [of thair] baners clere   *shining, bright*
  Lyghtenes all that lande.

815 Thus Charls with his chevalrye
Unto he come at Lumbardy
  In no place wolde he hone.   *stay*
And to the Sarazenes was it tolde
That Charls make werre appon tham wolde
820   To venge that are was done.   *formerly*
The grete lordes than togedir spake:
'It is better that we sir Garcy take
  And crownn hym the sowdane sonne.'
Than sent thay to many an hethyn knyghte,
825 Thay badde that alle solde come that myghte,
  By the heghten day at nonne.   *eighth, ninth hour*

---

793 do what you want me to. *795* Take your rest and recreation. *798* And set up magnificent tents. *799* With abundance of wine and other good things. *805* They all put themselves at his disposal. *810* went to arm. *813 of thair:* not now visible. *814* followed by: *Passus a ffitt.*

When thay were semblede, sekerly,   *truly*
Thay crownnede the sowdane sir Garcy,
   That solauce was to see[ne].
830 Sexty knyghtis of dyverse lande
Ilkon sent hym sere presande,   *various gifts*
   To witt withowtten wene.
Thay dressede on hym a dyademe,   *set*
And made hym emperour so hym seme,
835   Those knyghtis that were kene.
Syne present hym with golde,   *and then*
And stones of vertu that was holde,   *true*
   The beste in erthe myghte bene.

The kynge of Massedoyne lande
840 Sent the sowdane a presande,
   The meryeste one molde:
Sexty maydyns faire of face,
That cheffeste of his kyngdome was,   *most important*
   And faireste appon folde;   *earth*
845 Sexty fawcouns faire of flyghte,
And sexti stedis noble and wyghte,
   In everilke journay bolde,
And appon ilke a stede a knyghte sittande   *sitting*
With a fawcon appon his hande,
850   And a cowpe full of golde.

Sexty grewhondes unto the gamen   *for, sport*
And sexti raches rynnande in samen,
   The beste in erthe myghte bee.
He come hymselfe with this presande
855 And broghte in his awenn hande,
   That was worthe theise three:
In visebill a full riche stone,   *?*
A safre the beste that myghte be one,   *sapphire*
   To seke alle Crystiantee.   *throughout all*
860 The sowdane was full fayne of this
And kyndely gan his cosyn kysse   *lovingly*
   With mekill solempnytee.   *ceremony*

829 It was a delightful spectacle. *829 seene: see* M. *834* as might be fitting
for him. *841* The most delightful on earth. *847* every day's fighting. *852*
hunting dogs running as a pack.

When he his powere semblede hade,
A ryalle feste the sowdan made
865　Of worthy men in wede.
Of alle the damesels bryghte and schene,   *beautiful*
The sowdane hade hymselfe, I wene,
　　Thaire althere maydynhede;
By tham ilkone he laye a nyghte,
870 And sythen mariede hir unto a knyghte:
　　Thay leffed one haythen lede.
So mekill luste of lechery
Was amange that chevalry
　　That thay [mygh]te noghte wele spede.

875 To Charls now will I torne agayne   *return*
That passes over mountayne and playne,   *crosses*
　　At [Me]layne wolde he bee;
And when he come into that stede   *place*
Where als the Cristyn men byfore weren dede,   *killed*
880　Off Fraunce so grete plentee,   *numbers*
There heghe appon an hill appon highte
Turpyn garte an awtre dyghte,
　　That alle the folke myghte see;
And off the Trynytee a messe he says,
885 And hertly for the saules he prayes,   *devoutly*
　　And the bodyes that thare gan dye.

The bischopp sone gane hym revesche   *put on robes*
In gude entent he says a messe,   *devoutly, mass*
　　In the name of God almyghte:
890 He blyssede the awtere with his hande,
And a fayre oste of brede therappon he fande,
　　That ever he sawe with syghte.
His chalesse was so full of wyne   *chalice*
There myghte no more hafe gone therin,
895　It come fro heven on highte.   *high*
He dide his messe forthe to the ende   *celebrated*
And thankede Gode that it hym sende,
　　And Marie his modir bryghte.

867–8 I believe that the sultan himself took the virginity of every one of them. *871* They lived according to the heathen religion. *874* could never prosper. *874* and *877* [ ] not now visible. *882* Turpin had them set up an altar. *891–2* And found on it as fine consecrated bread as he had ever seen.

     The bischopp in his hert was fayne
900 And thankede God with all his mayne,
       And Marie his modir free.
     He tolde the hoste with lowde steven
     How brede and wyne was sent fro heven,
       Fro God of moste poustee:
905 'And all that ever hase sene this syghte,
     Yee are als clene of syn, I plyghte,
       Als that day borne were yee.
     And whoso endys in this felde
     In His byggynge sall he belde   *mansion, live*
910   Ever more in blysse to bee.'

     The bischopp than keste of his abytte   *robes*
     And aftir armours he askede tytte;   *for, quickly*
       For egernesse he loughe.
     A kirtill and a corsett fyne,   *body armour*
915 Therover he keste an acton syne,   *padded jacket*
       And it to hym he droughe;   *pulled*
     An hawbarke with a gesserante,
     His gloves weren gude and avenaunte;   *handsome*
       And als blythe als birde one boughe,   *happy*
920 He tuke his helme and sythen his brande,
     Appon a stede a spere in hande,
       Was grete and gud ynoghe.   *sufficiently*

     Sayse: 'I praye yow, all my cleregy here,
     Assembles undire my banere,
925   The vawarde will I have.   *vanguard*
     Charls and his knyghtis kene,
     Lete erles and barouns with hym bene,
       Bothe sqwyers and knave;
     I beseke [the] freschely forto fyghte,
930 That th[e le]wede [me]n may se with syghte   *the laity*
       And gud ensample have.
     Standi[s now baldly f]or youre trouthe;   *faith*
     Appon [yone Sarazen]es haves no rewthe: *pity*
       For golde in erthe, none save.'

905–6 And I swear that all of you who have witnessed this miracle are made
as free from sin. *913* He laughed ferociously. *917* A mail shirt and coat
of (scale) armour. *929 the:* omitted M. *930–3* [ ] not now visible.

935 Thus C[harls lede]th a faire menyhé   *company*
    Bifo[re Mela]yne, that riche cité,
      Braydes up baners yare.   *raises, ready*
    And when the sowdane hase tham sene,
    He comandes his knyghtis kene,
940   That thay solde make tham yare;
    And or he wolde passe owte of the townn,
    He made his offerande to Mahownn,
      The wars, leve Gode, thay fare.
    And sythen owt of that citee,
945 Off heythen men an hugge menyhee,
      That semyde als breme als bare.

    Sir Arabaunt, with ire and hete,   *rage*
    A furlange bifore the batelle grete,   *main army*
      Come and askede fighte;
950 And byfore oure folke had he slayne
      Bothe the lorde of Melayne
      And many another knyght.
    Than sayde the bischopp, 'So mot I spede,
    He sall noghte ruysse hym of this dede,   *boast about*
955   If I cane rede aryghte!'
    And or any knyght myght gete his gere
    The bischopp gart hym with a spere   *struck*
      Appon his tepet lighte.

    Turpyn strake hym so sekerly   *surely*
960 Thurgh the breste bone all plenerly,   *completely*
      A lange yerde and more,
    That dede he daschede to the grounde,   *fell violently*
    Grysely gronannde in that stownde,   *fearfully*
      Woundede wonderly sore.
965 The bischopp than lighte full apertly   *dismounted, boldly*
    And off he hewes his hede in hy,
      That are was breme als bare.
    His horse unto the Cristen oste gan spede;
    A sqwyere broghte agayne his stede,
970   And one he leppe righte thare.   *jumped*

935–6 [ ] not now visible. *943* May God grant that they have less success because of that. *946* Who looked as fierce as wild boars. *950 oure: of oure* M. *955* If I am a true prophet. *958* Upon his shining neck-armour. *961* The length of more than a yard. *966–7* And quickly cuts off the head of the man who before that.

    The bischopp sqwyere in the place   *there*
    Saw that the kynge dede was
        That had bene of grete powere;
    His helme and his hawberke holde,   *reliable*
975 Frette overe with rede golde,   *adorned*
        With stones of vertue dere;   *precious qualities*
    His gowere pendande on the grounde, *jewelled (?) pendant*
    It was worthe a thowsande pownde,
        Off rubys and safere:
980 He lowttede down, up wolde itt ta,   *bent, pick up*
    The bischopp bad hym fro it ga: *ordered*
        'Go fonnge the another fere.

    To wyn the golde thou arte a fole,   *take*
    Thou bygynnes sone forto spoyle:
985   Loo, yonder comes moo!
    Thou settis more by a littill golde,
    That thou seese lye appon the molde,
        Than to fighte one Goddes foo.
    Loo, yonder comes Sarazenes in the felde,
990 Go kill tham down under thi schelde,
        Slyk [w]orchippes were gude to do.' *honourable deeds*
    He tuke the pendande in his hande;
    The bishopp bett hym with his brande,
        [That] he keste it hym fro.

995 With that come girdande sir Darnadowse, *charging*
    A nobill knyghte and a chevallrouse,
        Prekande one a stede.
    He was the chefe of Famagose,   *lord*
    A Sarazene that fayne wolde wyn lose, *renown*
1000   And to the Cristen oste gan spede.
    He bad sende owte Charlyon:
    'If he dare come to wynn pardonn,
        A bofett forto bede.'   *blow, strike*
    He wolde noghte fighte bot with a kynge:
1005 He calde hymselfe, withowt lesynge,
        The chefe of hethyn thede.   *nation*

---

982 Go and find yourself another adversary. *984* You are quick to start
looting. *986* value more highly. *991* and *994* [ ] not now visible. *997*
Urging on his horse. *1001* He commanded that Charles should be sent out
(against him).

Then kyng Charls tuke his spere hym to; *hold of*
The bischopp Turpyn and other mo *many others*
 Prayede God solde hym spede. *give success*
1010 'A, dere lorde,' said Rowlande in heghe, *at once*
 'Late me fare to fighte for thee,
  For hym that one rode gan blede.'
 Than Charls sweris by saynt Paule:
 'Sen ilke a man feghtis for his saule,
1015 I sall for myn do mede.
 Slayne in the felde gif that I bee
 Kynge off Fraunce here make I the,
  With reghte the reme to lede.'

 Than withowtten any more habade *delay*
1020 Theis two kynges togedir rade,
  With ire and grete envy. *malice*
 And at the firste course that thay ranne
 Thies kynges two with horse and manne
  At the grounde bothe gun ly.
1025 Delyverly up sone bothe thay stirtt, *nimbly, jumped*
 And drewe thaire swerdis with noble hertt, *valiantly*
  Withowtten noyse or cry.
 Thay dalt so derfely with thaire brandes, *struck, boldly*
 Thay hewe theire scheldis to thaire handis
1030 In cantells hyngand by.

 So darfely bothe thaire dynttis thay driste, *struck*
 A littill while thay wolde tham riste,
  The Sarazene prayede hym styntt: *stop*
 'Nowe certis, sir,' he saide, 'me rewes of thee, *I am sorry*
1035 A Cristynn man that thou solde bee:
  Thou arte so stronge of dyntt.
 Bot torne unto oure lawes and take tham to,
 And I sall gyffe the rewmes two, *kingdoms*
  And elles will thou harmes hentt.'
1040 Bot the bischoppe Turpyn than cryes on heghte:
 'A, Charles, thynk appon Marie brighte,
  To whayme oure lufe es lentt. *on whom, set*

1014–15 Since every man is fighting for his salvation, I will profit my own soul (by doing the same). *1018* To rule the kingdom justly. *1024* Both of them fell to the ground. *1029–30* They hacked so at their shields that they hung in pieces from their hands. *1037* But be converted and accept our religion. *1039* Otherwise you will be destroyed.

And if ever that thou hade any myghte,
Latt it nowe be sene in syghte   *clearly seen*
1045   What pousté that thou hase.
Latte never oure kynge with dynt of brande
B[e] slayne with yone Sarazene hande,
      Ne ende, Lady, in this place.
A [.....] wote we sall be safe
1050 [......]y the l[...] wolde we hafe
Of oure comly kynge of face.
B[......]kere bathe of son and see,
[.........]he dole w[e d]ree for thee,   *misery, endure*
      And graunte us of thi grace!'

1055 [..........] saide, 'Sir b[is]chopp, nay,
[...........] forsake my lay'—
      And togedir gan thay goo.   *charge*
So stiffely aythere at othere strake,   *each*
Appon his helme sir Charles brake
1060   His nobill swerde in two.
Bot than the Franche folke with nobill stevenn   *outcry*
Thay cry up unto the kynge of hevenn,
      And for thaire lorde were wo.
The Sarazene was curtays in that fighte   *chivalrous*
1065 And lawses owt a knyfe full righte,   *draws*
      His swerde he keste hym fro.

And Charles voydede his broken brande;   *threw away*
Owte he hent a knyfe in hande,   *drew*
And samen thay wente full tytte.
1070 Thay daschede full darfely with thaire dynt;   *struck*
Mighte no steryn stele tham stynt,   *hard, withstand*
      So styffely bothe thay smyte.   *powerfully*
In sondre braste thay many a mayle,   *broke open*
Thaire hawberghes thurgh force gan fayle:
1075   To see had lordis delitte.   *joy*
Bot a felle stroke sir Charls gafe hym one   *fierce*
Evyn at the breste bone: *just*
      That strake his hert gan blende.   *trouble (?)*

1047–56 [ ] not now visible.   *1069* And they charged together vigorously..
1074 Their mail-shirts gave way under the force (of their blows).

    The Sarazene was dede of that strake,   *blow*
1080 And Charls gan this fende up take
     And with his awenn brande   *own*
    He broches hym so boldely   *stabs*
    That his hert blode, sekerly,
     Rane to oure kynges hande.
1085 And thare he wane the Sarazene swerde,   *acquired*
    And certis that with one this erthe
     He conquered many a lande.
    The Cristen folke were never so fayne;
    Bot by the kynge was horsede agayne,
1090   The batells were doande.

    And hawberkes sone in schredis were schorne,
    And beryns thorowe the bodys borne,   *pierced*
     And many a Sarazene slayne.
    Knyghtis one the bent bledis;   *battlefield*
1095 Many lay stekede undir stedis,   *stabbed*
     In gilten gere full gay[n]e.   *armour, excellent*
    Other with glafes were girde thurgh evyn:
    We may thanke Gode that is in heven,
     That lent us myghte and mayne.   *gave*
1100 Thay sloughe tham downn with swerdis bright; *struck (dead)*
    The Cristynnd faughte in Goddis righte,
     The bischopp loughe for fayne.   *joy*

    Bot als the cronakill yitt will telle
    Ther come a Sarazene fers and felle,
1105   And to the bischoppe glade.   *came up*
    And stroke hym righte thorowe the thee,   *thigh*
    And agayne to the hethen oste gane flee,
     And Turpyn after hym rade.
    The bischoppe folouede hym so ferre
1110 That the Sarazene hade the werre   *worst (of it)*
     For the maystrie that he [made].
    He stroke hym so in the sowdane syghte,
    He fande never man that after myghte
     Hele the hurt [he hade].   *wound*

1080 raised up this (diabolical) enemy. *1089–90* But by the time the king
had remounted, the main fighting had started again. *1091* were soon hacked
to pieces. *1096 gayne: gaye* M. *1097* Others were pierced right through
with swords. *1111* For the feat that he had performed. *1111* and *1114* [ ]
not now visible.

1115 Bot they helde in the bischoppe in that rowtte   *throng*
    That he ne myghte noghte wyn owte,   *get away*
      And th[. .]he[. . . . .]
    The kynge of Massedoyne land with a spere
    The bischop fro his horse gane bere,   *knock*
1120   And s[. . . . .]
    The Sarazenes sware he solde be dede,
    And the kynge sayde naye in that stede,   *no*
      For no Sarazene liffande.   *alive*
    And righte als thay solde oure bischopp slo,
1125 Thay smote the kynge of Massaydoyne fro,   *cut off*
      Clenly of his reghte hande.

    Bot th[e] kynges men of Massaydoyne weren wo,
    When thay saughe thaire lorde was wondede soo,
      And trowede he walde be dede.
1130 Thay braydede owte swerdes full bryghte   *drew*
    Agaynes the sowdane folke to fighte,
      Full styffely in that stede;
    For that gane fyfetene thowsandez dy,
    Of the sowdans chevalry:
1135   Laye bledande than full rede.   *bleeding*
    And with that Turpyn gatt awaye
    To Charls oste—full fayne were thay;
      A horse thay to hym lede.

    Bot when the bischoppe was horsede agayne,
1140 Alle the cleregy weren full fayne
      And presede into the place.
    So depe wondes that day thay dalt
    That many on wyde opyn walt,
      That wikkidly wondede was.
1145 Thay sloughe so many an heythen kynge   *killed*
    That at the laste thay tuke to flyinge,   *flight*
      Als God us gaffe the grace.
    Many a Sarazene garte thay falle,   *made*
    And Turpyn with his clergy alle
1150   Folowede faste one the chase.

1117 and *1120* [ ] not now visible.   *1127 the: than* M.   *1129* And were certain that he must die.   *1141* And charged as a body there.   *1143–4* That many terrible wounds split open.

And Charls on the tother syde
Sloughe tham downn with wondis wyde:
The doughty garte tha[m] dy.   *valiant (king)*
The sowdane hymselfe so harde was stedde   *pressed*
1155 That with ten thowsande away he fledde,
And faste to Melayne gatt he.
The Cristen men chasede tham to the barres,   *ramparts*
And sloughe righte there fele folke and fresche,
All that there walde byde and bee.   *remain*
1160 Bot than kynge Charls tuke the playne   *field*
And semblede all his folke agayne,
To luke how beste myghte [the]   *see, prosper*

Thay myghte noghte the cité wynn,   *take*
The strenghe of the Sarazenes that were within;
1165   The bischoppe said, 'I rede: *say*
Of oure knyghtes in the felde
Es many woundede under schelde,
And also some are dede;
And yone Sarazenes full of tresone es,
1170 There I concelle bothe more and lesse
We stirre noghte of this stede,   *move, from*
Ne or to-morne serche never a wounde,
Bot luke than who may be sownde;
Lete Criste wirke'—and forthe he yede.

1175 Here to a[c.]ordes everilkon,   *agrees*
Lordes [h]af thaire horses tone,
And comen es the nyghte.
Fo[......]f the Sarazenes there,
Th[.......]ste no forthir fare,
1180   Bot bydis in brenys bryghte.
Ch[..........] als thay rade,
Al[..........]e the bent thay bade,
With standardes even up streghte.   *upright*
The kynge prayede the bischoppe fre
1185 His wonde that he wolde late hym see,
That he hade tane in that fighte.   *received*

1153 tham: thay M.   *1162 the:* omitted M.   *1162* Because of the strength
of its Saracen garrison.   *1172–4* Do not attend to any of the wounded before
morning; then see who is uninjured, and leave everything to Christ.   *1175–82*
[ ] not now visible.

Bot the bischoppe saide, 'A vowe to God make I here,
There sall no salve my wonde come nere,   *ointment*
   Ne no hose of my thee,
1190 Ne mete ne drynke my hede come in,
The cité of Melayne or we it wyn,
   Or ells therfore to dye.'
He garte dele his vetells then,   *divide, provisions*
Furthe amanges oure wonded men,
1195   Bot no mete neghe wolde hee.   *food, touch*
Bot als so sore wondede als he was,
Knelande he his prayers mase   *says*
   To Gode of most pousté.

Oure folke hade done so doughtily
1200 That many of tham weren ful wery,
   So hade thay foghten than.
Bot one the morne the Cristen stode
A thowsande over theire fete in theire blode,
   Of theire awenn wondes wanne.   *livid*
1205 Othere refreschynge noghte many hade
Bot blody water of a slade,   *(steep) valley*
   That thurghe the oste ran.   *encampment*
The sowdanne sent a messangere
To kynge Charles als ye may here,
1210   And that sawe many a man.

The messangere bare a wande   *branch*
Of ane olefe in his hande,
   In takynnynge he come of pece;   *as a sign*
And lowde he cryede appon Charls the kynge,   *to*
1215 And saide he myghte his handis wrynge,
   'Appon lyfe if that he es,
For oure sowdane hase by Mahownn sworne
That he salle mete hym here to-morne,
   With full prowde men in prese;   *battle*
1220 With fowrty thowsande of helmes bryghte,
Was never yitt frekkere men to fighte   *bolder*
   Sene in hethynnesse.'

1189 Nor my hose be drawn from my leg. *1205* Many of them had nothing
else to revive them. *1215* he had (good) reason to lament. *1216* If he is
still alive.

And Charles ansuerde at that tide:
  'In faythe I sall tham here habyde, *wait for*
1225   Wode giffe that thay were. *mad, if*
  If that he brynge alle the Sarazenes
  That es alle heythynnesse within,
    Hyne will I noghte fare.'
  The messangere agayne than rade,
1230 And thay sett wache and still habade *did not move*
    Whills pryme was passede and mare. *until*
  Bot or the nonnee neghede nee, *drew near*
  To tham than soughte a felle semblé
    With baners breme als bare.

1235 Bot than sir Charles spekes full gudely *fairly*
  To Rowlande his nevewe that stode hym by,
    And seid, 'Sir, so God the spede,
  This day wirke thou manfully *conduct yourself*
  With thi nobill chevalry,
1240   And of the Sarazens hafe [thou no dre]de. *fear*
  Thou sall see that I sall noghte be sparede,
  Myselfe sall have the vawarde,
    There Jesu [Crist the sp]ede.'
  The trumpetes trynes one righte than;
1245 To joyne so jolyly thay bygane, *encounter, boldly*
    Oure worthy men in wede. *armour*

  Thay ruysschede samen with swilke a rake
  That many a Sarazene laye one his bake,
    And one the lawnde righte ther thay lay; *grass*
1250 Full grisely gronande one the grete, *gravel*
  Stekyde undir stedis fete,
    And liste nothynge of playe.
  So darfely than thay dynge tham downn,
  Thay saide the myghte of saynt Mahownn *power*
1255   Was clenely all awaye.
  'A, Mountjoye!' oure lordes gane crye,
  And Charles with his chevalrye
    Full freschely faughte that day.

1228 I will not move from here. *1233* A fearful army moved against them.
1237 As you hope God to give you success. *1240* and *1243* [ ] not now
visible. *1244* At that the trumpeters strike up. *1247* They charged together at such speed. *1252* And were not inclined to jest. *1255* Had
completely vanished.

They hewe of hethen hedis in hye;
1260 Oure Cristen men so sekirly,   *positively*
    Of tham hade littill drede,
Bot brittenesse tham with brandis bare   *massacre, swords*
And Sarazenes thurghe the schuldirs schare   *cut*
    That to the girdill it yode.   *waist*
1265 Thay tuke none hede of gudes nore golde,
    (Lay never so mekill appon the molde)
      Oure worthy men in wede;   *armour*
Bot beris abake the batells brade:
Fowrty thowsande in a slade,
1270   Laye stekede under stede.

And so harde bystade was the sowdane,
Hymselfe with ten thowsande than
    To Melayne tuke the gate.
Oure Cristen knyghtis with thaire speres
1275 The hyndirmaste fro thaire blonkes beres,
    And chacede tham to the yate.
The owte barres hew thay downn,
And slewe hethynn kynges with crownn,
    And thaire powere therate.   *there*
1280 To sawtte the cité sadly thay bygann,   *attack, vigorously*
Off Cristyn men many a cruelle man:
    The hethyn wex all mate.   *were confounded*

With speris and with spryngaldes faste,   *missiles*
With dartis kenely owte thay caste,   *fiercely*
1285   Bothe with myghte and mayne.
With gownnes and with grete stones: *engines (of war)*
Graythe gounnes stoppede those go[m]es
    With peletes, us to payne.   *missiles, harm*
Oure Cristyn men that were of price   *excellent*
1290 Bendis up bowes of devyce,
    And bekirs tham agayne.
Appon bothe the sydis so freschely thay fighte   *vigorously*
That by it drewe unto the nyghte
    Fele folke of Fraunce were slayne.

1265–6 However much equipment or gold was lying about, they paid no attention to it.   *1268* But force the great divisions back.   *1275* knock the stragglers off their horses.   *1287 gomes: gones* M; Men loaded the engines which were ready (to fire).   *1290–1* Get ready their ballistas and return their fire.   *1293* by the time that it began to grow dark.

1295 There were of oure clergy dede
And other lordes in that stede,
   Or thay of sawte walde sesse.   *desist from*
By than thay sawe it was no bote to byde,
And fro the cité warde thay ryde,   *away from*
1300   Oure prynces provede in presse.   *trusty*
The bischoppe es so woundede that tyde,
With a spere thoroweowte the syde,
   That one his ribbis gan rese.   *spring out*
Thurgh the schelde and the brow[n]e bare,
1305 A schaftemonde of his flesche he schare: *handbreadth*
   Lordynnges, this es no lese.   *sirs, lie*

He pullede it owte, keste it hym fro,
And weryde the handis that it come fro,   *cursed*
   And that it lete forthe glyde.   *hurled*
1310 The sowdane over the wallis byhelde
And sawe the Cristen in the felde,
   Frowarde the cité ride.   *away from*
And appon kynge Charls than cryes he:
 'What, Charls, thynkes now to flee?   *do you intend*
1315   I trowe th[ou] most habyde.
I sall the mete to-morne in felde
With fourty thowsand under schelde,
   Sall fonde to felle thi pryde.'   *strive, humble*

Says Charls, 'Thou false hethyn hownde,
1320 Thou ne dare noghte byde appon the grounde
   (Ther ever more worthe the woo);
Bot aythire of thies dayes ilyke   *each, alike*
Hase thou stollen awaye lyke a tyke: *hound*
   The develle myghte with the goo!
1325 That cité bot thou yelde to me   *unless, surrender*
And fully trowe and Cristyn be,
   Appon one God and no moo;   *in*
In felde yif ever I see the mare,
I sall by myghtfull God,' he sware,   *almighty*
1330   'Hewe thi bakke in twoo.'

1298 there was no point in staying. *1.304 browne: browe* M; Through the tough skin and unprotected flesh. *1.315 thou: the* M. *1.321* May you always have sorrow on that account. *1.326* And turn Christian and believe completely.

    Then of oure Cristen men in the felde
    Many semblede under schelde,   *formed up*
       And some ware wondede sare.
    Thay that were bothe hale and sownnde   *uninjured*
1335 Comforthed tham that were evyll wounde, *badly wounded*
       So als Criste wolde it were.
    The kynge than of his helme tase   *takes*
    And to the bischoppe swythe he gase,
       And sayde, 'Fadir for Goddes are,   *grace*
1340 Thy woundes that thou walde late me see;
    If any surgeoun myghte helpe thee,
       My comforthe ware the mare.'   *would be*

    'What, wenys thou, Charls,' he said, 'that I faynte bee,
    For a spere was in my thee,
1345   A[nd] glace thorowte my syde?   *shot*
    Criste for me sufferde mare;
    He askede no salve to his sare,
       Ne no more sall I this tyde.
    I sall never ette ne drynke,
1350 Ne with myn eghe slepe a wynke,
       Whate bale als ever I byde,
    To yone cité yolden bee,   *until, surrendered*
    Or ells therfore in batelle dye,   *for it*
       The sothe is noghte to hyde.'

1355 Als thay stode spekande of this thynge,
    To Charls come a newe tydynge
       That blenkede all his blee:
    Thay saide that one sir Tretigon,
    That was the sowdane syster son   *nephew*
1360   And the beste of Barbarye,
    'Certys, Charls, he comes at hande   *close by*
    With men of armes a sexty thowsande,
       To strenghe with yone cité.'   *reinforce*

. . . .
    'Now sone, when I hafe foughten my fill,
1365 I sall avise me gif that I will   *consider*
       One thi message to wende.'   *errand*

1336 Just as Christ would have wished.   *1343* Do you suppose, Charles,
that I have been made a coward.   *1345 And: A* M.   *1351* Whatever injury
I may suffer.   *1357* That made his expression change.   *1363* originally
followed by one or more leaves, now lost.

'Now sir Bawdwyne, buske and make the bownn.'   *get ready*
He saide, 'Allas, thou Charelyoun,
   That ever I tuke thi fee!
1370 For yitt myselfe es saffe and sownnde,
My body hole withowttyn wounde,
   Als thou thiselfe may see;
I walde noghte, for all thi kyngdome,
That ever that worde unto France come
1375   I solde so feyntly flee   *like a coward*
Gett the a currour whare thou may,   *messenger*
For, by God that awe this day,
   Thou sall have none of mee.'

'A, sir Ingelere, for a knyghte thou art kyde!'   *renowned*
1380 'Whi, sir Charls, what walde thou that I dide?'
   'I pray the wende thi waye.'
'Bi Jesu Criste that sittis aboffe,
Me thynke thou kydde me littill luffe,   *showed*
   When thou that worde wolde saye.
1385 Bot me sall never betyde that taynte;
I hope thou wenys myn herte be feynte,   *believe, suppose*
   I say the schortly, naye.
That I sall never so fremdly flee,
God lett me yif it his will[e] bee,
1390   Never habyde that daye.'

The duke Berarde was wondede sare,
Thurgh the schelde into the body bare
   He was borne with a brande.   *pierced*
Of this message thay gun hym frayne,
1395 Bot he hade no worde to speke agayne,
   Bot grymly stude lukande.   *glaring*
Than Turpyn gan to Charls say,
'Here arte thou servede bi my fay,   *paid out*
   Thou fayles of that thou fande.
1400 The duke es woundede so wonder sare,
It ware grete syn to greve hym mare;   *trouble*
   Gude sir, thou late hym stande.'

1369 That ever I became your vassal. 1385 I will never be guilty of that
sin. 1387 I absolutely refuse. 1388 flee in a way so contrary to my
nature. 1389 *wille: wills* M. 1394 They asked him to go on this mission.
1399 You have failed in your attempt.

Thay prayede a banare[r] than of pryce,   *standard bearer*
One sir Barnarde of Parische,
1405   For grete gyftis he wolde wende.
And he saide, 'Lordynges by my faye,
I ame over symple to yow to saye,   *humble*
    Where ever ye will me sende.
I aske ordir of knyghte thertill,
1410 Bot giffe your giftis where ye will,
    Elles ye [ne] be my frende.'
Thay made hym knyghte with full gud chere;   *very willingly*
He tuke leve at the twelve dugepere,
    This curtayse knyghte and he[nde]

1415 He saide than, 'Have gud daye, Charls, in this stede,
For thou sall never gyffe me brede,   *provide for me*
    Ne in thy burdynge say,   *sport*
If I be pore of golde and fee,   *even though*
That I fro this grete journee
1420   Fayntly fledde away.'
He rydis even to the yatis of Melayne
And there with Sarazenes was he slayne;
    He dide full wele that day.
And Charls for hym in hert was woo,
1425 Bischoppe Turpyn and othere moo
    For his dede sore murnede thay.   *death*

Thus have thay prayede everylkone,   *implored*
Bot there wolde goo never one;
    The symple thay bade none sende.
1430 The bischoppe Turpyn cryede appon highte:
'Sen ye are so frekke forto fighte,   *eager*
    God of his myghte yow mende!
Yitt are we ten thowsande here
That are yitt bothe hole and fere,   *uninjured, sound*
1435   That wele for kene are kende.   *as, known*
And of gude men that none will flee,
To fourty thowsande or we dye,
    In the felde to make thaire ende.'

1403 banarer: banarett M.   *1407 to yow to saye* for **to saye yow naye?*
1409 On condition that I be made a knight.   *1411 ne:* omitted M.   *1414*
[ ] not now visible.   *1419–20* That I ran away like a coward from this great
battle today.   *1428* They did not ask that any of low rank should be sent.

    Bot als Turpyn lenys hym on his brande,   *rests*
1440 Over an hill he saw comande   *advancing*
      Ful many a brade banere;
    The duke of Bretayne, sir Lyonelle,   *Brittany*
    That Charls was thare he herde telle,
    And hade mystere of powere.   *need, reinforcements*
1445 He broghte hym thirty thowsande fyne,   *excellent men*
    Vetaylls gude and nobill engyne,
      This bolde, with full blythe chere.   *gladly*
    Than Turpyn gan to Charls say,
    'I see a felle hoste, bi my fay,
1450   That sone will neghe us nere.   *come close to*

    Yone are the Sarazenes mekill of mayne,
    The full powere owt of Spayne,
      That sone sall full ill spede.
    For by hym that swelt on tree,   *died*
1455 This day no Sarazene sall I see
      Sall gerre me torne my stede.'   *make*
    And in his hande he caughte a launce: *seized*
    'Have gud day, Charls, and grete wele Fraunce'—
    And agayne that hoste he yede.
1460 In fewter sone he keste his spere
    And thoghte the boldeste down to bere
      That batelle walde hym bede.

    So blody was that bischoppis wede,
    His conysaunce ne yit his stede   *coat of arms*
1465   The Bretons ne couthe noghte knawe.   *recognize*
    Bot als an harawde hym byhelde   *herald*
    He lukede up into his schelde   *at*
    And sayde to alle one rawe:
    'If bischoppe Turpyn appon lyve be,
1470 In faythe, lordynges, yone es he,
      That ye se hedirwarde drawe.'
    Thay ferlyde why he fewterde his spere;
    'A, Mountejoye!' cryes one that he myghte here:
    He was glade of that sawe.   *cry*

1452 The whole of their army from Spain. *1458* and salute France (for me,
after my death). *1462* Who would offer to fight with him. *1468* as they
were all lined up. *1471* coming in this direction. *1472* They marvelled
why he should put his lance in rest.

1475 The wardayne rydis hym agayne   *commander*
     And said, 'Sir bischoppe, for Goddis payne,
         Who hase greved the?'   *angered*
     He tuke his spere owt of reste adownn
     And gaffe tham alle his benysoun,   *blessing*
1480   The Bretonns when he tham see.
     The bischoppe tolde tham of his care
     Bot than the Bretonns hertis were sare,
         For the dole oure oste gun dryee.   *distress, suffer*
     A messangere went to telle the kynge;
1485 So fayne was Charles never of thynge
         With eghe that he gan see.

     And or Turpyn myghte his tale halfe telle
     He sawe come hovande over a felle   *moving, hill*
         Many a brade banere;
1490 Standardis grete with stalworthe men,   *valiant*
     Sexti thowsande wele myghte thay ken,
         In brenyes burnescht clere.
     Under the cante of an hille   *side*
     Oure Bretonns beldis and bydis still,
1495   When thay wiste whate they were.
     The bischoppe saide, 'Bi Goddis myghte,
     Thaym sall rewe or it be nyghte,   *regret*
         The tyme that thay come here!

     Go we to yone company,
1500 With 'Mountjoye' baldly tham ascrye,
         Late ther be no lettynge.'   *holding back*
     An hawrawde said, 'To fewe are we
     To fighte with slyke a grete menyé;   *such*
         It is better wende to the kynge;
1505 A, sir, whare thay are sexti thowsande men!'
     'And if thay were mo bi thowsandis ten,
         [Bi] God that made all thynge,
     The more powere that thay be,
     The more honour wyn sall we:
1510   We dowte noghte tham to dynge.'

1492 In brightly polished shirts of mail.   1494 see to their defences and
remain behind them.   1500 tham: and tham M; Attack them boldly shouting
'Mountjoy'.   1505 See, lord, there are.   1507 Bi: omitted M.   1510 We
are not afraid to fight with them.

The bischoppe to the kyng sent
And prayes hym to byde appon the bent,   *stay in the field*
  The cité forto kepe;   *watch over*
That there no Sarazene solde come owte,
1515 To thay had rekkenede with that rowte,
  Thay sawe come overe the depe.   *from the interior*
Oure Bretonns kyndely comforthes he;   *graciously encourages*
Sayse: 'Alle the Sarazenes ye yonder see
  Thaire frendis sore may wepe: *lament*
1520 We sall wirke tham wondis full wyde;   *inflict upon*
I hete tham be thaire lemans syde,   *promise, mistresses'*
  Sowndely never sall thay slepe.'

For isschuynge owte of the cité,
Kynge Charles with his menyé
1525   Helde his batelle still.   *divisions firm*
Oure Bretons bolde that fresche come in
Thoghte that thay wolde wirchipp wyn,   *renown*
  And gatt the cante of the hill.   *won, slope*
The Sarazenes were so strange and stowte, *bold*
1530 Thay late no lede that thay wolde lowte:
  Thay were so wykkede of w[ill].   *evil, nature*
Oure Bretonns dide so doughtyly
That lange or none sekerly
  The Sarazenes lykede full ill.

1535 Samen than strake that grete stowre
Als it were aftire the none ane houre:
  It was noghte mekill[e] mare;   *time*
Bot many a Sarazene in that stownde
Lay grysely gronande on the grownde,   *terribly*
1540   Woundede wonderly sore.
Bot there God will helpe ther es no lett; *where, obstacle*
So stronge strokes thay one tham sett,   *laid*
  With burneschede bladis bare,
That fourty thowsande Sarazenes kene
1545 With brandis lay brettenyde one the grene: *massacred, grass*
  So bolde oure Bretonns were.

1515 settled accounts with that army.   *1523* So that no-one could get out
of the city.   *1530* They would not acknowledge any nation as their superior.
1531 [ ] no longer visible.   *1535* They came violently together in a great
battle.   *1537 mekille: mekills* M.

And to the cité the tother wolde have flede,
And Rowlande thoghte he wolde tham stedde,   *give help*
   Ten thowsande was with hym.
1550 And when he with the Sarazenes mett,
Full grym stokes he on tham sett,   *cruel*
   With growndyn speris and grym.   *sharp*
Charles appon the tothere syde
Sloughe tham downn with woundis wyde,
1555   And made thaire dedis full dyme.
And thus thay chase tham here and thare,
Als the howndes dose the hare,   *do*
   And refte tham lyfe and lyme.   *took from*

Rowlande rydis to Letygon,
1560 That was the sowdane sister sone,
   And stroke hym with a spere,
That dede he daschede in the felde: *crashed down*
Helme ne hawberke he myghte none welde,   *make use of*
   Ne never after none bere.
1565 Of sexti thowsande, sothely to say,
Passede never one qwyke away,
   Bot evyll thay endide there.
The Cristenyde knelide down in that place
And thankede God that gaffe tham grace,
1570   So worthily tham to were.   *nobly, defend*

The false in the felde thus gun thay felle,   *infidels*
The kynge callede sir Lyonelle,
   And avauncede hym full heghe.   *advanced, greatly*
The duke of Burgoyne bifore was dede,
1575 He sessede hym in his stede,
   And gafe hym his doughter free.
And to the bischoppe than swythe he gase,   *promptly*
That wery and sore woundede was,
   And fastande dayes three.
1580 Be that tyme he myghte note wele a worde owt-wyn,   *get out*
The teris rane over Charles' chynn,
   That sorowe it wa[s to] see:

1555 And effaced (the memory of) their prowess. 1566 Not one escaped
with his life. 1575 He invested him with the lands that had been (the duke's).
1579 had been fasting for. 1582 [ ] not now visible.

'And thou dy, than dare I saye
The floure of presthode es awaye,   *has passed*
1585   That ever hade schaven crownn.   *the tonsure*
For there ne is kynge ne cardynere
In Cristyndome may be thi pere,   *equal*
   Ne man of religiownn.   *the church*
He will no man his wondes late see,
1590 Ne mete ne drynke none neghe hym ne,
   For prayer ne for pardownn.'
Oure oste for the bischoppe mournes alle,
And graythes tham to Melayne walle,   *make their way*
   With baners buskede bownn.

1595 New vetailles the Bretons broghte than   *fresh*
That refresschede many of oure men,
   Of brede, brawne and wyne.
A nobill hurdas ther was graythede
And baners to the walles displayede,
1600   And bendis up thaire engyne.

. . . .

1589 He will not let anyone see to his wounds.   *1598* They set up an elaborate palisade there.   *1600* was originally followed by one or more leaves containing the end of the romance.

Emaré

Jesu that ys kyng in trone,
As thou shoope bothe sonne and mone,   *created*
   And all shall dele and dyghte,   *apportion, control*
Now lene us grace such dedus to done,
5 In thy blys that we may wone: *dwell*
   Men calle hyt heven lyghte;
And thy modur Mary, hevyn qwene,
Bere our arunde so bytwene
   (That semely ys of syght)   *beautiful, to see*
10 To thy sone that ys so fre,
In heven wyth Hym that we may be,
   That lord ys most of myght.

Menstrelles that walken fer and wyde,   *travel, everywhere*
Her and ther in every a syde,   *all parts*
15   In mony a dyverse londe,
Sholde at her bygynnyng
Speke of that ryghtwes kyng   *invoke*
   That made both see and sonde.
Whoso wyll a stounde dwelle,
20 Of mykyll myrght Y may you telle
   (And mornyng theramonge):
Of a lady fayr and fre,
Her name was called Emaré,
   As I here synge in songe.

25 Her fadyr was an emperour
Of castell and of ryche towre,
   Syr Artyus was hys nome.
He hadde bothe hallys and bowrys,   *private chambers*
Frythes fayr, forestes wyth flowrys;   *(wood)lands*
30   So gret a lord was none.
Weddedde he had a lady
That was both fayr and semely,   *gracious*
   Whyte as whales bone.
Dame Erayne hette that emperes;   *was called*
35 She was full of love and goodnesse,
   So curtays lady was none.

3 all: all that L.   *4* Grant us now grace to act in such a way.   *8* So intercede for us.   *16* Ought at the beginning (of their performance).   *19* stay (to hear me) for a time.   *21* Which is mingled with sadness.

Syr Artyus was the best manne
In the worlde that lyvede thanne;   *at that time*
   Both hardy and therto wyght.   *valiant, strong*
40 He was curtays in all thyng   *respects*
Bothe to olde and to yynge,
   And well kowth dele and dyght.
He hadde but on chyld in hys lyve,
Begeten on hys weddedde wyfe,
45   And that was fayr and bryght.
Forsothe, as Y may telle the,
They called that chyld Emaré,
   That semely was of syght.

When she was of her modur born,
50 She was the fayrest creature borne
That yn the lond was thoo.
The emperes, that fayr ladye,
Fro her lord gan she dye,
   Or hyt kowthe speke or goo.
55 The chyld that was fayr and gent   *gracious*
To a lady was hyt sente
   That men kalled Abro;
She thawghth hyt curtesye and thewe,   *good manners*
Golde and sylke forto sewe,
60   Amonge maydenes moo.   *other*

Abro tawghte thys mayden small
Nortur that men useden in sale,   *courtly behaviour, hall*
   Whyle she was in her bowre.
She was curtays in all thynge,
65 Bothe to olde and to yynge,
   And whythe as lylye flowre.
Of her hondes she was slye,   *with, clever*
All he[r] loved that her sye,
   Wyth menske and mychyl honour.   *respect*
70 At the mayden leve we,
And at the lady fayr and fre,
   And speke we of the emperour.

53–4 Was taken from her husband by death, before the child could speak or walk. *68 her: he* L. *70–1* Now let us stop talking about the girl and the beautiful and noble lady.

The emperour of gentyll blode   *noble lineage*
Was a curteys lorde and a gode,
75 In all maner of thynge.   *every respect*
Aftur, when hys wyf was dede,
A ledde hys lyf yn weddewede,
    And myche loved playnge.

Sone aftur yn a whyle,
80 The ryche kynge of Cesyle
    To the emperour gan wende;   *journey*
A ryche present wyth hym he browght,
A cloth that was wordylye wroght: *excellently made*
    He wellcomed hym as the hende.   *graciously*

85 Syr Tergaunte that nobyll knyght,
He presented the emperour ryght,
    And sette hym on hys kne,
Wyth that cloth rychyly dyght,   *contrived*
Full of stones ther hyt was pyght,   *set*
90   As thykke as hyt myght be;
Off topaze and rubyes
And other stones of myche prys,
    That semely wer to se;
Of crapowtes and nakette,   *toadstones, agates (?)*
95 As thykke ar they sette,
    Forsothe, as Y say the.

The cloth was dysplayed sone;   *unfolded*
The emperour lokede therupone,
    And myght hyt not se;
100 For glysteryng of the ryche ston
Redy syght had he non,
    And sayde, 'How may thys be?'
The emperour sayde on hygh,   *in haste*
'Sertes thys ys a fayry,
105   Or ellys a vanyté!'   *illusion*
The kyng of Cysyle answered than,
'So ryche a jwell ys ther non
    In all Crystyanté.'

77 A: And L; He led the life of a widower. *79* A short time after that.
85 knyght: knyght hyghte L. *86* in the proper manner. *101* He was
dazzled for a moment. *104* something made by enchantment. *107* So
splendid and precious an object.

The amerayle dowghter of hethennes
110 Made thys cloth wythouten lees,   *truly*
   And wrowghte hyt all wyth pryde,
And purtreyed hyt wyth gret honour
Wyth ryche golde and asowr   *asure*
   And stones on ylke a syde.
115 And as the story telles in honde
The stones that yn thys cloth stonde
   Sowghte they wer full wyde.   *searched out*
Seven wynter hyt was yn makynge
Or hyt was browght to endynge,   *before*
120   In herte ys not to hyde.

In that on korner made was   *represented*
Ydoyne and Amadas,
   Wyth love that was so trewe;
For they loveden hem wyth honour,
125 Portrayed they wer wyth trewe-love-flour,
   Of stones bryght of hewe: *colour*
Wyth carbunkull and safere,   *rubies, sapphires*
Kassydonys and onyx so clere,   *chalcedonies*
   Sette in golde newe;
130 Deamondes and rubyes
And othur stones of mychyll pryse,
   And menstrellys wyth her gle[we].   *music*

In that othur corner was dyght   *represented*
Trystram and Isowde so bryght,
135   That semely wer to se.
And for they loved hem ryght,
As full of stones ar they dyght,
   As thykke as they may be;
Of topase and of rubyes
140 And othur stones of myche pryse,
   That semely wer to se;
Wyth crapawtes and nakette,
Thykke of stones ar they sette,
   Forsothe as Y say the.

109 The daughter of the heathen emir.   *112* And formed splendid pictures on it.   *115 in honde* for **in londe?*   *120* The truth cannot be hidden.   *125–6* Their portraits were adorned with brightly jewelled love-knots.   *132 glewe: gle* L.   *136* truly loved one another.

145 In the thrydde korner, wyth gret honour,
    Was Florys and Dam Blawncheflour,
       As love was hem betwene.
    For they loved wyth honour,
    Purtrayed they wer wyth trewe-love-flour,
150   Wyth stones bryght and shene:
    Ther wer knyghtus and senatowres,
    Emerawdes of gret v[alowr]es,   *value*
       To wyte wythouten wene;
    Deamonndes and koralle,
155 Perydotes and crystall,   *chrysolite*
       And gode garnettes bytwene.

    In the fowrthe korner was oon,   *a (picture)*
    Of Babylone the sowdan sonne,
       The amerayles dowghtyr hym by.
160 For hys sake the cloth was wrowght;
    She loved hym in hert and thowght,
       As testymo[n]yeth thys storye.   *bears witness*
    The fayr mayden her byforn   *in front of*
    Was portrayed an unykorn,
165   Wyth hys horn so hye.   *tall*
    Flowres and bryddes on ylke a syde,   *birds*
    Wyth stones that wer sowght wyde:
       Stuffed wyth ymagerye.

    When the cloth to ende was wrowght,   *was finished*
170 To the sowdan sone hyt was browght,
       That semely was of syghte.
    'My fadyr was a nobyll man;
    Of the sowdan he hyt wan,   *from*
       Wyth maystrye and wyth myghth.
175 For gret love he yaf hyt me;
    I brynge hyt the in specyalté:
       Thys cloth ys rychely dyght.'
    He yaf hyt the emperour;
    He receyved hyt wyth gret honour,
180   And thonkede hym fayr and ryght.

151 There were (depicted). *152 valowres: vertues* L. *162 testymonyeth: testymoyeth* L. *168* (It was) full of pictorial representations. *176* as a sign of special affection.

The kyng of Cesyle dwelled ther   *remained*
As long as hys wyll wer,
   Wyth the emperour forto play;   *take his ease*
And when he wolde wende
185 He toke hys leve at the hende
   And wente forth on hys way.
Now remeveth thys nobyll kyng:
The emperour aftur hys dowghtur hadde longyng,
   To speke wyth that may.
190 Messengeres forth he sent
Aftyr the mayde fayr and gent,
   That was bryght as someres day.

Messengeres dyghte hem in hye;
Wyth myche myrthe and melodye,
195   Forth gon they fare,
Both by stretes and by stye,   *highways, lane(s)*
Aftur that fayr lady,
   Was godely unthur gare.   *robe*
Her norysse that hyghte Abro,   *nurse*
200 Wyth her she goth forth also,
   And wer sette in a chare.   *litter*
To the emperour gan the[y] go;
He come ayeyn hem a myle or two;
   A fayr metyng was there.

205 The mayden whyte as lylye flour
Lyghte ayeyn her fadyr the emperour;
   Two knyghtes gan her lede.
Her fadyr that was of gret renowne,
That of golde wered the crowne,
210   Lyghte of hys stede.   *dismounted*
When they wer bothe on her fete,   *their*
He klypped her and kyssed her swete,   *embraced*
   And bothe on fote they yede.
They wer glad and made good chere,   *rejoiced*
215 To the palys they yede in fere,   *together*
   In romans as we rede.

---

187 And so this noble king takes his leave. *193* quickly got themselves ready. *202 they: the* L. *203* He came a mile or two of the way to greet them. *206* Got down to greet.

Then the lordes that wer grete,
They wesh and seten don to mete,
   And folk hem served swyde.   *promptly*
220 The mayden that was of sembelant swete,   *appearance*
Byfore her owene fadur sete,
   The fayrest wommon on lyfe;   *alive*
That all hys hert and all hys thowghth   *mind*
Her to love was y-browght: *moved*
225   He byhelde her ofte sythe.
So he was anamored hys thowghtur tyll,
Wyth her he thowghth to worche hys wyll,   *do*
   And wedde her to hys wyfe.

And when the metewhyle was don,
230 Into hys chambur he wente son
   And called hys counseyle nere.
He bad they shulde sone go and come
And gete leve of the pope of Rome,
   To wedde that mayden clere.
235 Messengerres forth they wente,
They durste not breke hys commandement,
   And erles wyth hem yn fere.
They wente to the courte of Rome,
And browghte the popus bullus sone,
240   To wedde hys dowghter dere.

Then was the emperour gladde and blythe,
And lette shape a robe swythe   *had made*
   Of that cloth of golde;
And when hyt was don her upon,   *put*
245 She semed non erthely wommon,   *mortal*
   That marked was of molde.   *created, earth*
Then seyde the emperour so fre,   *noble*
'Dowghtyr Y woll wedde the,
   Thow art so fresh to beholde.'   *fair*
250 Then sayde that wordy unthur wede,   *honourable lady*
'Nay syr, God of heven hyt forbede,
   That ever do so we shulde!

---

224 y-browght: yn browght L.   *226* He was so infatuated with his daughter.
229 the meal was over.   *231* And summoned his advisers to him.   *232–3*
should pass between him and the Pope of Rome and obtain his consent.
236 They dared not refuse his bidding.

Yyf hyt so betydde that ye me wedde   *came about*
And we shulde play togedur in bedde,   *make love*
255   Bothe we were forlorne!   *damned*
The worde shulde sprynge fer and wyde:
In all the worlde on every syde   *part*
  The worde shulde be borne.   *carried*
Ye ben a lorde of gret pryce,   *honour*
260 Lorde, lette nevur such sorow aryce:
  Take God you beforne!
That my fadur shulde wedde me,
God forbede that I hyt so se,
  That wered the crowne of thorne!'

265 The emperour was ryght wrothe   *very*
And swore many a gret othe,
  That deed shulde she be.   *must die*
He lette make a nobull boot,
And dede her theryn, God wote,
270   In the robe of nobull ble.   *brilliantly coloured*
She moste have wyth her no spendyng,
Nothur mete ne drynke,
  But shote her ynto the se.   *launched*
Now the lady dwelled thore,
275 Wythowte anker or ore,
  And that was gret pyté.

Ther come a wynd, Y unthurstonde,   *am told*
And blewe the boot fro the londe,
  Of her they lost the syght.
280 The emperour hym bethowght   *realized*
That he hadde all myswrowht,   *sinned greatly*
  And was a sory knyghte.
And as he stode yn studyynge,   *meditation*
He fell down in sowenynge,   *faint*
285   To the yrthe was he dyght.
Grete lordes stode therby
And toke u[p] the emperour hastyly,   *raised*
  And comforted hym fayr and ryght.

256 The report of it would spread everywhere.   261 Keep God's will before you.   269 And put her in it.   271 She was not allowed to take any money with her.   285 He fell to the ground.   287 *up: un* L.

When he of sownyng kovered was,
290 Sore he wepte and sayde, 'Alas,
   For my dowhter dere!
Alas that Y was made man,
Wrecched kaytyf that I hyt am!'   *miserable wretch*
   The teres ronne by hys lere.   *down, cheeks*
295 'I wrowght ayeyn Goddes lay   *contrary to, law*
To her that was so trewe of fay:
   Alas, why ner she here!'
The teres lasshed out of hys yghen;   *gushed*
The grete lordes that hyt syghen   *saw*
300   Wepte and made yll chere.   *were distressed*

Ther was nothur olde ny yynge
That kowthe stynte of wepynge,   *stop*
   For that comely unthur kelle.   *robe (?)*
Into shypys faste gan they thrynge   *rush*
305 Forto seke that mayden yynge,
   That was so fayr of flesh and fell.   *skin*
They her sowght ovurall yn the see   *everywhere*
And myghte not fynde that lady fre,
   Ayeyn they come full snell.   *quickly*
310 At the emperour now leve we,
And of the lady yn the see
   I shall begynne to tell.

The lady fleted forth alone,   *floated*
To God of heven she made her mone   *complaint*
315   And to hys modyr also.
She was dryven wyth wynde and rayn
Wyth stronge stormes her agayn,   *against*
   Of the watur so blo.   *dark*
As Y have herd menstrelles syng yn sawe,
320 Hows ny lond myghth she non knowe,   *discern*
   Aferd she was to go.
She was so dryven fro wawe to wawe,   *wave*
She hyd her hede and lay full lowe,
   For watyr she was full woo.   *distressed*

289 came out of his swoon.   319 tell in their songs.

325 Now thys lady dwelled thore
    A good sevennyghth and more, *fully a week*
      As hyt was Goddys wylle.
    Wyth carefull herte and sykyng sore, *sorrowful*
    Such sorow was here yarked yore,
330   And ever lay she styll. *motionless*
    She was dryven ynto a lond,
    Thorow the grace of Goddes sond, *dispensation*
      That all thyng may fulfylle. *do*
    She was on the see so harde bestadde, *grievously afflicted*
335 For hungur and thurste almost madde:
      Woo worth wederus yll!

    She was dryven into a lond
    That hyghth Galys, Y unthurstond: *was called*
      That was a fayr countré.
340 The kyngus steward dwelled ther bysyde, *nearby*
    In a kastell of mykyll pryde: *great splendour*
      Syr Kadore hyght he.
    Every day wolde he go,
    And take wyth hym a sqwyer or two,
345   And play hym by the see. *exercise*
    On a tyme he toke the eyr
    Wyth two knyghtus gode and fayr;
      The wedur was lythe of le.

    A boot he fond by the brym *water's edge*
350 And a glysteryng thyng theryn:
      Therof they hadde ferly. *were astonished*
    They went forth on the sond
    To the boot, Y unthurstond,
      And fond theryn that lady.
355 She hadde so longe meteles be *without food*
    That hym thowht gret dele to se;
      She was yn poyn[t] to dye.
    They askede her what was her name;
    She chaunged hyt ther anone, *at once*
360   And sayde she hette Egaré. *was called*

---

329 was destined for her long before.   *336* Accursed be all evil storms!
348 The weather was calm and the place sheltered.   *356* That it greatly
distressed him to see it.   *357 poynt: poyn* L; at the point of death.

Syr Kadore hadde gret pyté;
He toke up the lady of the see
   And hom gan he[r] lede.
She hadde so longe meteles be,
365 She was wax lene as a tre,
   That wordy unthur wede.   *robe*
Into hys castell when she came,
Into a chawmbyr they her namm   *took*
   And fayr they gan her fede,
370 Wyth all delycyus mete and drynke
That they myghth hem on thynke,   *could devise*
   That was yn all that stede.

When that lady fayr of face
Wyth mete and drynke kevered was,   *recovered*
375   And had colour agayne,
She tawghte hem to sewe and marke   *fashion*
All maner of sylky[n] werke:
   Of her they wer full fayne.
She was curteys yn all thyng,
380 Bothe to olde and to yynge,
   I say yow for certeyne.
She kowghthe werke all maner thyng
That fell to emperour or to kyng,   *were worn by*
   Erle, barown or swayne.   *squire*

385 Syr Kadore lette make a feste
That was fayr and honeste,   *noble*
   Wyth hys lorde the kynge.
Ther was myche menstralsé,
Trommpus, tabours and sawtré,
390   Bothe harpe and fydyllyng.
The lady that was gentyll and small   *slender*
In kurtull alone served yn hall,   *robe*
   Byfore that nobull kyng.
The cloth upon her shone so bryghth
395 When she was theryn y-dyghth,   *dressed in it*
   She semed non erdly thyng.

---

363 her: he L.   *365* She had become as thin as a stick.   *377 sylkyn: sylky*
L.   *378* They were very glad to have her.   *389* (Playing on) trumpet,
drum and psaltery.

    The kyng loked her upon;
    So fayr a lady he sygh nevur non:
      Hys herte she hadde yn wolde.   *under her power*
400 He was so anamered of that syghth,
    Of the mete non he myghth,
      But faste gan her beholde.   *fixedly*
    She was so fayr and gent,   *gracious*
    The kynges love on her was lent,   *set*
405   In tale as hyt ys tolde.
    And when the metewhyle was don,
    Into the chambur he wente son,
      And called hys barouns bolde.

    Fyrst he calle[d] syr Kadore
410 And othur knyghtes that ther wore,
      Hastely come hym tyll.   *to*
    Dukes and erles wyse of lore,
    Hastely come the kyng before
      And askede what was hys wyll.
415 Then spakke the ryche ray;   *king*
    To syr Kadore gan he say
      Wordes fayr and stylle:
    'Syr, whenns ys that lovely may   *from where*
    That yn the halle served thys day?
420   Tell my yyf hyt be thy wyll.'

    Then sayde syr Kadore, Y unthurstonde,
    'Hyt ys an erles thowghtur of ferre londe,   *daughter, distant*
      That semely ys to sene.
    I sente aftur her certeynlye
425 To teche my chylderen curtesye,   *etiquette*
      In chambur wyth hem to bene.
    She ys the konnyngest wommon,   *most skilled*
    I trowe, that be yn Crystendom,
      Of werk that Y have sene.'   *embroidery*
430 Then sayde that ryche raye,
    'I wyll have that fayr may
      And wedde her to my quene.'

---

401 He could not eat anything.   *409 called:* calle L.   *412* skilled in giving
counsel.   *415 ray: yn ray* L.   *417* Graciously and quietly.

The nobull kyng, verament,
Aftyr hys modyr he sent
435   To wyte what she wolde say.   *hear*
They browght forth hastely
That fayr mayde Egarye—
    She was bryghth as someres day.
The cloth on her shon so bryght
440 Whenn she was theryn dyght,
    And herself a gentell may,
The olde qwene sayde anon,
'I sawe never wommon
    Halvendell so gay!'   *half*

445 The olde qwene spakke wordus unhende   *mischievous*
And sayde, 'Sone, thys ys a fende,   *evil spirit*
    In thys wordy wede!   *splendid*
As thou lovest my blessynge,
Make thou nevur thys weddynge,
450   Cryst hyt de forbede!'   *thee*
Then spakke the ryche ray,
'Modyr I wyll have thys may!'
And forth gan her lede.
The olde qwene, for certayne,
455 Turnede wyth ire hom agayne,
    And wolde not be at that dede.   *ceremony*

The kyng wedded that lady bryght;
Grete purvyance ther was dyghth,
    In that semely sale.   *stately hall*
460 Grete lordes wer served aryght,   *as was fitting*
Duke, erle, baron and knyghth,
    Both of grete and smale.
Myche folke forsothe ther was,
And therto an huge prese,   *throng*
465   As hyt ys tolde in tale.
Ther was all maner thyng
That fell to a kyngus weddyng,   *belonged*
    And mony a ryche menstrall.

448 As you wish to have.   *453* And led her away.   *458* Great preparations
were made there.

When the mangery was done,   *feast*
470 Grete lordes departed sone,
  That semely were to se.
The kynge belafte wyth the qwene;   *remained*
Moch love was hem betwene,
  And also game and gle.   *sport, joy*
475 She was curteys and swete,
Such a lady herde Y nevur of yete:
  They loved both wyth herte fre.
The lady that was both meke and mylde
Conceyved and wente wyth chylde,
480 As God wolde hyt sholde be.

The kyng of France yn that tyme
Was besette wyth many a Sarezyne,   *harassed*
  And cumbered all in tene;
And sente aftur the kyng of Galys   *for*
485 And othur lordys of myche prys,
  That semely were to sene.
The kyng of Galys in that tyde
Gedered men on every syde,   *called together*
  In armour bryght and shene.
490 Then sayde the kyng to syr Kadore
And othur lordes that ther wore,
  'Take good hede to my qwene.'   *care of*

The kyng of Fraunce spared none,
But sent for hem everychone,
495 Both kyng, knyghth and clerke.
The st[e]ward bylaft at home
To kepe the qwene whyte as fome,   *look after*
  He com not at that werke.
She wente wyth chylde yn place
500 As longe as Goddus wyll was,
  That semely unthur serke;   *robe*
Thyll ther was of her body
A fayr chyld borne and a godelé;   *handsome*
  Hadde a dowbyll kyngus marke. *birthmark*

---

483 And greatly harmed and hurt. *496 Steward : stward* L. *498* He took
no part in that action.

505 They hyt crystened wyth grete honour
    And called hym Segramour:
       Frely was that fode.   *noble, child*
    Then the steward, syr Kadore,
    A nobull lettur made he thore
510   And wrowghte hyt all wyth gode.
    He wrowghte hyt yn hyghynge   *haste*
    And sente hyt to hys lorde the kynge,
       That gentyll was of blode.
    The messenger forth gan wende
515 And wyth the kyngus modur gan lende,   *tarry*
       And ynto the castell he yode.   *went*

    He was resseyved rychely
    And she hym askede hastyly   *at once*
       How the qwene hadde spedde.   *fared*
520 'Madame, ther ys of her y-borne
    A fayr man-chylde, Y tell you beforne,   *now*
       And she lyth in her bedde.'
    She yaf hym for that tydynge
    A robe and fowrty shylynge
525   And rychely hym cladde.
    She made hym dronken of ale and wyne
    And when she sawe that hyt was tyme,
       Tho chambur she wolde hym lede.   *to*

    And when he was on slepe browght,
530 The qwene that was of wykked thowght,   *evil intention*
       Tho chambur gan she wende.
    Hys letter she toke hym fro,
    In a fyre she brente hyt do: *burned, then*
       Of werkes she was unhende.
535 Another lettur she made wyth evyll   *composed, malice*
    And sayde the qwene had born a devyll,
       Durste no mon come her hende.   *near*
    Thre heddes hadde he there,
    A lyon, a dragon and a beere:
540   A fowll feltred fende.   *shaggy*

---

510 And wrote it with complete good will.   *517* He was given a splendid
welcome.   *525* She gave him magnificent clothes.   *527* that the time was
ripe.   *529* *he: she* L.

On the morn when hyt was day
The messenger wente on hys way,
   Bothe by stye and strete.
In trwe story as Y say,
545 Tyll he come theras the kynge laye,   *where, was*
   And speke wordus swete.
He toke the kyng the lettur yn honde,
And he hyt redde, Y unthurstonde:
   The teres downe gan he lete.   *shed*
550 And as he stode yn redyng,
Downe he fell yn sowenyng,
   For sorow hys herte gan blede.

Grete lordes that stode hym by
Toke up the kyng hastely,   *raised*
555   In herte he was full woo.
Sore he grette and sayde, 'Alas,
That Y evur man born was!
   That hyt evur shullde be so.
Alas, that Y was made a kynge
560 And sygh wedded the fayrest thyng   *then*
   That on erthe myght go.   *walk*
That evur Jesu hymself wolde sende
Such a fowle lothly fende
   To come bytwene us too.'

565 When he sawe hyt myght no bettur be,
Anothur lettur then made he
   And seled hyt wyth hys sele.
He commanded yn all thynge   *respects*
To kepe well that lady yynge   *look after*
570   Tyll she hadde her hele.   *had recovered*
Bothe gode men and ylle
To serve her at her wylle,
   Bothe yn wo and wele.
He toke thys lettur of hys honde
575 And rode thorow the same londe,
   By the kyngus modur castell.

---

547 He gave the letter into the king's hands. *558 so* before *shullde* L. *565* When he saw that nothing could be done about it. *571–2* All kinds of servants (were) to be at her disposal.

And then he dwelled ther all nyght;
He was resseyved and rychely dyght   *nobly treated*
    And wyste of no treson.   *did not know*
580 He made hym well at ese and fyne,
Bothe of brede, ale and wyne,
    And that berafte hym hys reson.   *took away*
When he was on slepe browght,
The false qwene hys lettur sowghte: *examined*
585   Into the fyre she kaste hyt downe.
Another lettur she lette make,   *did*
That men sholde the lady take,
    And lede her out of towne,

And putte her ynto the see,
590 In that robe of ryche ble,   *colour*
    The lytyll chylde her wyth;
And lette her have no spendyng,
For no mete ny for drynke,
    But lede her out of that kygh.   *land*
595 'Upon payn of chylde and wyfe
And also upon your owene lyfe,
    Lette her have no gryght!'   *shelter*
The messenger knewe no gyle,
But rode hom mony a myle,
600   By forest and by fryght.   *wilderness*

And when the messenger come home,
The steward toke the lettur sone
    And began to rede.
Sore he syght and sayde, 'Alas,
605 Sertes thys ys a fowle case,   *detestable business*
    And a de[l]full dede!'   *cruel*
And as he stode yn redyng,
He fell downe yn swonynge;
    For sorow hys hert gan blede.
610 Ther was nothur olde ny yynge,
That myghte forbere of wepynge   *keep from*
    For that worthy unthur wede.

---

580 He made himself perfectly at home.   *595–6* For fear of your own death
and those of your wife and children.   *598* did not suspect any treachery.
606 *delfull: defull* L.

The lady herde gret dele yn halle;   *lamentation*
On the steward gan she calle
615   And sayde, 'What may thys be?
Yyf anythyng be amys,   *wrong*
Tell me what that hyt ys,
    And lette not for me.'
Then sayde the steward, verament,   *truly*
620 'Lo, her a lettur my lord hath sente,
    And therfore woo ys me!'
She toke the lettur and bygan to rede,
Then fonde she wryten all the dede   *details*
    How she moste ynto the see.

625 'Be stylle, syr,' sayde the qwene,
    'Lette syche mornynge bene;
    For me have thou no kare.
Loke thou be not shente,
But do my lordes commaunndement,
630   God forbede thou spare.
For he weddede so porely
On me a sympull lady,
    He ys ashamed sore.
Grete well my lord fro me,
635 So gentyll of blode yn Crystyanté,
    Gete he nevur more.'

Then was ther sorow and myche woo,
When the lady to shype shulde go;   *had to*
    They wepte and wronge her hondus.
640 The lady that was meke and mylde
In her arme she bar her chylde,
    And toke leve of the londe.
When she wente ynto the see
In that robe of ryche ble,
645   Men sowened on the sonde.
Sore they wepte and sayde, 'Alas,
Certys thys ys a wykked kase.
    Wo worth dedes wronge!'

618 Do not hold back on my account. *621* Which has caused me great distress. *628* Do not incur your own ruin. *631-2* Because he made such a wretched marriage to a lady of humble birth, like myself. *635 blode: blolde* L. *635-6* He will never get (a child) of more noble birth in the whole of Christendom. *648* Accursed be evil actions!

  The lady and the lytyll chylde
650 Fleted forth on the watur wylde,
   Wyth full harde happes.
  Her surkote that was large and wyde,   *robe*
  Therwyth her vysage she gan hyde,
   Wyth the hynthur lappes;   *back folds*
655 She was aferde of the see
  And layde her gruf uponn a tre,
   The chylde to her pappes.
  The wawes that were grete and strong
  On the bote faste they thonge,   *dashed*
660 Wyth mony unsemely rappes.   *blows*

  And when the chyld gan to wepe
  Wyth sory herte she songe hyt aslepe,
   And putte the pappe yn hys mowth,   *breast*
  And sayde, 'Myghth Y onus gete lond, *reach*
665 Of the watur that ys so stronge,   *cruel*
   By northe or by sowthe,
  Wele owth Y to warye the, see,   *curse*
  I have myche shame yn the!'
   And evur she lay and growht.   *lamented*
670 Then she made her prayer
  To Jesu and hys modur dere,
   In all that she kowthe.

  Now thys lady dwelled thore
  A full sevenenyght and more,
675 As hyt was Goddys wylle;
  Wyth karefull herte and sykyng sore,
  Such sorow was her yarked yore,
   And she lay full stylle.
  She was dryven toward Rome,
680 Thorow the grace of God yn trone,
   That all thyng may fulfylle.
  On the see she was so harde bestadde,
  For hungur and thurste allmost madde,
   Wo worth chawnses ylle!

---

651 They endured severe misfortunes. 656 face downwards on a plank.
667 I have good reason to curse you, sea. 672 To the full extent of her
powers. 684 Accursed be (such) tribulations!

685 A marchaunte dw[el]led yn that cyté,
    A ryche mon of golde and fee,   *property*
      Jurdan was hys name.
    Every day wolde he
    Go to playe hym by the see,   *take his recreation*
690   The eyer forto tane.
    He wente forth yn that tyde,
    Walkynge by the see sythe,   *side*
      All hymselfe alone.
    A bote he fonde by the brymme
695 And a fayr lady therynne,
      That was ryght wo-bygone.

    The cloth on her shon so bryth
    He was aferde of that syght,
      For glysteryng of that wede;
700 And yn hys herte he thowghth ryght
    That she was non erdyly wyght;   *mortal creature*
      He sawe nevur non such yn leede.   *(any) land*
    He sayde, 'What hette ye, fayr ladye?'
    'Lord,' she sayde, 'Y hette Egarye,
705   That lye her yn drede.'   *fear*
    Up he toke that fayre ladye
    And the yonge chylde her by,
      And hom he gan hem lede.

    When he come to hys byggynge   *house*
710 He welcomed fayr that lady yynge
      That was fayr and bryght;
    And badde hys wyf yn all thynge   *told*
    Mete and drynke forto brynge
      To the lady ryght.
715 'What that she wyll crave   *desire*
    And her mowth wyll hyt have,
      Loke hyt be redy dyght.
    She hath so longe meteles be
    That me thynketh grette pyté:
720   Conforte her yyf thou myght.'   *restore*

685 [ ] not now visible.   *688* Every: Eevery L.   *702* such: schuch L.

Now the lady dwelles ther
Wyth alle mete[s] that gode were: *kinds of food*
   She hedde at her wylle.
She was curteys yn all thyng,
725 Bothe to olde and to yynge;
   Her loved bothe gode and ylle.
The chylde bygan forto thryfe;
He wax the fayrest chyld on lyfe,
   Whyte as flour on hylle.
730 And she sewed sylke werk yn bour
And tawghte her sone nortowre,   *courtesy*
   But evyr she mornede stylle.   *in secret*

When the chylde was seven yer olde
He was bothe wyse and bolde,
735   And wele made of flesh and bone;
He was worthy unthur wede
And ryght well kowthe pryke a stede;   *urge on*
   So curtays a chylde was none.
All men lovede Segramowre,
740 Bothe yn halle and yn bowre,
   Whersoevur he gan gone.
Leve we at the lady clere of vyce,   *bright, face*
And speke of the kyng of Galys,
   Fro the sege when he come home.

745 Now the sege broken ys,
The kyng come home to Galys,
   Wyth mykyll myrthe and pryde;
Dukes and erles of ryche asyce,   *rank*
Barones and knyghtes of mykyll pryse,
750   Come rydynge be hys syde.
Syr K[a]dore hys steward thanne,
Ayeyn hym rode wyth mony a man,   *towards*
   As faste as he myght ryde.
He tolde the kyng aventowres
755 Of hys halles and hys bowres
   And of hys londys wyde.

722 metes: mete L. *745* Now that the siege has been raised. *751 Kadore: Kodore* L. *754-5* all that had happened concerning his properties.

The kyng sayde, 'By Goddys name,
Syr Kadore, thou art to blame
   For thy fyrst tellynge!
760 Thow sholdest fyrst have tolde me
Of my lady Egaré,
   I love most of all thyng!'
Then was the stewardes herte wo,
And sayde, 'Lorde, why sayst thou so?
765   Art not thou a trewe kynge?
Lo her, the lettur ye sente me,
Yowr owene self the sothe may se;
   I have don your byddynge.'

The kyng toke the lettur to rede,   *began reading*
770 And when he sawe that ylke dede,
   He wax all pale and wanne.
Sore he grette and sayde, 'Alas,   *wept*
That evur born Y was,
   Or evur was made manne!
775 Syr Kadore, so mot Y the,
Thys lettur come nevur fro me;
   I telle the her anone!'   *at once*
Bothe they wepte and yaf hem ylle.
'Alas,' he sayde, 'Saf Goddys wylle!'
780   And both the[y] sowened then.

Grete lordes stode by
And toke up the kyng hastyly;
   Of hem was grete pyté;
And when they both kevered were,
785 The kyng toke hym the letter ther
   Of the heddys thre.
'A, lord,' he sayde, 'be Goddus grace,
I sawe nevur thys lettur in place!   *anywhere*
   Alas, how may thys be?'
790 Aftur the messenger ther they sente;
The kyng askede what way he went:
   'Lor[d], be your modur fre.'   *past*

758–9 are wrong to tell me of these things first. *765* a king who is true to
his word. *779* if it were not the will of God. *780* they: *the* L. *783* They
were filled with compassion. *792* Lord: *Lor* L.

'Alas!' then sayde the kynge,
'Whethur my modur wer so unhende
795   To make thys treson?
By my krowne she shall be brent,
Wythowten any othur jugement: *further trial*
    That thenketh me best reson!'   *course*
Grete lordes toke hem betwene
800 That they wolde exyle the qwene
    And berefe her hyr renowne.   *deprive, honour(s)*
Thus they exiled the false qwene
And byrafte her hyr lyflothe clene,   *maintenance, absolutely*
    Castell, towre and towne.

805 When she was fled ovur the see fome,
The nobull kyng dwelled at hom,
    Wyth full hevy chere;
Wyth karefull hert and drury mone,
Sykynges made he many on
810   For Egarye the clere;   *fair*
And when he sawe chylderen play
He wepte and sayde, 'Wellawey,
For my sone so dere!'
Such lyf he lyved mony a day,
815 That no mon hym stynte may,
    Fully seven yere.

Tyll a thowght yn hys herte come
How hys lady whyte as fome,
    Was drowned for hys sake.
820 'Thorow the grace of God yn trone,
I woll to the Pope of Rome,
    My penans forto take!'   *receive*
He lette ordeyne shypus fele
And fylled hem full of wordes wele,   *worldly riches*
825 Hys men mery wyth to make.
Dolys he lette dyghth and dele,
Forto wynnen hym sowles hele;   *salvation*
    To the shyp he toke the gate.   *made his way*

---

795 As to act so treacherously. *799* determined between themselves.
809 He sighed very often. *815* could persuade him to stop (mourning).
823 He commanded that many ships should be got ready. *826* Alms were
got ready and distributed.

  Shypmen that wer so mykyll of pryce
830 Dyght her takull on ryche acyse,   *gear, manner*
   That was fayr and fre.
  They drowgh up sayl and leyd out ore;
  The wynde stode as her lust wore,
   The wethur was lythe on le.
835 They sayled over the salt fome,
  Thorow the grace of God in trone,
   That most ys of powsté.
  To that cyté when the[y] come
  At the burgeys hous hys yn he nome,   *citizen's*
840 Theras woned Emarye.   *where*

  Emaré called he[r] sone,
  Hastely to her come,
   Wythoute ony lettynge;
  And sayde, 'My dere sone so fre,
845 Do a lytull aftur me,
   And thou sha[l]t have my blessynge.
  Tomorowe thou shall serve yn halle
  In a kurtyll of ryche palle,   *tunic*
   Byfore thys nobull kyng;
850 Loke, sone, so curtays thou be   *see to it*
  That no mon fynde chalange to the   *fault with*
   In no manere thynge!   *any respect*

  When the kyng ys served of spycerye, *last course*
  Knele thou downe hastylye
855 And take hys hond yn thyn.
  And when thou hast so done
  Take the kuppe of golde sone,
   And serve hym of the wyne.
  And what that he speketh to the
860 Cum anon and tell me,   *at once*
   On Goddus blessyng and myne!'
  The chylde wente ynto the hall,
  Among the lordes grete and small,
   That lufsumme wer unthur lyne.

---

829 of such great excellence. *833* blew in the direction they wanted.
838 they: the L. *841 her: he* L. *845* Conduct yourself for a time as I
shall tell you (to do). *846 shalt: shat* L. *848* In a tunic of the finest cloth.
864 handsome in their linen (clothes).

865 Then the lordes that wer grete
  Wysh and wente to her mete,   *washed*
   Men[s]trelles browght yn the kowrs.
  The chylde hem served so curteysly
  All hym loved that hym sy,   *saw*
870 And spake hym gret honowres.
  Then sayde all that loked hym upon
  So curteys a chyld sawe they nevur non,
   In halle ny yn bowres.
  The kynge sayde to hym yn game,   *cheerfully*
875 'Swete sone what ys thy name?'
   'Lorde,' he seyd, 'Y hyghth Segramowres.'

  Then that nobull kyng
  Toke up a grete sykynge   *sighed deeply*
   For hys sone hyght so;
880 Certys wythowten lesynge
  The teres out of hys yen gan wryng;   *were forced*
   In herte he was full woo.
  Neverthelese he lette be   *controlled himself*
  And loked on the chylde so fre,
885 And mykell he lovede hym thoo.
  The kyng sayde to the burgeys anon,
  'Swete syr, ys thys thy sone?'
   The burgeys sayde, 'Yoo.'   *yes*

  Then the lordes that wer grete
890 Whesshen ayeyn aftyr mete
   And then come spycerye.
  The chyld that was of chere swete
  On hys kne downe he sete
   And served hym curteyslye.
895 The kynge called the burgeys hym tyll
  And sayde, 'Syr yf hyt be thy wyll
   Yyf me thys lytyll body!   *fellow*
  I shall hym make lorde of town and towr
  Of hye halles and of bowre:
900 I love hym specyally."

---

*867 Menstrelles: Mentrelles L. 870 And paid him great compliments.
879 Because that was what his son had been called. 900 I feel a particular
affection for him.*

When he had served the kyng at wylle,   *voluntarily*
Fayr he wente hys modyr tyll
   And tellys her how hyt ys.
'Soone when he shall to chambur wende
905 Take hys hond at the grece ende,
   For he ys thy fadur, ywysse.
And byd hym come speke wyth Emaré,
That changed her name to Egaré,
   In the londe of Galys!'
910 The chylde wente ayeyn to halle
Amonge the grete lordes alle
   And served on ryche asyse.   *worthily*

When they wer well at ese afyne,   *finally*
Bothe of brede, ale and wyne,
915   They rose up, more and myn.   *less*
When the kyng shulde to chambur wende,
He toke hys hond at the grece ende,
   And fayre he helpe hym yn;
And sayde, 'Syr yf your wyll be,
920 Take me your honde and go wyth me,   *give*
   For Y am of yowr kynne!
Ye shull come speke wyth Emaré,
That chaunged her nome to Egaré,
   That berys the whyte chynne.'   *has*

925 The kyng yn herte was full woo
When he herd mynge tho
   Of her that was hys qwene;
And sayde, 'Sone, why sayst thou so?
Wherto umbraydest thou me of my wo?   *reproach*
930   That may never bene!'
Nevurtheles wyth hym he wente;
Ayeyn hem come the lady gent,
   In the robe bryght and shene.   *shining*
He toke her yn hys armes two,
935 For joye they sowened, both to,
   Such love was hem bytwene.

904 Soone for **Sone* (son)? *905* foot of the steps. *926* was reminded by
these words.

A joyfull metyng was ther thore,
Of that lady, goodly unthur gore,   *robe*
   Frely in armes to folde.
940 Lorde, gladde was syr Kadore,
And othur lordes that ther wore,
   Semely to beholde.
Of the lady that wa[s] put yn the see,
Thorow grace of God in Trinité,
945   That was kevered of cares colde.
Leve we at the lady whyte as flour,
And speke we of her fadur the emperour,
   That fyrste the tale of Y tolde.

The emperour her fadyr then
950 Wa[s] woxen an olde man,   *had become*
   And thowght on hys synne,
Of hys thowghtyr Emaré
That was putte ynto the see,
   That was so bryght of skynne.   *fair*
955 He thowght that he wolde go
For hys penance to the Pope tho,
   And heven forto wynne.
Messengeres he sente forth sone
And they come to the kowrt of Rome
960   To take her lordes inne.

Emaré prayde her lord the kyng,
'Syr, abyde that lordys komyng
   That ys so fayr and fre.
And, swete syr, yn all thyng
965 Aqweynte you wyth that lordyng,
   Hyt ys worshyp to the.'   *to your honour*
The kyng of Galys seyde than,
'So grete a lord ys ther non,
   Yn all Crystyanté.'
970 'Now, swete syr, whatevur betyde   *happens*
Ayayn that grete lord ye ryde,   *up to*
   And all thy knyghtys wyth the.'

---

939 A fair lady to embrace. *943* was: wat L. *945* Who had seen the end of her grievous sorrows. *950* *Was: Wax* L. *960* To prepare lodgings for their master. *962* Sir, wait until the lord (himself) arrives. *965* Make yourself known.

Emaré thawghte her sone yynge
Ayeyn the emperour komynge,
975 How that he sholde done:
'Swete sone yn all thyng
Be redy wyth my lord the kyng   *alert*
    And be my swete sone!
When the emperour kysseth thy fadur so fre,
980 Loke yyf he wyll kysse the,
    Abowe the to hym sone;   *bow*
And bydde hym come speke wyth Emaré
That was putte ynto the see:
    Hymself yaf the dome.'

985 Now kometh the emperour of pryse;
Ayeyn hym rode the kyng of Galys,
    Wyth full mykull pryde.
The chyld was worthy unthur wede,
A satte upon a nobyll stede,   *he*
990   By hys fadyr syde;
And when he mette the emperour,
He valed hys hode wyth gret honour   *took off, headdress*
    And kyssed hym yn that tyde;
And othur lordys of gret valowre   *worth*
995 They also kessed Segramowre;
    In herte ys not to hyde.

The emperours hert anamered gretlye
Of the chylde that rode hym by,
    Wyth so lovely chere.
1000 Segramowre he s[t]ayde hys stede;   *reined in*
Hys owene fadur toke good hede,
    And othur lordys that ther were.
The chylde spake to the emperour
And sayde, 'Lord, for thyn honour,
1005   My worde that thou wyll here:
Ye shull come speke wyth Emaré
That changede her name to Egaré
    That was thy thowghthur dere.'   *daughter*

973-5 Emaré told her young son how he was to behave when the emperor
arrived. *984* It was he who passed the sentence. *997* felt great affection
for. *1000 stayde: sayde* L. *1005* Listen to what I have to say.

The emperour wax all pale,
1010 And sayde, 'Sone, why umbraydest me of bale,
      And thou may se no bote?'
   'Syr, and ye wyll go wyth me,   *if*
   I shall the brynge wyth that lady fre,   *to*
      That ys lovesom on to loke.'
1015 Nevurthelesse, wyth hym he wente;
   Ayeyn hym come that lady gent,
      Walkynge on her fote.
   And the emperour alyghte tho,
   And toke her yn hys armes two,
1020   And clypte and kyssed her sote.   *sweetly*

   Ther was a joyfull metynge
   Of the emperour and of the kynge,
      And also of Emaré;
   And so ther was of Syr [S]egramour,
1025 That aftyr was emperour:
      A full gode man was he.
   A grette feste ther was holde,
   Of erles and barones bolde,
      As testymonyeth thys story.   *bears witness*
1030 Thys ys on of Brytayne layes
   That was used by olde dayes,
      Men callys 'Playn[t] Egarye.'
   Jesus that settes yn thy trone,
   So graunte us wyth the to w[o]ne
1035   In thy perpetuall glorye!

1010–11 Why do you reproach me with my evil action, when you can see no way of setting right (its effects)?   *1024 Segramour: Egramour* L.   *1032 Playnt Egarye: playn the garye* L.   *1034 wone: wene* L.

Octavian

Lytyll and mykyll, olde and yonge,
Lystenyth now to my talkynge,   *speech*
  Of whome Y wyll yow [k]ythe;   *tell*
Jesu lorde, of hevyn kynge,
5 Grawnt us all hys blessynge
  And make us gladd and blythe.   *joyful*
Sothe sawys Y wyll yow mynge
Of whom the worde wyde can sprynge,   '*did*'
  Yf ye wyll lystyn and lythe;   *hear*
10 Yn bokys of ryme hyt ys tolde
How hyt befelle owre eldurs olde,
  Well oftyn sythe.

Some tyme felle aventure
In Rome ther was an emperowre,
15   In romans as we rede;
He was a man of grete favour,   *esteem*
He levyd in yoye and gret honour
  And doghty was in dede.   *valiant, actions*
In turnament and yn fyght,
20 Yn the worlde was not a bettur knyght
  Then he was undur wede.   *than, armour*
Octavyan hys name hyght;   *was called*
He was a man of moche myght,   *great*
  And bolde at every nede.   *in, crisis*

25 An emperes he had to wyfe,   *as*
The feyrest that myght bere lyfe: *live*
  These clerkys seyn soo;   *scholars, say*
Sevyn yere togedur had they ben,
Wyth yoye and game them betwene,   *delight*
30   And othur myrthys moo.
Tho the sevyn yerys were all goon,   *when*
Chylde myght they gete noon,   *beget*
  That tyme betwene them twoo,
That aftur hym hys londys schulde welde: *rule over*
35 Therfore grete sorowe drewe them to elde:
  Yn herte he was full woo.   *very distressed*

---

3 kythe T: *lythe* C. *7–8* I will remind you of true stories of people of great renown. *10 ryme: Rome* T. *11–12* What adventures very often happened to our ancestors. *13* It once happened that. *35 When that thay drewe till elde* T.

The emperowre, on a day,   *one day*
In hys bedd as he lay,
   Wyth hys lady bryght,   *fair*
40 He behelde hur feyre lere   *face*
That was bryght os blossom on brere   *briar*
   And semely in hys syght.
A sorowe to hys herte ranne   *pang, shot*
That chylde togedur they myght noon han,
45 Hys londe to ye[m]e and ryght.   *rule, govern*
Be hys lady as he sete,
For woo hys chekys waxe all wete,
   That was so hende a knyght.   *courteous*

When the lady can hyt see,
50 Chaunge sche dud hur feyre blee   *complexion*
   And syghyd wondur sare: *very deeply*
Sche felle on kneys hym agayne   *before him*
And of hys sorowe sche can hym frayne,
   And of hys mekyll care: *great grief*
55 'For yf that hyt were yowre wylle,
Yowre counsell forto schewe me tyll
   Of yowre lyvys fare;
Ye wott, Y am youre worldys fere,
Youre thoght to me ye myght dyskever: *reveal*
60 Youre comfort were the mare.'   *greater*

In hys armes he can hur folde   *embrace*
And hys cownsell to hur tolde,   *secret thoughts*
   And of hys hertys wownde.   *anguish*
'Now have we sevyn yere togedur byn,
65 And we no chylde have us betwen,
   And here we schall not leve but a stownde;   *(brief) space*
Y wott not how thys londe schall fare,
But leve in warre, in sorowe and care,
   When we are broght to grownde;
70 Therfore Y have so mekyll thoght   *grief*
That when Y am to bedd broght
   I slepe but selden sownde.'

45 *yeme: yene* C; *rewle* T. 53 And asked him the reason for his grief.
56–7 To make known to me what is (secretly) troubling you about your way
of life. 58 You know that I am your wife in this world. 66 *For fay* (truly)
we sall hythen fownde (must leave this world) T. 67–9 I cannot see that
anything but strife and grief will come to this land after we are dead.

Than answeryd that lady bryght,
'Syr, Y can yow rede aryght:
75   Yf yow nothyng [ill]!
    A ryche abbey schall we make   *splendid, build*
    For owre dere lady sake,
        And londys geve thertylle.
    Sche wyll prey hur sone feyre
80 That we togedur may have an heyre,
        Thys londe to welde at wylle.'
    They let make an abbey thoo;   *had built, then*
    The lady was wyth chyldren twoo,
        As hyt was Goddys wylle.

85 Wyth chylde waxe the lady thore;
    Grete sche was wyth peynys sore,
        That was bothe hende and free;   *gracious, noble*
    Tyll tyme felle that hyt was soo,   *came*
    The lady had men chyldren two,
90   That semely were to see.
    Tythyngys come to the emperowre,   *news*
    As he lay in hys towre: *was*
        A gladd man was hee.
    Two maydenys the errande hym broght;   *message*
95 Wythowt gyftys yede they noght: *left*
        Eyther he gafe townys three.   *to each*

    The emperowre was full blythe of mode;   *joyful*
    To hys chapell swythe he yode   *quickly, went*
        And thanked God of hys sonde.   *gift*
100 Yerly when the day can sprynge,   *early, dawn*
    A preest he dud a masse synge;
        Hys modur there he fonde.
    'Sone,' sche seyde, 'Y am blythe   *glad*
    That the emperes schall have lyve
105   And leve wyth us in londe;
    But moche sorowe deryth mee   *great, afflicts*
    That Rome schall wrong-heyred bee,
        In unkynde honde.'

74 I can give you sound advice. *75* Do not upset yourself; *ill* T: *to ylle* C.
78 And endow it with lands. *81* To rule over the country as pleases him;
at wylle: with skyll (as is right) T. *105* And go on living here with us.
107–8 That Rome shall pass into the hands of an unworthy stranger.

'Modur,' he seyde, 'why sey ye soo?   *this*
110 Now have we men chyldren two;
  Y-thankyd be Goddys wylle!'
'Nay,' sche seyde, 'sone myne;
Ther ys never neythyr of them thyn:
  That lykyth me full ylle!
115 For thou mygt no chylde have,   *beget*
Thy wyfe hath take a cokys knave, *kitchen boy*
  That wyll Y prove be skylle.'
A sorowe to the emperowrs herte ranne,
That worde cowde he speke noon,
120 But yede awey full stylle.   *went, silently*

To hys chapell forthe he yode
And at hys masse stylle he stode,
  As man that was in care.
The emperowrs modur let calle a knave
125 And hym behett grete mede to have: *promised, reward*
  An thowsande pownde and mare.
To the chaumbur the knave toke the way,
There as the emperes in chylde-bedd lay: *where*
  All slepte that there ware,
130 Forwhy they had wakyd longe, *because, kept watch*
In peynys and in sorowe stronge, *intense*
  Or sche were delyvyrd thare. *before*

'Haste the, knave, wyth all thy mygt:
Prevely that thou were dygt
135 And that thou were uncladd. *undressed*
Softly be hur yn thou crepe
That thou wake hur not of hur slepe, *so that*
  For seke sche ys bestadd!'
Hastyly was the knave uncladd;
140 In he went as sche hym badd
  Into the ryche bedde.
And evyr he drewe hym away; *shrank*
For the ryches that he in lay, *splendid cloths*
  Sore he was adredd. *afraid*

---

114 That displeases me greatly. *117* I will give you reasonable proof of it.
124 had a boy brought to her. *127 the knave: bothe thay* T. *132* followed
in T by three extra verses: see Commentary. *134* Get yourself ready
stealthily. *138* Because she is seriously ill.

145 The emperowrs modur awey went than;   *then*
   To hur sone swythe sche wan,   *quickly, went*
     At masse there as he stode.
   'Sone,' sche seyde, 'thou trowest not me;   *will not believe*
   Now thou mayste the sothe see.'   *truth*
150   To the chaumbur wyth hur he yode.   *went*
   When he sawe that syght than,
   Sorowe to hys herte ranne
     And nerehonde waxe he wode.
   The knave he slewe in the bedd:
155 The ryche clothys were all bebledd   *saturated*
     Of that gyltles blode.

   Evyr lay the lady faste aslepe;   *all the time*
   A dylfull swevyn can sche mete,
     That was so swete a wyght.
160 Sche thoght sche was in wyldyrnes,
   Yn thornes and in derkenes,
     That sche myght have no syght.
   There come fleyng ovyr the stronde
   A dragon all wyth fyre brennand,   *blazing*
165   That all the londe was bryght.
   In hys palmes, all brennyng bloo,
   Up he toke hur chyldren twoo
     And away he toke hys flyght.

   When the lady can awake
170 A dylfull gronyng can sche make: *anguished*
     The lasse was hur care.
   The emperowre toke up the grome,   *boy*
   The herre in hys honde he nome: *took*
     The hede smote of thare.
175 He caste hyt ageyne into the bedd: *back*
   The ryche clothys were all bebledd,   *made bloody*
     Of redd golde there they ware.
   The grete treson that there was wroght,   *act of treachery*
   The lady slept and wyste hyt noght:
180   Hur comfort was the mare.   *greater*

153 And he very nearly went mad.   158 She had a terrifying dream.   162
So that she could not see anything.   163 From over the sea.   166 In his
claws that were blazing with a dark flame; *bloo: so* T.   171 Which relieved
her grief; 169–80 very different in T: see Commentary.   179 and knew
nothing about it.

Wordys of thys were spoke no moo
Tyll the emperes to churche was goo,
   As lawe was in lede.
The emperowre made a feste, Y undurstonde,   *that land*
185 Of kyngys that were of ffarre londe   *am told*
   And lordys of dyvers stede.   *various regions*
The kyng of Calabur, wythowt lees,   *truly*
That the ladys ffadur was,
   Thethur was he bede.   *invited*
190 All they semblyd on a day,   *gathered*
Wyth myrthe, game and wyth play,
   Whan the lady to churche yede.

Kyngys dwellyd then all in same;   *remained, together*
There was yoye and moche game
195   At that grete mangery,   *feast*
Wyth gode metys them amonge,   *dishes*
Harpe, pype, and mery songe,
   Bothe lewte and sawtre.   *lute, psaltery*
When the sevyn nyght was all goon,
200 Wyth all kyn welthe in that won   *all manner of, place*
   And mery mynstralsy,
Ther was nevyr so ryche a getherynge   *splendid, assembly*
That had so sory a pertynge:
   I wyll yow telle forwhy.   *the reason*

205 Grete dele hyt ys to telle   *sorrow*
On the nynethe day what befelle:
   Lystenyth and ye schall here.
The emperowre to chaumbur yode,
All the kyngys abowte hym stode,
210   Wyth full gladd chere.
The emperowre seyde, there he can stonde,   *where*
Soche aventure felle in that londe   *chance, came about*
   Of a lady in that yere,
Wyth soche a treson was take and teynt;
215 He askyd wh[at] maner jugement
   That sche worthy were.

181–2 No more was said about this until the churching of the empress.
187 *wythowt lees: allas* T. *191* With all kinds of delight. *196 metys:
myrthis* T. *203* That broke up so sorrowfully. *206 nynethe: haghten*
(eighth) T. *214* Had been caught and proved guilty of just such a crime.
215 what: when C.

When the emperowre had hys tale tolde,   *finished speaking*
The kyng of Calabur answere wolde:
   (He wyste not what hyt mente);
220 He seyde, 'Hyt ys worthy for hur sake
Wythowt the cyté a fyre to make,   *kindle*
   Be ryghtwyse yugement;   *just decree*
When the fyre were brennyng faste,   *fiercely*
Sche and hur two chyldren therin to be caste,
225   And to dethe to be brente.'   *burnt*
The emperowre answeryd hym full sone: *at once*
   'Thyn own doghtur hyt hath done:
   Y holde to thyn assent.'

There was dele and grete pyté;
230 A feyre they made withowt the cyté
   Wyth brondys brennyng all bryght.   *logs*
To the fyre they ledd that lady thare,
Two squyers hur chyldren bare,
   That semely were in syght;
235 In a kyrtull of scarlett redd   *gown*
In the fyre to take hur dedd   *die*
   Redy was sche dyght.   *was got ready*
The kyng of Calabur made evyll chere: *looked wretched*
For dele he myght not stonde hys doghtur nere;
240   There wept bothe kynge and knyght.

The lady sawe no bettur redd
But that sche schulde be dedd
   That day upon the fylde;
Wyth sory hert, the sothe to telle,
245 Before the emperowre on kneys sche felle
   And bothe hur hondys uphelde.   *raised up*
'Grawnt me, lorde, for Jesus sake,
Oon oryson that Y may make   *prayer*
   To hym that all may welde;   *rule over*
250 And sythen on me do yowre wylle: *afterward, with*
What dethe that ye wyll put me tyll,   *to*
   Therto Y wyll me yelde.'   *to that, submit*

219 He did not know what the emperor had in mind.   *228* I shall be guided
by your opinion.   *241–2* The lady saw no way of avoiding death.   *241–3*
replaced in T by three lines after *252*: see Commentary.

The lady on her kneys hur sett;   *went on*
To Jesu Cryste full sore sche wepte:
255   What wondur was hyt thogh she were woo!
'Jesu,' sche seyde, 'kynge of blysse,
Thys day thou me rede and wysse,   *counsel, guide*
      And hevene qwene alsoo.
Mary, mayden and modur free;
260 My preyer wyll Y make to thee
      For my chyldren twoo;
As thou lett them be borne of mee,
Grawnt that they may crystenyd bee,
      To dethe or that they goo.'   *before*

265 Kyngys and qwenys abowte hur were;   *around*
Ladys felle in swownyng there
      And knyghtys stode wepande;
The emperowre hur lorde stode hur nere,
The terys tryllyd downe on hys lere: *ran, cheeks*
270   Full sory can he stande.
The emperowre spake a worde of pyté: *compassion*
'Dame, thy dethe Y wyll not see,
      Wyth herte nothur wyth hande.'
The emperowre gaf hur leve to goo
275 And wyth hur to take hur chyldren two
      And flee owt of hys londe.

The emperowre gaf hur fowrty pownde
Of fflorens that were rownde,
      In yeste as we rede;   *story*
280 And betoke hur knyghtys twoo
And gaf hur the golde and badd hur goo
      Owt of hys londe to lede.
The knyghtys the chyldren bare
There the hye weyes ware,
285   And forthe full swythe they yede.   *quickly*
The kyngys from the parlement,
Eche man to hys own londe went:
      For sorowe ther hertys can blede.

254 *wepte: grette* T.   265 *Than lordis that abowte hyr ware* T.   272-3 I will
neither kill you nor consent to have you killed.   283 *The knyghtys: Two
sqwyers* T.   284 *In stede* (place) *ther thay were never are* (before) T.   285
And intill uncouthe thede (unknown country) T.   286 *When scho was flemyd*
(exiled) *that was so gent* T.

    Tho the lady come to a wyldurnes
290 That full of wylde bestys was:
      The wode was grete and streyght.   *upright*
    The knyghtys toke hur there the chyldren twoo,   *handed over*
    And gaf hur the golde and badd hur goo
      The way that lay forthe ryght.
295 They badd hur holde the hye strete   *keep to, main*
    For drede of wylde beestys for to mete
      That mekyll were of myght.   *very powerful*
    Ageyne they went wyth sory mode;
    The lady aloon forthe sche yode,
300   As a wofull wyght.   *creature*

    So had sche wepte there beforne
    That the ryght wey had sche lorne
      (So moche sche was in thoght).
    Ynto a wode was veryly thykk,
305 There clevys were and weyes wyck,   *steep rocks, difficult*
      And hur wey fonde sche noght.
    Yn a clyff undur an hylle
    There sche fonde a full feyre welle   *spring*
      In an herber redy wroght;
310 Wyth olyfe treys was the herber sett: *planted*
    The lady sett hur downe and wepte,
      Further myght sche noght.   *could not go*

    The lady by the welle hur sett,
    To Jesu Cryste sore sche grett: *cried*
315   No further myght sche gone.
    'Lorde kynge,' sche seyde, 'of hevyn blys,
    Thys day thou me rede and wysse:
      Full weyle Y am of won.
    Mary modur, maydyn free,
320 My preyer wyll Y make to the,
      Thou mende my sorowfull mone.   *set right*
    So full Y am of sorowe and care
    That thre dayes are goon and mare,
      That mete ete Y noon.'   *food*

291 And all wylsom (desolate) *it semed to syghte* T. *293–4* and told her to
follow the path that lay straight ahead of her. *303* Her distress was so
great. *304 veryly: ferly* (remarkably) T. *307 clyff: greve* (grove) T.
309 In a patch of cleared ground. *311 wepte: grette* T. *318* I am absolutely lost and homeless; *weyle: will* T.

325 Be that sche had hur chyldren dyght,   *seen to*
    Hyt was woxe derke nyght,   *become*
        As sche sate be the welle;
    In the erber downe sche lay
    Tyll hyt was dawnyng of the day
330   That fowlys herde sche yelle.   *cry out*
    There came an ape to seke hur pray;
    Hur oon chylde sche bare away
        On an hye hylle.
    What wondur was, thogh sche were woo?
335 The ape bare the chylde hur froo!   *away from*
        In swownyng downe sche felle.

    In all the sorowe that sche in was,
    There come rennyng a lyenas,   *lioness*
        Os wode as sche wolde wede;
340 In swownyng as the lady lay,
    Hur wodur chylde sche bare away,   *second*
        Hur whelpys wyth to fede.   *cubs*
    What wondur was thogh sche woo ware?
    The wylde beestys hur chyldyr away bare;
345   For sorowe hur herte can blede.
    The lady sett hur on a stone
    Besyde the welle and made hur mone,   *complaint*
        And syghyng forthe sche yede.

    There came a fowle that was feyre of flyght   *excellent in*
350 (A gryffyn he was callyd be ryght)
        Ovyr the holtys hore;   *grey woods*
    The fowle was so moche of myght
    That he wolde bare a knyght
        Well armyd thogh he ware.
355 The lyenas wyth the chylde up toke he
    And into an yle of the see
        Bothe he them bare.
    The chylde slept in the lyenas mowthe;
    Of wele nor wo nothyng hyt knowyth,   *good fortune*
360   But God kepe hyt from care!   *protect*

337 While she was still overwhelmed with grief.   *339* In a frenzied rush.
345 In swoghe scho lay for drede T.   *346-8* very different in T: see Commentary.   *359 knowyth: kouthe* T.

Whan the lyenas had a fote on londe,
Hastyly sche can upstonde,
   As a beste that was stronge and wylde.   *fierce*
Thorow Goddys grace the gryffyn she slowe   *killed*
365 And sythen ete of the flesche ynowe   *afterwards, plenty*
   And leyde hur downe be the chylde.
The chylde soke the lyenas,
As hyt Goddys wylle was,
   Whan hyt the pappys feled;   *teats*
370 And when the lyenas began to wake,
Sche lovyd the chylde for hur whelpys sake
   And therwyth sche was full mylde.   *gentle*

Wyth hur fete sche made a denne   *scraped out*
And leyde the lytull chylde theryn
375 And kepte hyt day and nyght;   *guarded*
And when the lyenas hungurd sore,
Sche ete of the gryffyn more,
   That afore was stronge and wyght.   *formerly*
As hyt was Goddys owne wylle,
380 The lyenas belafte the chylde stylle: *left, unmolested*
   The chylde was feyre and bryght.
The lady sett hur on a stone,
Besyde the welle and made hur mone   *complaint*
   As a wofull wyght.

385 'Jesu,' sche seyde, 'Kynge of blys,
Thys day thou me rede and wysse: *counsel, guide*
   Of all kyngys thou art flowre.   *supreme*
As Y was kyngys doghtur and qwene
And emperes of Rome have bene,
390   Of many a ryche towre,
Thorow the lesyng that ys on me wroght
To moche sorowe Y am broght
   And owt of myn honowre;   *dishonoured*
The worldys wele Y have forlorne
395 And my two chyldren be fro me borne:
   Thys lyfe Y may not dewre!   *endure*

361–2 As soon as the lioness touched the ground, she sprang up. *370 The lyones gan it wake* (watch over) T. *374 That lyttill childe in broghte scho then* T. *381 With that barne so bryghte* T. *388* As certainly as I was. *391* Because of the false accusation brought against me. *394* All prosperity on earth.

  Lorde, the sorowe that Y am ynne,
  Well Y wot hyt ys for my synne:
   Welcome be thy sonde.
400 To the worlde Y wyll me nevyr yeve,   *as long as*
  But serve the, lorde, whyll Y leve,   *in*
   Into the Holy Londe.'   *took*
  Downe be an hylle the wey she name
  And to the Grekeysch See sche came
405 And walkyd on the stronde;   *shore*
  Beforne hur an haven there she sye   *harbour*
  And a ceté wyth towrys hye,
   All redy there sche fonde.

  When sche come to the ryche towne
410 A schyppe sche fonde all redy bowne,   *prepared*
  Wyth pylgrymys forthe to fare;   *voyage*
  Sche badd the schyppman golde and fee *promised, master, wealth*
  In hys schypp that sche myght bee,
   Yf hys wylle ware.
415 A bote they sende ovyr the flode
  To the lady there sche stode,
   A wyght man in hur bare;   *strong, carried*
  By the maste they badd hur sytte,
  Of hur wo myght no man wytt,
420 But evyr sche wept full sare.   *bitterly*

  The schypp come be an yle syde,
  The schyppman bade them there abyde: *anchor*
   'Fresche watur have we none.'
  Besyde them was a roche hye,   *cliff*
425 A well feyre welle there they sye,   *stream*
  Come strykyng ovyr a stone.   *rushing*
  Two men to the londe they sente,
  Up by the streme they wente,
   The welle they fonde anone.   *source*
430 A lyenas lay in hur denne
  And was full fayne of tho two men: *glad*
   Anon sche had them slon.

399 whatever (fortune) you may send. *400* I will never (again) devote myself to worldly pursuits. *408 A redy waye there scho fand* T. *413–14* If he would agree to let her come aboard his ship. *419* No-one could discover the reason for her sorrow. *425 well feyre welle: welle streme* T.

So long on ankyr can they ryde,
The two men forto abyde,   *wait for*
435 Tyll none was on the day.   *ninth hour*
Twelve men anon can they dyght   *get ready*
Wyth helmes and hawberkys bryght;   *mailshirts*
To londe than wente they.
They fonde the lyenas denne,
440 A man-chylde lyeng therynne   *in it*
Wyth the lyenas to pley.
Sometyme hyt soke the lyenas pappe,
And sometyme they can kysse and cleppe: *embrace*
For fere they fledd away.

445 They yede and tolde what they sye: *went (back)*
They fonde on the roche on hye
A lyenas in hur denne;
A man-chylde therin lay,
Wyth the lyenas to play,
450 And dedd were bothe ther men.
Than spake the lady mylde:
'Mercy, lordyngys, that ys my chylde!   *sirs*
On londe ye let me renne.'
The bote they sente ovyr the flode,
455 To londe allone the lady yode,
Sore wepeyd the schypman than.

When sche came on the roche on hyght   *high*
Sche ranne whyll sche myght
Wyth full sory mode:
460 The lyenas, thorow Goddys grace,
When sche sye the ladyes face,
Debonerly stylle sche stode.   *meekly quiet*
Thorow the myght of Mary mylde
Sche suffurd hur to take up the chylde,   *allowed*
465 And wyth the lady to the see she yode.
When the schypmen the lyenas sye,   *sailors*
The londe durste they not come nye: *near*
For feere they were nye wode!

435 on: of T.   *440 A knave childe laye sowkand hir then* T.   *453* Let me go quickly to land.   *459* In great distress.   *468* Their fear nearly drove them mad.

Some hente an oore and some a sprytt,   *seized, spar*
470 The lyenas forto meete: *encounter*
    Owt of ther schyppe to were;   *repel from*
The lady ynto the schyp wente;
Thyrty fote the lyenas aftur sprente,   *leaped*
    Ther durste no man hur yn bere.   *bring*
475 There men myght game see!
Fowrty men lepe ynto the see,
    So ferde of the lyenas they were.   *afraid*
By the lady the lyenas downe lay
And wyth the chylde can sche play,
480   And no man wolde sche dere.

They drewe up seyle of ryche hewe;   *bright colours*
The wynde owt of the havyn them blewe,
    Ovyr the wanne streme.   *dark sea*
The furste londe that they sye
485 Was a ceté wyth towrys hye,
    That hyght Jerusalem.
As glad they were of that syght,
As fowlys be of day lyght   *birds*
    And of the sonne leme.   *ray*
490 When hyt was ebbe and not flode,
The schypmen and the lady to londe yode
    Into that ryche realme.   *kingdom*

Ovyr all the cyté wyde and longe
Of thys lady worde ther spronge,
495   That there on londe was lende: *had arrived*
How sche had a lyenas
Broght owt of wyldurness:
    The kynge aftur hur sende.   *for*
The kynge bad hur lett for nothynge
500 And the lyenas wyth hur brynge,
    To the castell there nerehonde.   *close by*
When that sche before hym come,
For the emperyce of ryche Rome   *as*
    Full well he hur kende.   *recognized*

---

472 wente: thay hente T.   *475 There was than bot lyttill glee* T.   *489 sonne
leme: dayes gleme* T.   *493–4 The fame of this lady spread to every part of
the city.   499 not to delay for any consideration.   501 To the castelle es
scho went* T.   *503 He kende hir for* T.   *504 And by the hande he hir hente* T.

505 The kynge frayned hur of hur fare,
And sche hym tolde of moche care,
 As a wofull wyght.
Wyth hys quene he made hur to dwelle,
And maydenys redy at hur wylle,   *bidding*
510 To serve hur day and nyght.   *at all times*
The chylde that was so feyre and free,
The kynge let hyt crystenyd bee: *had it*
 Octavyon he hyght.
When the chylde was of elde   *an age*
515 That he cowde ryde and armys welde,   *manage*
 The kynge dubbyd hym knyght.

The lyenas that was so wylde
Sche levyd with the lady mylde:
 Hur comfort was the more.   *greater*
520 The lady was wyth the quene,
With myrthe and game them betwene,
 To covyr hur of hur care.
Eche oon servyd hur day and nyght
To make hur gladd wyth all ther myght,
525 Tyll hyt bettur ware.
In Jerusalem can the lady dwelle,
And of hur odur chylde Y can yow telle
 That the ape away bare.

Now comyth the ape that was wylde
530 Thorow the forest wyth the chylde
 Be the holtys hoore.
As the ape come ovyr the strete   *path*
Wyth a knyght can sche meete,
 That chylde as sche bare.   *was carrying*
535 There faght the knyght wondur longe
Wyth the ape that was so stronge,
 Hys swyrde brake he thare.
The ape then awey ranne,
The knyght there the chylde wanne,   *took*
540 And on hys way can he fare.   *go*

505 The king questioned her about her state. *507 And of hir grete unryghte* (the great wrong done her) T. *518 Belefte* (remained) *with the lady and the childe* T. *520 was: byleved* T. *522* To make her forget her sorrow. *523–4* Everyone did their utmost, at all times, to cheer her up. *527 Y can yow: now will I* T.

Forthe rode the knyght wyth the chylde then,
And yn the foreste he mett owtlawys ten,
   That moche were of myght;
The knyght yyt was nevyr so wo,
545 For hys swerde was brokyn yn two,   *so that*
   That he ne myght wyth them fyght.
Thogh the knyght were kene and thro,   *bold, fierce*
The owtlawys wanne the chylde hym fro   *got*
   That was so swete a wyght.
550 The knyght was woundyd so that day,
Unnethe hys hors bare hym away:
   So delefully was he dyght.   *wretchedly, served*

The owtlawys set them on a grene
And leyde the lytyll chylde them betwene:
555   The chylde upon them loghe.
The maystyr owtlawe seyde then: *chief*
'Hyt were grete schame for hardy men,   *bold*
   Thys chylde here and we sloghe.   *if*
I rede we bere hyt here besyde
560 To a ryche cyté wyth grete pryde,
   And do we hyt no woghe;   *harm*
Hyt ys so feyre and gentyll borne,
That we myght have therforne   *for it*
   Golde and sylvyr ynoghe.   *plenty of*

565 Then two of them made them yare
And to the cyté the chylde they bare,
   That was so swete a wyght.
Ther was no man that the chylde sye,
But that they wepte wyth ther eye:
570   So feyre hyt was be syght.   *to see*
A burges of Parys came them nere   *citizen, up to*
That had be palmer sevyn yere,   *pilgrim*
   Clement the Velayn he hyght:
'Lordyngys,' he seyde, 'Wyll ye thys chylde selle?'
575 'Ye, who wyll us golde and sylvyr telle,   *pay out*
   Floryns brode and bryght.'

544 Never before had the knight been so distressed. 550–1 The knight
was then so badly wounded that he could hardly get away on his horse.
555 The child laughed up at them. 559–60 My advice is to take it
honourably to the great city close at hand. 567 *Thay couthe the way full
ryghte* T. 570 *be: of* T. 575 *The golde will I for hym telle* T.

For fowrty pownde the chylde selle they wolde;
Clement seyde, 'Longe y[e] may hym holde,   *keep*
   Or y[e] hym selle may.   *before*
580 Y swere yow, lordyngys, be my hode,
I trowe ye can full lytyll gode,
   Soche wordys forto say.
Golde and sylvyr ys to me full nede;
Twenty pownde Y wyll yow bede,   *offer*
585   And make yow redy paye.'   *down payment*
The chylde they to Clement yolde;   *handed over*
Twenty pownde he them tolde,   *counted out*
   And wente forthe on hys way.

When Clement had the chylde boght,
590 A panyer he let be wroght,   *basket*
   The chylde yn to lede;   *carry*
A nurse he gate hym also,
Into Fraunce wyth hym to go,
   The chylde forto fede.
595 Home he toke the wey full ryght   *directly*
And hastyd hym wyth all hys myght;
   That was hys beste rede.
Burgeys of Parys were full fayne;
Many wente Clement agayne: *to meet*
600   A sklavyn was hys wede.

They callyd Clement and kyssyd hym all
And broght hym home to hys halle.
   Hys wyfe therof was blythe.
Sche askyd hym the ryght dome,   *true explanation*
605 How he to the chylde come;
   He tolde hur full swythe: *promptly*
'In Jerusalem there Y hym gete,
For there wolde Y hym not lete: *abandon*
   The sothe Y wyll the kythe.'   *make known*
610 The wyfe answeryd wyth herte mylde:
'Hyt schall be myn own chylde!'
   And kyssyd hyt many a sythe.

578, 579 ye T: *y* C. *581–2* If you can talk in this way, I don't believe you
know what is to your advantage. *583* are very scarce with me. *597* That
seemed to him the best thing to do; *And unto Paresche he yede* T. *600* He
was dressed in a pilgrim's mantle. *601 callyd: haylse[d]* (greeted) T.

'Dame,' seyde Clement, 'whyll Y palmer was,
Thys chylde Y gate wyth my flesche
615   In the hethen thede.   *nation*
Into thys londe Y have hym broght:
Forwhy that thou wylt greve the noght,   *if*
    Full ryche schall be thy mede.   *reward*
The wyfe answeryd wyth herte fre,   *generous*
620 'Full welcome, syr, hyt ys to me;
    Full well Y schall hym fede;
And kepe hym wyth my chylde
Tyll that he come of elde,   *age*
    And clothe them yn oon wede.'

625 Clement than was full blythe
And let crysten hym full swythe;   *straightway*
    Hyt was [not] taryed that nyght.   *put off*
In the jeste as hyt ys tolde,
The ryght name he hym calde: *proper, gave*
630   Florent be name he hyght.
Whan the chylde was sevyn yere olde
Hyt was feyre, wyse and bolde,
    T[o] man that redyth aryght.
Thorow the realme of Fraunce wyde and longe,
635 Of thys chylde the worde spronge,   *fame spread*
    So feyre he was be syght.

Evyr the burges and hys wyfe   *always*
Lovyd the chylde as ther lyfe,
    To them he was full dere.
640 Tyll the chylde was sevyn yere olde and more,
The burges set hym to lore   *apprenticed him*
    To be a chaungere.   *money-changer*
Clement toke the chylde oxen two
And bad hym to the brygge go,
645   To be a bochere;
To lerne hys crafte forto do,   *practise*
And hys kynde was nevyr therto,
    Soche games forto lere.   *proceedings*

---

624 And give them exactly the same clothes. 627 *not* T: omitted C.
633 To anyone with proper understanding; *To: The* CT. 641–2 *He sett
his ownn son to the lore/To be a chawndelere* (chandler) T. 647 But it was not
in his nature. 648 *To use* (practise) *swylke mystere* (profession) T.

As Florent to the brygge can go,
650 Dryvyng forthe hys oxen two,
    He sawe a semely syght: *fair*
A squyer, as Y schall yow telle,
A jentyll ffawcon bare to selle,   *noble*
    Wyth ffedurs folden bryght.
655 Florent to the squyer yede,   *went*
Bothe hys oxen he can hym bede   *offer*
    For the ffawcon lyght.   *swift*
The squyer therof was full blythe   *delighted*
Forto take the oxen swythe,
660   And gave hym the ffawcon ryght.   *directly*

The squyer therof was full gladd
When he tho oxen taken had,
    And hyed owt of syght;   *hurried*
And Florent to fle was full fayne,
665 He wende he wolde have had hys hawk agayne,
    And ranne wyth all hys myght.
Home he toke the ryght way   *shortest*
To Clementys hows, as hyt lay,   *where it was*
    And yn he went full ryght;   *at once*
670 He fedde the hawke whyll he wolde,
And sythen he can hys fedurs folde,
    As the squyer had hym teyght.   *instructed*

Clement came yn full sone: *soon afterwards*
'Thefe, where haste thou my oxen done,   *put*
675   That Y the begyfte?'   *entrusted to*
Grete dele myght men see thore:
Clement bete the chylde sore,
    That was so swete a wyght.
'Wyth odur mete shalt thou not leve   *on*
680 But that thys glede wyll the yeve,   *kite, give*
    Neythur day ne nyght.'   *at no time*
As sore beton as the chylde stode,
Yyt he to the ffawcon yode,   *went*
    Hys fedurs forto ryght.   *set in order*

662–84 missing in T.   664–5 And Florent was very glad to get away; he thought that the squire would have demanded his hawk back.   670 as long as it wanted food.   672 *hym: hym hym* C.   676 That was a very distressing sight.

685 The chylde thoght wondur thore
    That Clement bete hym so sore,
      And mekely he can pray:
    'Syr,' he seyde, 'for Crystys ore,   *mercy*
    Leve and bete me no more,   *stop*
690   But ye wyste well why.
    Wolde ye stonde now and beholde
    How feyre he can hys fedurs folde
      And how lovely they lye,   *gracefully*
    Ye wolde pray God wyth all your mode   *heart*
695 That ye had solde halfe your gode,   *possessions*
      Soche anodur to bye.'

    The burgeys wyfe besyde stode,
    Sore sche rewyd yn hur mode   *pitied (him), mind*
      And seyde, 'Syr, thyn ore!
700 For Mary love, that maydyn mylde,
    Have mercy on owre feyre chylde
      And bete hym no more!
    Let hym be at home and serve us two
    And let owre odur sonys go
705   Eche day to lore;
    Soche grace may God for the chylde have wroght,
    To a bettur man he may be broght
      Than he a bocher were.'

    Aftur all thys tyme befelle   *it happened*
710 Clement fowrty pownde can telle
      Into a pawtenere;   *purse*
    Clement toke hyt chylde Florent   *gave to*
    And to the brygge he hym sente,
      Hys brothur hyt to bere.   *take*
715 As the chylde thorow the cyté of Parys yede,
    He sye where stode a feyre stede,
      Was stronge yn eche werre;   *every battle*
    The stede was whyte as any mylke,
    The brydyll reynys were of sylke,
720   The molettys gylte they were.   *bosses (on bit)*

685–720 missing in T.   *685* It seemed strange to the child then.   *690*
Unless you have good reason for it.   *691* If you would only now stop and
look.   *696* To buy another like it.   *705* Every day to learn their trade.
706–7 God in his mercy may have intended the child to achieve a higher
station in life.

Florent to the stede can gone, *went up to*
So feyre an hors sye he nevyr none,
   Made of flesche and felle; *skin*
Of wordys the chylde was wondur bolde *speech*
725 And askyd whedur he schoulde be solde; *was for sale*
   The penyes he wolde hym telle.
The man hym lovyd for thyrty pownde,
Eche peny hole and sownde,
   No lesse he wolde hym selle. *for no*
730 Florent seyde: 'To lytull hyt were,
But never the lees thou schalt have more':
   Fowrty pownde he can hym telle.

The merchaund therof was full blythe, *glad*
Forto take the money swythe, *promptly*
735   And hastyd hym away.
Chylde Florent lepe up to ryde
To Clementys hows wyth grete pryde,
   He toke the ryght way;
The chylde soght noon odur stalle *looked for*
740 But sett hys stede yn the halle
And gave hym corne and haye,
And sethyn he can hym kembe and dyght
That every heer lay aryght,
   And nevyr oon wronge lay.

745 Clement comyth yn full sone:
'Thefe,' he seyde, 'what haste thou done?
   What haste thou hedur broght?' *here*
'Mercy, ffadur for Goddys peté!
Wyth the money that ye toke me, *gave*
750   Thys horse have Y boght.'
The burges wyfe felle on kne thore:
'Syr, mercy,' sche seyde, 'for Crystys ore: *grace*
   Owre feyre chylde bete ye noght!
Ye may see, and ye undurstode,
755 That he had never kynde of thy blode,
   That he these werkys hath wroght.'

721–56 missing in T. *727–8* valued it at thirty pounds of good coin. *730* that would be too little. *742* And afterwards he groomed it thoroughly. *754–6* If you took careful heed you would see that his actions show he could never have been your son.

Aftur thys hyt was not longe
In Fraunce felle a werre stronge;
 An hondryd thousande were there y-lente,
760 Wyth shyldys brode and helmys bryght,
Men, that redy were to fyght,
 Thorowowt the londe they went.
They broke castels stronge and bolde: *battered down*
Ther myght no hye wallys them holde,   *withstand*
765 Ryche townys they brente!   *burned*
All the kyngys, ferre and nere,   *from all parts*
Of odur londys that Crysten were,
 Aftur were they sente.

Octavyon the emperour of Rome
770 To Parys sone he come,
 Wyth many a mody knyght;   *brave*
And othur kyngys kene wyth crowne: *bold*
All they were to batell bowne,   *ready to fight*
 Wyth helmys and hawberkys bryght.   *mailshirts*
775 In Parys a monyth the oost lay,
For they had takyn a day   *fixed upon*
 Wyth the sowdon moche of myght.
The sowdon wyth hym a gyaunt broght;
The realme of Fraunce durste noght
780 Agenste hym to fyght.

The sowdon had a doghtur bryght,
Marsabelle that maydyn hyght:
 Sche was bothe feyre and free;   *noble*
The feyrest thynge alyve that was
785 In Crystendome or hethynnes,
 And semelyest of syght.
To the kynge of Fraunce the maydyn sende
To lye at Mountmertrous there nerehonde,
 From Parys mylys thre.
790 At Montmertrous besyde Borogh Larayn,
That stondyth ovyr the banke of Sayne,
 For aventours wolde sche see.

757-92 missing in T. *758* That violent war broke out in France. *759* invaded the country. *771* Wyth: Wyth a C. *775* the army was quartered. *779* No-one in the whole kingdom. *788* For permission to encamp at Montmartre, close at hand. *792* Because she wished to see the fighting.

The kyng of Fraunce the maydyn hyght,   *promised*
As he was trewe kyng and knyght,
795   And swere hur be hys fay,   *word*
That she m[ygh]t savely come therto:
Ther schulde no man hur mysdo,   *molest*
    Neythur be nyght ne day.   *at any time*
The mayde therof was full blythe;   *glad*
800 To the castell sche went swythe,   *quickly*
    And sevyn nyghtys there sche lay;   *stayed*
For sche thoght yoye and pryde
To see the Crystyn knyghtys ryde,
    On fylde them forto play.   *exert*

805 The gyauntys name was Aragonour;
He lovyd that maydyn par amour,   *as his mistress*
    That was so feyre and free;
And sche had levyr drawyn bene
Than yn hur chaumbur hym to sene:
810   So fowle a wyght was he!
The gyaunt came to Mountmertrous on a day,
For to comfort that feyre may,   *please*
    And badd hur blythe bee;
He seyde: 'Lemman, or Y ete mete,
815 The kyngys hed of Fraunce Y wyll the gete,
    For oon cosse of the.'

Than spake the mayde mylde of mode   *manner*
To the gyaunt there he stode   *where*
    And gaf hym answere:
820 'The kyngys hed when hyt ys broght,
A kysse wyll Y warne the noght,   *refuse*
    For lefe to me hyt were.'   *dear*
The gyaunt armyd hym full well,
Bothe yn yron and yn stele,
825   Wyth schylde and wyth spere.
Hyt was twenty fote and two
Betwyx hys hedd and hys too:
    None hors myght hym bere.

793–804 *missing in* T.   796 *myght: must* C.   802 It gave her a feeling of.
805 *preceded in* T *by a defective stanza: see Commentary.*   808–9 And she
would rather have been dismembered than have him in her bedroom.   815–16
get for you in exchange for a single kiss.

  The gyaunt toke the ryght way
830 To the cyté of Parys, as hyt lay,   *where*
   Wyth hym went no moo.   *others*
  The gyaunt leynyd ovyr the walle
  And spake to the folkys all
   Wordys kene and thro;   *bold, fierce*
835 And bad them sende hym a knyght   *told*
  To fynde hym hys fylle of fyght,   *fighting*
   Or the londe he wolde ovyrgo.   *overrun*
  And he ne wolde leve alyfe
  Man, beste, chylde ne wyfe,
840   But that he wolde them brenne and slo. *burn*

  All the folke of that cyté
  Ranne that gyaunt forto see,
   At the walle there he stode;
  As farre as they sye hys blee,
845 They were fayne forto flee,   *anxious*
   For fere they were nye wode.
  Owt went armyd knyghtys fyve:
  They thoght to aventour ther lyve; *hazard*
   The gyaunt thoght hyt gode:
850 Full hastely he had them slayne,
  Ther came nevyr oon quyk agayne, *alive*
   That owt at the yatys yode.   *gates*

  Chylde Florent askyd hys fadur Clement,
  Whodur all that people went,
855   That to the yatys dud renne.   *run*
  Clement tolde Florent hys sone:
  'Soche a gyaunt to the walle ys come'—
   The chylde harkenyd hym then—
  'Sone, but yf he may fynde a man
860 That he may fyght hys fylle upon,
   Thys cyté wyll he brenne;
  And sythen thys londe ovyrgone:
  Quykk wyll he leve noon
   Alyve that ys therynne.'

---

843 walle: bretage (parapet) T. *844* Once they could see his face. *852*
followed by two extra stanzas in T: see Commentary. *854* Where all the
people were going. *858 Hase slayne fyve of oure men* T.

865 'Fadur,' he seyde, 'sadull my stede
 And lende me somedele of your wede,   *some, armour*
  And helpe that Y were dyght;   *ready*
 Yf that hyt be Goddys wylle,
 I hope to fynde hym hys fylle,
870   Thogh he be stronge and wyght.'
 Clement seyde: 'And thou oon worde more speke,
 Thys day Y wyll thy hedd breke,
  I swere be Mary bryght!'
 'For nothynge, fadur, wyll Y byde,   *delay*
875 To the gyaunt wyll Y ryde
  And prove on hym my myght.'

 For sorowe Clementys herte nye braste   *nearly broke*
 When he on Florent hacton caste;   *(padded) jacket*
  The chylde was bolde and kene.
880 An hawberke above let he falle,
 Rowsty were the naylys all   *rivets*
  And hys atyre bedeene.
 Clement broght forthe schylde and spere
 That were uncomely for to were: *disgusting*
885   All sutty, blakk and unclene.
 A swyrde he broght the chylde beforne
 That sevyn yere afore was not borne,   *carried (to battle)*
  Ne drawe—and that was seene.   *drawn, obvious*

 Clement the swyrde drawe owt wolde,   *wanted to*
890 Gladwyn his wyfe schoulde the scabard holde,   *had to*
  And bothe faste they drowe;   *pulled hard*
 When the swyrde owt glente,   *shot*
 Bothe to the erthe they wente: *fell*
  There was game ynowe!
895 Clement felle to a benche so faste
 That mowth and nose all tobraste,   *were cut open*
  And Florent stode and loghe.   *laughed*
 Hyt ys gode bowrde to telle   *jest*
 How they to the erthe felle,
900   And Clement lay in swoghe.   *unconscious*

876 And give proof of my strength against him; followed by two extra stanzas in T: see Commentary. *882* And all the rest of his equipment too. *894* That was a great joke.

Chylde Florent yn hys onfayre wede,   *unprepossessing armour*
When he was armyd on a stede,
  Hys swyrde y-drawyn he bare;
Hys ventayle and hys basenett,   *beaver, round helmet*
905 Hys helme on hys hedd sett:
  Bothe rowsty they were.
Bothe Clement and hys wyfe
Lovyd the chylde as ther lyfe;
  For hym they wept full sore.
910 To Jesu Cryste faste can they bede,   *pray*
To sende hym grace well to spede—
  They myght do no more.

For hys atyre that was so bryght,
Hym behelde bothe kynge and knyght
915 And moche wondur thoght;
Many a skorne there he hent
As he thorow the cyté went,
  But therof roght he noght.   *cared*
The people to the wallys can go
920 To see the batell betwene them two,
  When they were togedur broght.
Clement hys fadur wo was he,
Tyll he wyste whych schulde maystyr be,
  Gladd was he noght.

925 The chylde came to the yatys sone
And bad the portar them ondone   *unbar*
  And opyn them full wyde.
All that abowt the chylde stode
Laghed as they were wode,
930 And skornyd hym that tyde.   *jeered at, time*
Every man seyde to hys fere,   *companion*
  'Here comyth an hardy bachelere: *young knight*
  Hym besemyth well to ryde.
Men may see be hys bre[ni]e bryght
935 That he ys an hardy knyght,
  The gyaunt to abyde.'   *face*

906 rowsty: soyty T.   *913–15* All the people stared at him on account of
his 'dazzling' armour and thought it very strange; *so bryght: unbryghte* T.
916 He was the butt of many insults.   *923* which of them was going to win.
933 He will make a splendid knight.   *934 brenie: breme* C; *brene* T.

The gyaunt upryght can stonde
And toke hys burdon yn hys honde,   *club*
   Of stele that was unryde;   *huge*
940 To the chylde smote he so
That the chyldys shylde brake yn two
   And felle on every syde.
The chylde was nevyr yyt so wo,
That hys schylde was brokyn yn two:
945   More he thoght to byde.
To the gyaunt he smote so sore
That hys ryght arme flye of thore:
   The blode stremyd wyde.   *shot out*

Clement on the wallys stode;
950 Full blythe was he yn hys mode
   And mende can hys chere.
'Sone, for that Y have seene,
Thy noble stroke that ys so kene,
   To me art thou full dere;
955 Now me thynkyth yn my mode
Thou haste well besett my gode,
   Soche playes forto lere.   *procedures*
Jesu that syttyth yn Trynyté,
Blesse the fadur that gate the,
960   And the modur that the dud bere.'

Chylde Florent yn hys feyre wede
Sprange owt as sparkyll on glede,   *from ember*
   The sothe Y wyll yow say.
He rode forthe wyth egur mode   *angry*
965 To the gyaunt there he stode:
   There was no chyldys play.
The gyaunt to the chylde smote so
That hys hors and he to grounde dud go; *fell*
   The stede on kneys lay.
970 Clement cryed wyth egur mode,
'Sone, be now of comfort gode   *heart*
   And venge the yf thou may.'

---

943 had never before been so distressed. *944 That: Als when* T. *945* He
determined to go on fighting; *More: Bot more* T. *951* And became more
cheerful. *956* You have made good use of what I have given you. *961 feyre:
unfaire* T. *970 egur: sory* T. *972* And take your revenge if you can.

As evyll as the chylde farde,
When he Clementys speche harde,   *heard*
975   Hys harte beganne to bolde;   *grow bold*
Boldely hys swyrde he lawght,   *took hold of*
To the gyaunt soche a strok he raght   *struck*
    That all hys blode can colde.
He hytt the gyaunt on the schouldur boon,
980 That to the pappe the swyrde ranne: *breast, cut*
    To grounde can he folde.   *fall*
Thus hyt was thorow Goddys grace:
The gyaunt swownyd yn that place,
    In geste as hyt ys tolde.

985 The kyngys on the wallys stode;
Whan the gyaunt to grounde yode,   *fell*
    All gladd they were.
All the people at the chylde loghe,
How he the gyauntys helme of droghe   *pulled*
990   And hys hedd he smote of there.
The chylde lepe upon hys stede
And rode awey a gode spede;
    Wyth them spake he no more.
The chylde toke the ryght way
995 To Mountmertrous there the mayde lay,
    And the hedd wyth hym he bare.

When he came to the maydyns halle,
He fonde the boordys covyrde all,   *tables*
    And redy to go to mete;
1000 The maydyn that was so mylde of mode,
In a kyrtull there sche stode
    And bowne sche was to sete.   *ready*
'Damysell,' he seyde, 'feyre and free
Well gretyth thy lemman the
1005   Of that he the behete;
Here an hedd Y have the broght,
The kyngys of Fraunce ys hyt noght:
    Hyt ys evyll to gete.'   *difficult*

---

973 As badly off as the boy was.   *983 He slewe the geaunt in that place* T.
1004–5 Your lover salutes you fairly, in accordance with his promise to you.

ring

The byrde bryght as golde [b]ye

1010 When sche the gyauntys hedd sye,

Well sche hyt kende.   *knew*

'Me thynkyth he was trewe of hete:

The kyngys when he myght not gete,

Hys own that he me sende.'

1015 'Damysell,' he seyde, 'feyre and bryght,

Now wyll Y have that thou hym hyght.'   *promised*

And ovyr hys sadull he leynyd;

Ofte sythys he kyste that may,   *many times*

And hente hur up and rode away,   *lifted*

1020 That all the brygge can bende.

Crye and noyse rose yn the towne;

Sone ther was to batell bowne

Many an hardy knyght,

Wyth sperys longe and schyldys browne;   *shining*

1025 Florent let the maydyn adowne

And made hym bowne to fyght.

Her skarlet sleve he schare of then,   *cut*

He seyde, 'Lady, be thys ye shall me ken,   *recognize*

When ye me see by syght.'

1030 Soche love waxe betwene them two,   *grew*

That the lady wepte for wo,

When he ne wynne hur myght.

Chylde Florent yn onfeyre wede   *unsightly*

Sprange owt as sparkyll on glede,

1035 The sothe forto say;

Many hethen men that stownde   *time*

In dede he broght to the grounde:

There was no chyldys play.

When Florent beganne to fownde,   *leave*

1040 Wythowt any weme of wownde,

To Parys he toke the way;

The hethyn men were so fordredd,   *terrified*

To Cleremount wyth the mayde they fledd,

There the sowdon lay.

1009 bye: hye C; *bey* T.   *1012* It seems to me that he kept his word.
1019 rode: wolde T.   *1020 Bot thay alle the brigges did fende* (guard) T.
1024 schyldys: swerdes T.   *1034 Full many a Sarazene made he to blede* T.
1040 Without having received the slightest wound.

1045 In hur ffadur pavylon
         There they let the maydyn downe,
             And sche knelyd on knee;
         The sowdon was full blythe:
         To hys doghtur he went swythe
1050   And kyssyd hur sythys thre.   *times*
         He set hur downe on a deyse,
         Rychely, wythowt lees,   *lie*
             Wyth grete solempnyté;   *reverence*
         Sche tolde hur ffadur and wolde not layne   *hide (anything)*
1055 How Aragonour, the gyaunt, was slayne:
             A sory man was he.

         'Leve ffadur,' sche seyde, 'thyn ore: *I beg you*
         At Montmertrous let me be no more,
             So nere the Crysten to bene;
1060 In soche aventure Y was today   *danger*
         That a rybawde had me borne away,
             For all my knyghtys kene.
         Ther was no man yn hethyn londe
         Myght sytte a dynte of hys honde,   *endure*
1065   The traytur was so [b]reme.   *violent*
         As oftyn as Y on hym thenke,
         Y may nodur ete nor drynke,
             So full Y am of tene.'   *anger*

         When the sowdon thes tythyngys herde,
1070 He bote hys lyppys and schoke hys berde,   *bit*
             That h[ydo]us hyt was to see;
         He swere be egur countynawns
         That hange he wolde the kyng of Fraunce
             And brenne all Crystyanté.
1075 'I schall neythur leve on lyve
         Man ne beste, chylde ne wyve,
             Wyth eyen that Y may see.
         Doghtur go to chaumbur swythe
         And loke thou make the glad and blythe;
1080   Avengyd schalt thou be.'

1052 That full riche was withowttyn lese T. *1061–2 That a ruffian would*
have carried me off in spite of all my brave knights (could do). *1065 breme:*
preme C; *That he ne fellede tham bydene* T. *1071 hydous: hodyus* C. *1072*
be: with T.

Full rychely was the chaumbur spradd;   *covered*
Therto was the maydyn ladd
  Wyth maydenys that sche broght.
On softe seges was sche sett: *seats*
1085 Sche myght nodur drynke ne ete,
  So moche on hym sche thoght.
Odur whyle on hys feyre chere   *another time*
And of the colour of hys lere: *face*
  Sche myght forgete hym noght.
1090 Stylle sche seyde wyth herte sore: *quietly*
'Allas, wyth my lemman that Y ne were,
  Where he wolde me have brought!'

On hur bedd as sche lay
To hur sche callyd a may,
1095   Full prevely and stylle;   *secretly*
The maydyn hyght Olyvan,
The kyngys doghtur of Sodam,
  That moost wyste of hur wylle.
Sche seyde, 'Olyvan, now yn prevyté
1100 My councell wyll Y schewe the,   *secret, reveal to*
  That grevyth me full ylle:
On a chylde ys all my thoght
That me to Parys wolde have broght,
  And Y ne may come hym tylle!'

1105 Olyvan answeryd hur tho:
'Sethyn, lady, ye wyll do so,
  Drede ye no wyght;
I schall yow helpe bothe nyght and day,
Lady, all that evyr Y may,
1110   That he yow wynne myght.
Yyt may soche aventour be,
Lady, that ye may hym see,
  Or this ffourtenyght.   *before the end of*
At Mountmertrous Y wolde ye were,
1115 The sothe of hym there shulde ye here,
  Be he squyer or knyght.'

1092 Wherever he wanted to take me. *1097 That was full faire of blode
and bane* T. *1098* In whom she most confided. *1104* And I cannot get
to him. *1106–7* Since, lady, you are determined, do not be at all afraid.
1111 It may come about by chance.

The Crysten men were full blythe
When they sye Florent on lyve:
   They wende he had be lorne;   *had thought*
1120 [And when he come nere the ceté,
Agayne hym wente kynges thre,   *towards*
   And the emperoure rode byforne.
And to the palayse the childe was broghte,
Full riche atyre thay for hym soghte
1125   Of golde and sylver schene;   *bright*
Men callede hym Florent of Paresche,   *Paris*
   For thus in romance tolde it es,
    Thoghe he ther were noghte borne.

And Clement, for the childes sake,
1130 Full faire to courte thay gan take
   And gaffe hym full riche wede;   *clothes*
One softe seges was he sett
Amonge grete lordes at the mete
   And servede of many riche brede!
1135 The childe was sett with grete honowre
Bytwixe the kynge and the emperoure:
   His mete thay gan hym schrede.   *carve for*
He was so curtayse and so bolde
That alle hym lovede, yonge and olde,
1140   For his doghety dede.

Noghte longe after, als I yow saye,
The childe solde be knyghte that other daye: *was to, next*
   No lenger wolde thay habyde.   *delay*
His atyre of golde was wroghte,
1145 Byfore the emperoure the childe was broghte,
   A kyng one aythir syde.   *each*
The kyng of Fraunce byfore hym yode
With mynstralles full many and gode,
   And lede hym up with pryde.
1150 Clement to the mynstralles gan go
And gaf some a stroke and some two:
   There durste noghte one habyde.   *stay*

1120–52 missing in C; supplied from T.   *1124* They furnished him with
very splendid clothing.   *1125 schene:* for *(y-)corne* (excellent)?   *1134* with
many kinds of roast meat.

Clement so sorye was that daye
For alle thaire costes, that he solde paye,
1155   That he gane wepe wele sore;
And whills the kynges dauwnsede in the halle,
Clement tuke thaire mantills alle   *took, cloaks*
    And to his howse tham bare.
Than the kynges gan thaire mantills myse,
1160 And ilke man askede after his,
    Where thay bycomen were.
Than swore Clement: 'By Goddes daye,
For youre mete moste ye paye,   *food*
    Or ye gete tham no more!'

1165 Thereatt all the kynges loghe;   *laughed*
There was joye and gamen ynoghe   *much*
    Amonges tham in the haulle.
The kynge of Fraunce with hert ful fayne   *joyful*
Said: 'Clement, brynge the mantils agayne,
1170   For I sall paye for alle!'
Clement thoreof was full blythe
And home he rane alsso swythe   *immediately*
    To his owen haulle;
And to the palays [t]he mantils bare,
1175 And bade tham take tham alle thare
    And downe he lette tham falle.

The burdes were sett and coverd alle;   *tables*
Childe Florent was broghte into the haulle,
    With full mekill presse;]   *throng*
1180 The chylde was set wyth honour
Betwyx the kyng of Fraunce and the emperour,
    Sothe wythowten lees.
The emperour the chylde can beholde:
He was so curtes and so bolde,
1185   But he ne wyste what he was.
The emperour thoght ever yn hys mode   *heart*
The chylde was comyn of gentyll blode;
    He thoght ryght as hyt was.

1153–79 missing in C; supplied from T.   1154 That he would have to meet all their expenses.   1161 What had happened to them.   1174 *the: he* T.   1188 And he had hit upon the truth of it.

When the folke had all eton,
1190 Clement had not all forgeton,
 Hys purce he openyd thore.
Thyrty florens forthe caste he:
'Have here for my sone and me;   *take this*
 I may pay for no more.'
1195 Clement was so curtes and wyse,
He wende hyt had ben merchandyse,
 The pryde that he sawe thore.
At Clement logh the kyngys all,
So dud the knyghtys yn that halle,
1200 And chylde Florent schamyd sore.

The emperour than spekyth he
To Florent that was feyre and fre,
 Wordys wondur stylle: *very quietly*
'Yonge knyght, Y pray the,
1205 Ys he thy ffadur? Telle thou me.'
 The chylde answeryd thertylle: *to that*
'Syr, love Y had nevyr hym to
As Y schulde to my ffadur do,
 In herte ne yn wylle;   *mind*
1210 Of all the men that evyr Y sye,
Moost yevyth my herte to yow trewly:
 Syr, take hyt not yn ylle.'

The emperour let calle Clement there; *had*
He hym sett hym full nere
1215 On the hygh deyse.
He bad hym telle the ryght dome, *explanation*
How he to the chylde come,
 The sothe wythowten lees.
'Syr, thys chylde was take yn a forest *snatched away*
1220 From a lady wyth a wylde beest,   *by*
 In a grete wyldurnes;
And Y hym boght for twenty pownde,
Eche peny hole and sownde,
 And seyde, my sone he was.'

1196–7 He supposed that all the ceremony that he saw there had been for
sale. 1207–8 Sir, I never felt the kind of love for him that I should have for
my father. 1210–11 Indeed, my heart goes out to you more than to anyone
else I ever saw. 1212 Do not be offended by this, sir.

1225 The emperour than was full blythe,
 Of that tythynge for[to] lythe,   *hear*
  And thankyd God almyght.
 The emperour felle on kne full swythe
 And kyste the chylde an hondryd sythe
1230 And worschyppyd God full ryght.   *praised*
 Well he wyste, wythowt lees,
 That he hys own sone was;
  All gamyd, kyng and knyght.   *rejoiced*
 The chyldys name was chaungyd wyth dome,   *by law*
1235 And callyd hym syr Florent of Rome,
  As hyt was gode ryght.   *perfectly proper*

 The emperour was blythe of chere,
 The terys traylyd downe on hys lere;
  He made full grete care.   *displayed, grief*
1240 'Allas,' he seyde, 'my feyre wyfe,
 The beste lady that evyr bare lyfe,   *lived*
  Schall Y hur see no more?   *must*
 Me were levyr then all the golde
 That evyr was upon molde,
1245 And sche alyve wore.'   *if*
 The emperour gave Clement townys fele,   *many*
 To leve yn ryches and yn wele,   *live, prosperity*
  Inowe for evyrmore.

 On a nyght as the chylde yn bedd lay,
1250 He thoght on hys feyre may;   *maiden*
  Mekyll was he yn care.
 The chylde had nodur reste ne ro   *peace*
 For thoght how he myght come hur to,   *thinking*
  And what hym beste ware;
1255 The chylde thoght for the maydyns sake
 A message that he wolde make
  And to the sowdon fare.   *go*
 On the morne he sadulde hys stede
 And armyd hym yn ryche wede;   *armour*
1260 A braunche of olefe he bare.   *olive*

1226 forto T: *for that* C. *1230 Thoghe he ne wiste whate he highte* T. *1243–5* I would rather she were alive than possess all the gold that ever was on earth. *1246 townys: welthis* T. *1254* And what would be best for him to do. *1256* That he would act as a messenger.

Hyt was of messengerys the lawe   *custom*
A braunche of [o]lefe for to have
    And yn ther honde to bere;
For the ordynaunce was so,   *observance*
1265 Messengerys schulde savely come and go,
    And no man do them dere.   *harm*
The chylde toke the ryght way
To Cleremount as hyt lay,   *where it was*
    Wyth hym hys grete heere;   *army*
1270 At the halle dore he reynyd hys stede
And on hys fete yn he yede,
    A messengere as he were.   *as if*

Than spake the chylde wyth hardy mode,
Before the sowdon there he stode,   *where*
1275   As a man of moche myght:
'The kynge of Fraunce me hedur sende
And byddyth the owt of hys londe thou wynd,   *orders, go*
    Thou werryst ageyn the ryght.   *are making war*
Or he wyll brynge agenste the   *if not*
1280 Thyrty thousande tolde be thre,   *multiplied (?)*
    Wyth helmys and hawberkys bryght;
Eche knyght schall thyrty squyers have,
And every squyer a fote-knave
    Worthe an hethyn knyght.'

1285 Than began the sowdon to speke,
There he sate at hys ryche mete,   *feast*
    Amonge hys knyghtys kene:
'The kyng of Fraunce shall welcome be,
Agenste oon he schall have thre,
1290   I wot wythowten wene,   *know, doubt*
That also fayne are of fyght   *glad, battle*
As fowle of day aftur nyght,
    To schewe ther schyldys schene.   *display*
To prove to-morne be my lay,   *tomorrow, faith*
1295 I wyll nevyr set lenger day,
    Than schall the sothe be sene.'

1262 *olefe: clefe* C; *olyve* T.   1271 And walked in.   1289 For every one
(of his men) he shall find three (of ours).   1292 *Als fowle es of dayes lyghte*
T.   1295 I will not put it off longer than that.

Than spekyth the mayde wyth mylde mode
To feyre Florent there he stode,
 That was so swete a wyght:
1300 'Messengere, Y wolde the frayne,   *ask*
Whedur he be knyght or swayne,
 That ys so moche of myght,
That hath my ffadurs gyaunt slayne
And ravyschyd me fro Borogh Larayn   *carried off*
1305 And slewe there many a knyght.'
Thogh sche monyd hym to ylle,
Yyt were hyt mykull yn hur wylle
 To have of hym a syght.

'Lady,' he seyde, 'nodur lesse nor more,
1310 Than yf hyt myselfe wore,   *since*
 Syth thou wylt of me frayne;   *recogniʒe*
Thou schalt me knowe yn all the heere:
Thy sleve Y wyll bere on my spere,   *open*
 In the batell playne.'   *by that then*
1315 All they wyste therby than
That he was the same man
 That had the gyaunt slayne;
Wythowt ony odur worde   *leaped up*
All they start fro the borde,
1320 Wyth swyrdys and knyvys drawyn.

Florent sawe none odur bote
But that he muste fyght on fote
 Agenste the Sarsyns all;
And evyr he hyt them amonge
1325 Where he sawe the thykest thronge: *many, made*
 Full fele dud he the[n] falle.   *seiʒed*
Some be the armys he nome   *came away*
That all the schouldur wyth hym come,
 The prowdyst yn the halle;   *blows, dealt*
1330 And some soch bofettys he lente
That the hedd fro the body wente,
 As hyt were a balle.

1306 Though she spoke evil of him; *Alle thoghe scho nevenede hym with ille*
T. 1307 Yet she greatly desired. 1309–10 He does not differ more from
me than I from myself. 1311, 1312 *me: hym* T. 1313 *Y, my: he, his* T.
1324 And he went on striking blows in the midst of them. 1326 *then:
them* C; *to* T.

Whan hys swyrde was y-brokyn,
A Sarsyns legge hath he lokyn   *taken hold of*
1335   Therwyth he can hym were.   *defend*
To the grounde he dud to go
Sevyn skore and somedele moo,
  That hethyn knyghtys were.
The chylde made hym wey full gode
1340 To hys stede there he stode,
  Tho myght hym no man dere.   *injure*
The chylde toke the ryght way
To the cyté of Parys as hyt lay,
  Thorowowt all the heere.

1345 The Crysten men were full blythe
When they sye Florent come alyve:
  They wende he lorne had bene.
When he come nye the cyté,
Agenste hym rode kyngys thre,   *towards*
1350   And the emperour rode them betwene.
The folke presyd hym to see: *thronged*
Every man cryed, 'Whych ys he?'
  As they hym nevyr had sene.
To the pales was he ladd
1355 And tolde them how he was bestadd   *hard pressed*
  Amonge the Sarsyns kene.

'Lordyngys, loke that ye ben yare   *ready*
To the batell for[to] fare,
  And redy forto ryde.
1360 To-morne hyt muste nede be sene
Whych ys hardy man and kene;   *which of you*
  We may no lenger byde.'   *put it off*
The folke seyde they were blythe
To wynde to the batell swythe,   *go, quickly*
1365   In herte ys noght to hyde.
A ryche clothe on borde was spradde
To make the chylde blythe and gladd;
  A kynge on aythur syde.

1333 was y-brokyn: broken was T. *1334 A mete-forme* (bench) *he gatt par
cas* (chance) T. *1336* He made fall to the earth. *1339* cut a clear way
through. *1347* They supposed him to have been killed. *1358 forto* T:
for that C.

On the morne when hyt was day lyght,
1370 The folke can them to batell dyght; *got ready*
All that wepyn myght welde. *bear*
There men myght see many a knyght
Wyth helmys and wyth hawberkys bryght,
Wyth sperys and wyth schylde;
1375 Wyth trumpys and wyth moche pryde, *show*
Boldely owt of the borowe they ryde *city*
Into a brode fylde. *wide plain*
The downe was bothe longe and brode, *hill*
There bothe partyes odur abode,
1380 And eyther on odur behelde.

Marsabelle the maydyn fre
Was broght the batell forto see,
To Mountmertrous ovyr Seyn.
Florent hur sleve bare on hys spere,
1385 In the batell he wolde hyt were,
And rode forthe yn the playne:
For that men schulde see by than *so that*
That he was that ylke man *very*
That had the gyaunt slayne;
1390 And also for the maydyn free,
That sche schulde hys dede see: *prowess*
Therof sche was fayne.

That whyle was moche sorowe yn syght, *time, to see*
When the batell[s] began to smyte *battalions*
1395 Wyth many a grevys wounde.
Fro the morne that day was lyght *when*
Tyll hyt was evyn derke nyght,
Or eythur party wolde fownde. *before, leave*
Florent can evyr among them ryde
1400 And made there many a sore syde
That afore were softe and sownde. *before, unwounded*
So moche people to dethe yode *many*
That the stedys dud wade yn blode
That stremyd on the grounde.

1378 *downe: felde* T. 1379–80 The two sides faced each other and waited for the fighting to begin. 1391 *Was broghte that batelle forto see* T. 1393 *syght* (perhaps *fyght*): *syte* (grief) T. 1394 *batells* T: *batell* C. 1397 Right up to when it was pitch dark; *To it was even and dirke nyghte* T.

1405 There men myght see helmys bare: *empty (?)*
    Hedys that full feyre ware,
      Lay to grounde lyght.   *clearly*
    The Crystyn party become so th[y]n
    That the fylde they myght not wynne,
1410   All arewyd hyt, kynge and knyght.   *regretted*
    Florent smote wyth herte gode,
    Thorow helme ynto the hed hyt wode;   *cut*
      So moche he was of myght.
    Thorow Godys grace and Florent there
1415 The Crysten men the bettur were
      That day yn the fyght.

    The partyes were y-drawe away   *sides, withdrawn*
    And takyn was anodur day,   *appointed*
      That the batell schulde bee.
1420 Florent rode toward Borough Larayn,
    Be the watur banke of Seyne,
      Moo aventurs forto see.
    The maydyn whyte as lylly flowre
    Lay yn a corner of hur towre,   *battlement*
1425   That was ferly feyre and free.
    Florent sche sye on fylde fare;   *ride*
    Be the sleve that he bare,
      Sche knewe that hyt was he.

    Then spekyth the mayde wyth mylde mode
1430 To Olyvan that be hur stode
      And knewe hur prevyté: *secrets*
    'Olyvan how were beste to do
    A worde that Y myght speke hym to?
      Iwysse then wele were me.'   *truly*
1435 Sche seyde, 'Lady, we two
    Allone wyll be the rever go,
      Thereas he may yow see.   *where*
    Yf he yow love wyth herte gode,
    He wyll not let for the flode,   *refrain, water*
1440   For a full gode stede hath he.'

1407 *Full lawe to the grownde than lyghte* (fell) T.   1408 *thyn* T: *than C.*
1415 Things went better with the Christians.   1432–3 how might I best
arrange to converse with him?

Forthe went the maydyns two;
Be the rever syde can they goo, *walk*
   Themselfe allone that tyde. *time*
When Florent sawe that swete wyght,
1445 He sprange as fowle dothe yn flyght, *rushed forward*
   No lenger wolde he byde. *wait*
The stede was so wondur gode, *extremely*
He bare the chylde ovyr the flode,
   Hymselfe well cowde ryde.
1450 Grete yoye hyt was to see them meete
Wyth clyppyng and wyth kyssyng swete, *embracing*
   In herte ys not [to] hyde.

'Lady,' he seyde, 'well ys me,
A worde that Y may speke wyth the,
1455   So bryght thou art of hewe. *complexion*
In all thys worlde ys noon so fre;
Why ne wyll ye crystenyd be,
   And syth of herte be trewe?' *afterwards*
Sche seyde, 'If that ye myght me wynne,
1460 I wolde forsake all hethyn kynne, *renounce*
   As thogh Y them nevyr knewe;
And syth ye wolde me wedde to wyfe, *since*
I wolde leve yn Crysten lyfe;
   My yoye were evyr newe.'

1465 'Lady,' he seyde, 'wythowt fayle, *(say) truly*
How were beste yowre counsayle,
   That Y yow wynne myght?'
'Certys, ye nevyr wynne me may
But hyt were on that ylke day, *same*
1470   That ye have take to fyght: *agreed*
That ye wolde sende be the flode
Wyth men that crafty were and gode *skilful*
   A schyppe that well were dyght. *appointed*
Whyll that men are at that dere dede, *noble action*
1475 That whyle myght men me awey lede
   To yowre cyté ryght.

1452 to T: omitted C; It cannot be kept secret. *1463* I would keep to the Christian faith. *1464* My joy would never fade. *1466* What, in your opinion, would be the best way.

My fadur hath a noble stede;
In the worlde ys noon so gode at nede,
   In turnament ne yn fyght.
1480 Yn hys hedd he hath an horne,
Schapon as an unycorne,   *formed*
   That selkowth ys be syght.
Syr, yf that ye hym myght wynne
There were no man yn hethyn kynne   *race*
1485   That hym wythstonde myght.'   *stand against*
Florent kyste that feyre maye
And seyde, 'Lady have gode day:
   Holde that ye have hyght.'

Florent ynto the sadull nome   *jumped*
1490 And ovyr the rever soon he come;
   To Parys he toke the way.
He ne stynt ne he ne blanne,
To Clementys hows tyll that he came,
   Hys aventurs to say.
1495 He tolde hym of the noble stede
That gode was at every nede,
   And of that feyre maye.
'Sone,' seyde Clement, 'be doghty of dede,   *valiant*
And certys thou schalt have that stede,
1500   To-morne yf that Y may.'

On the morne when hyt was day lyght,
Clement can hymselfe dyght   *get ready*
   As an onfrely feere.
He dud hym ynto the hethen ooste
1505 There the prees was althermoost,
   A Sarsyn as thogh he were.
To the pavylown he can hym wynne,   *go*
There the sowdon hymselfe lay ynne,
   And bre[m]ely can he bere.
1510 Full well he cowde ther speche speke
And askyd them some of ther mete;   *food*
   The sowdon can hym here.

1482 That is astonishing to see. *1488* Keep the promise you have made.
1492 He did not stop at all. *1494* To tell how he had fared. *1500* if I
can do anything about it. *1503* As a wretched pilgrim. *1504–5* He made
his way into the thick of the Saracen army. *1509* bremely: brenely C;
brymly T; And assumed a fierce manner.

Octavian

Grete dole the sowdon of hym thoght,
And soon he was before hym broght,
1515   And wyth hym can he speke.
He seyde he was a Sarsyn stronge
That yn hys oost had be longe,
And had defawte of mete.   *was starving*
'Lorde, ther ys noon hethyn lede   *man*
1520 That so well cowde kepe a ryche stede,
Or othur horsys full grete.'
The sowdon seyde that ylke tyde,
'Yf thou can a stede well ryde,
Wyth me thou schalt be lete.'   *kept*

1525 They horsyd Clement on a stede,   *mounted*
He sprang owt as sperkull on gle[de],
Into a feyre fylde.
All that stodyn on ylke syde
Had yoye to see hym ryde
1530   Before the sowdon they tolde.
When he had redyn coursys three,
That all had yoye that can hym see,
The sowdon hym behelde.
Downe he lyght full soon
1535 And on a bettur was he done;   *set*
Full feyre he can hym welde.   *conducted*

Grete yoye the sowdon of hym thoght
And bad hys feyre stede forthe be broght,
And Clement shall hym ryde.
1540 When Clement was on that stede
He rode away a full gode spede,
No lenger wolde he byde.
When he was redy forthe to fou[nde]:   *get away*
'Beleve there,' he seyde, 'ye hethen ho[unde],
1545   For ye have lorne yowre pryd[e].'   *lost*
Clement toke the ryght way
Into Parys as hyt lay:
Full blythe was he that tyde.

1513 The sultan felt very sorry for him.   1519 *Sir there es no man in
heythen thede* (lands) T.   1520 knows how to look after a noble horse.
1526 *glede* T: *gle* C.   1530 *Byfore the sowdans telde* (tent) T.   1534 He
quickly dismounted.   1537 The sultan was delighted with him.   1543–5 [ ]
not now visible C.

'Florent sone, where art thou?
1550 That Y the hyght Y have hyt [nowe];   *promised*
I have broght thy stede.'
Florent blythe was that day
And seyde: 'Fadur, yf Y leve may,   *live*
I wyll the quyte thy mede.   *reward you*
1555 But to the emperour of Rome
Therwyth Y wyll hym present sone;
To the pales ye schall hym lede;
For evyr me thynkyth yn my mode
That Y am of hys own blode,
1560   Yf hyt so pouerly myght sprede.'

To the pales the stede was ladde,
And all the kyngys were ful gladd
Theron forto see.
The emperour before hym stode,
1565 Ravyschyd herte and blode,   *delighted*
So wondur feyre was he.
Then spekyth the chylde of honour
To hys lorde the emperour:
'Syr thys stede geve Y the.'
1570 All that abowte the chylde stode
Seyde he was of gentull blode: *noble*
Hyt myght noon odur be.

Aftur thys the day was nomyn   *fixed*
That the batell on schulde comyn
1575   Agenste the Sarsyns to fyght.
Wyth trumpys and wyth moche pryde,   *pomp*
Boldely owt of the borogh they ryde,
As men moche of myght.
Florent thoght on the feyre maye;
1580 To batell wente he not that day,
A schyppe he hath hym dyght.
Fro Mountmertrous there the lady lay
To Parys he broght hur away:
Ne wyste hyt kynge ne knyght.   *knew about*

1550 nowe T; not visible C.   *1560* If it could run in the veins of so humble
a person; *So prodly if I moghte spede* T.   *1565 And resceyvede hym with mylde
mode* T.   *1567–84* partially missing in T.   *1572* It could not be otherwise.

1585 That whyle was moche sorowe in syght,
　　 When the batell[s] began to smyght
　　　　 Wyth many a grymme gare;　　　　　　 *deadly spear*
　　 Fro morne that hyt was day lyght
　　 Tyll hyt was evyn derke nyght,
1590 　　 Wyth woundys wondur sore.
　　 Forwhy that Florent was not there　　　　 *because*
　　 The hethyn men the bettur were,　　　　　 *fared*
　　　　 The batell venquyscht they thore;　　　 *won*
　　 Or Florent to the felde was comyn,
1595 Emperour and kynge were y-nomyn,　　　　 *captured*
　　　　 And all that Crysten were.

　　 Florent was of herte so gode
　　 He rode thorow them [als] he was wode,　　 *mad*
　　　　 As wyght as he wolde wede.
1600 Ther was no Sarsyn so moche of mayn　　　 *strength*
　　 That myght hym stonde wyth strenkyth agayn,
　　　　 Tyll they had slayne hys stede.
　　 Of Florent there was dele ynow,　　　　　 *for*
　　 How they hys hors undur hym slowe,
1605 　　 And he to grounde yede.
　　 Florent was take yn that fyght;
　　 Bothe emperour, kynge and knyght,
　　　　 Woundyd they can them lede.　　　　　 *take away*

　　 The Sarsyns buskyd them wyth pryde
1610 Into ther own londys to ryde;
　　　　 They wolde no lenger dwelle.　　　　　 *delay*
　　 Takyn they had syr Florawns,
　　 The emperour and the kyng of Fraunce,
　　　　 Wyth woundys wondur fele;
1615 Othur Crystyn kyngys moo,
　　 Dewkys, erlys and barons also,
　　　　 That arste were bolde and swelle;　　　 *proud*
　　 And ladd them wyth yron stronge,　　　　 *fetters*
　　 Hur fete undur the hors wombe:　　　　　 *belly*
1620 　　 Grete dele hyt ys to telle.　　　　　　 *relate*

1585–1600 partially missing in T.　*1586 batells: batell* C.　*1597 of such
great courage. 1598 als* T: *omitted* C.　*1599 With frenzied valour.
1601 Who could stand against him with force of arms. 1608 Woundyd:
Bownden* T.　*1609–20 missing in* T.

Wyde the worde sprange of thys chawnce,   *misfortune*
How the sowdon was yn Fraunce,
    To warre agenste the ryght.
In Jerusalem men can hyt here,
1625 How the emperour of Rome was there
    Wyth many an hardy knyght.
Than spekyth Octavyon the yyng
Full feyre to hys lorde the kyng,   *graciously*
    As chylde of moche myght: *strength*
1630 'Lorde, yf hyt were yowre wylle,
I wolde wynde my ffadur tylle   *go to*
    And helpe hym yn that fyght.'

Than spekyth the kyng of moche myght   *power*
Full fayre unto that yong knyght;
1635   Sore hys herte can blede:
'Sone, thou schalt take my knyghtys fele,
Of my londe that thou wylle wele,   *choose*
    That styffe are on stede,
Into Fraunce wyth the to ryde,
1640 Wyth hors and armys be thy syde,
    To helpe the at nede;
When thou some doghtynes haste done   *deeds of valour*
Then may thou shewe thyn errande soone;
    The bettur may thou spede.'   *succeed*

1645 He bad hys modur make hur yare
Into Fraunce wyth hym to fare:
    He wolde no lenger byde.
Wyth hur she ladd the lyenas
That sche broght owt of wyldurnes,
1650   Rennyng be hur syde......

There men myght see many a knyght
Wyth helmys and wyth hawberkys bryght
    Forthe ynto the strete.
Forthe they went on a day;
1655 The hethyn ooste on the way
    All they can them meete.

1621–56 missing in T.   *1621* The news of this misfortune spread far and
wide.   *1635* His heart was greatly troubled.   *1643* You will be able at
once to show them why you have come.   *1653* Marching along the highway.

By the baners that they bare
They knewe that they hethyn ware,
   And stylle they can abyde.
1660 They dyght them wyth bre[nie]s bryght
And made them redy forto fyght,
   Ageyn them can they ryde.
They hewe the flesche fro the bone:
Soche metyng was nevyr none,   *encounter*
1665   Wyth sorow on ylke syde.
Octavyon the yong knyght,
Thorow the grace of God almyght,
   Full faste he fellyd ther pryde.   *cast down*

The lyenas that was so wyght,
1670 When she sawe the yong knyght
   Into the batell fownde,   *go*
Sche folowed hym wyth all hur myght
And faste fellyd the folke yn fyght:
   Many sche made onsownde!   *wounded*
1675 Grete stedys downe sche drowe   *pulled*
And many hethen men she slowe,
   Wythynne a lytull stownde!
Thorow God that ys of myghtys gode,
The Crysten men the bettur stode;
1680   The hethyn were broght to grownde. *laid low*

The Crysten prysoners were full fayne,   *rejoiced*
When the Sarsyns were y-slayne,
   And cryed, 'Lord, thyn ore!'   *glory to Thee!*
He ne stynt ne he ne blanne
1685 To the prysoners tyll that he wanne,
   To wete what they were.   *find out*
The emperour, wythowt lees,
That hys own ffadur was,
   Bowndon fownde he there;   *in fetters*
1690 The kyng of Fraunce and odur moo,   *many others*
Dewkys, erlys and barons also,
   Were woundyd wondur sore.   *grievously*

1657–85 missing in T.   *1659* And quietly awaited (their attack). *1660* brenies: bremus C. *1677* Within a short space of time. *1679* stood their ground more firmly. *1684–5* He did not stop at all until he had come up to the prisoners. *1686–92* partially missing in T.

Hys ffadur was the furste man
That he of bondys to lowse began,   *release*
1695   Ye wete wythowten lees;
And he lowsyd hys brodur Floraunce,
Or he dud the kynge of Fraunce,
      Yyt he wyste not what he was.
Be that hys men were to hym comyn,   *by the time that*
1700 Soon they were fro yrons nomyn,
      The pryncys prowde yn prees.
Whan he had done that noble dede,
The bettur he oght forto spede,
      To make hys modur pees.   *peace for*

1705 A ryche cyté was besyde;   *close by*
Boldely thedur can they ryde
      To a castell swythe;
Ryche metys were there y-dyght,
Kyngys, dewkys, erlys and knyght:
1710   All were gladd and blythe.
Syth came Octavyon the yong wyth honour   *respectfully*
And knelyd before the emperour,
      Hys errande forto kythe;   *declare*
That ylke tale that he tolde,
1715 Ryche and pore, yong and olde,
      Glad they were to lythe.

He seyde, 'Lorde, yn all thys londe Y have the soght;
My modur have Y wyth me broght:
      I come to make hur pees.
1720 For a lesyng that was stronge,
Sche was exylyd owt of yowre londe:
      I prove that hyt was lees.'
The emperour was nevyr so blythe:
He kyssyd that yong knyght swythe
1725   And for hys sone hym chees.   *acknowledged*
For yoye that he hys wyfe can see,
Sevyn sythys swownyd he,
      Before the hye deyse.

*1693–719 partially missing in T.   1695 You may take this as a fact.   1701
The noble leaders of the army.   1720 On account of a vicious slander.   1722
I am ready to prove that it was false.*

  Feyre Florent was full blythe
1730 Of thes tydyngys forto lythe,
   And hys modur to see.
  Than spekyth the lady of honowre   *noble*
  To hur lorde the emperour,
   Wordys of grete pyté: *very pitiable*
1735 'Lorde, yn all the sorow that me was wroght, *done to*
  Thyn own sone have Y wyth me broght,
   And kepyd hym wyth me.
  Thyn odur sone yn a foreste
  Was takyn wyth a wylde beste,
1740 That was ferly feyre and fre.   *marvellously*
  I wot hyt ys Godys grace,
  I knowe hym be hys face:
   Hyt ys that yong knyght by the!'

  There was moche yoye and game
1745 Wyth clyppyng and wyth kyssyng same;
   Into a chaumbur they yode.
  Grete yoye there was also,
  The metyng of the brethurn two,
   That doghty were yn dede.
1750 A ryche feste the emperour made there
  Of kyngys that were farre and nere, *from all parts*
   Of many londys thede.   *people*
  The tale whoso redyth ryght,
  The feste lastyd a fourtenyght,
1755 In jeste as we rede.

  Marsabelle that feyre maye
  Was aftur sente the sothe to say,   *sent for*
   Fro Parys there sche was;
  Crystenyd sche was on a Sonday,
1760 Wyth yoye and myrthe and moche play;
   Florent to wyfe hur chees.
  Soche a brydale ther was there
  A ryaller ther was nevyr noon here:
   Ye wot wythowten lees.
1765 Florent hymselfe can hur wedd
  And ynto Rome sche was ledd,   *escorted*
   Wyth pryncys prowde yn prees.

1732–4 not in T. *1748 The metyng: At the metyng* T. *1752 thede: lede*
(man) T. *1753* Whoever wishes to tell this story correctly (must report that).
1762–3 There was never on earth a more splendid wedding than this one.

Than hyt befelle on a day   *came about*
The emperour began to say,
1770   And tolde the lordys how hyt was.
The ryche kyngys gave jugement
The Emperours modur schulde be brent
   In a tonne of brasse.   *vessel*
As swythe as sche therof harde telle,   *soon*
1775 Swownyng yn hur chaumbur she felle,
   Hur heere of can sche race;   *tear*
For schame sche schulde be prouyd false,
Sche schare ato hur own halse   *cut, throat*
   Wyth an analasse.   *dagger*

1780 Therat all the kyngys loghe:
What wondur was thowe ther were no swoghe?
   They toke ther leve that tyde;
Wyth trumpys and wyth mery songe
Eche oon went to hys own londe,
1785   Wyth yoye and wyth grete pryde.
Wyth game and wyth grete honowre
To Rome went the emperour,
   Hys wyfe and hys sonys be hys syde.
Jesu lorde, hevyn kynge,
1790 Graunt us all thy blessyng,
   And yn hevyn to abyde.

1769–70 The emperor made a speech telling his lords all the details of the case. *1773 tonne: belle* T. *1781* Is it any wonder that no grief was displayed (by fainting or lamentation)?; *There was joye and gamen ynowghe* T. *1788–91* represented by ten lines in T: see Commentary.

Sir Isumbras

God that made both erthe and hevenne   *created*
And all this worlde in deyes seven,
   That is full of myghthe;
Sende us alle his blessynge,
5 Lasse and more, olde and yynge,
   And kepe us day and nyghte.   *watch over*

I wyll you tell of a knyghte
That dowghty was in eche a fyghte,   *valiant, every*
   In towne and eke in felde;   *also*
10 Ther durste no man his dynte abyde,
Ne no man ayeyn hym ryde,
   With spere ne with schelde.

A man he was ryche ynowghe
Of oxen to drawe in his plowghe,
15   And stedes also in stalle;
He was bothe curteys and hende,   *gracious*
Every man was his frende,
   And loved he was with all.

A curteys man and hende he was;
20 His name was kalled syr Isumbras,
   Bothe curteys and fre.   *generous*
His gentylnesse nor his curtesye   *nobility*
There kowthe no man hit discrye: *describe*
   A ffull good man was he.   *very*
25 Menstralles he hadde in his halle,
And yafe hem robes of ryche palle,   *cloth*
   Sylver, golde and fee.   *possession*
Of curtesye he was kynge;   *supreme*
His gentylnesse hadde non endyng,   *limits*
30   I[n] worlde was none so fre.   *noble*

1–30 represented by two stanzas in TEA: see Commentary.   *5* Humble and
great, old and young.   *10* There was no-one who dared meet him in battle.
13 He was a man who had great plenty.   *30 In: I* L.

A fayre wyfe then hadde he,
As any in erthe myghte be:
   The sothe as I telle yow;   *truth*
And manne children had they thre,
35 As fayre as any myghte be,   *handsome*
   For they were fayre ynow.   *very*

Into his herte a pryde was browghte
That of God yafe he ryghte nowghte,
   His mercy ones to nevenne.   *praise*
40 So longe he regned in that pryde
That Jesu wolde no lengur abyde: *endure (it)*
   To hym he sente a stevenne.   *(warning) voice*

So hit byfell upon a day,   *happened*
The knyghte wente hym to play,
45   His foreste forto se;   *inspect*
As he wente by a derne sty,   *secluded path*
He herde a fowle synge hym by,   *bird, beside*
   Hye upon a tre.
He seyde, 'Welcome, syr Isumbras:
50 Thow haste foryete what thou was,
   For pryde of golde and fee.
The kynge of hevenn the gretheth so,
In yowthe or elde thou schall be wo: *old age*
   Chese whedur hyt schall be.'   *choose which*

55 With carefull herte and sykynge sore,   *sorrowful, sighing*
He fell upon his knees thore;   *there*
   His hondes up he helde.
'Worldes welthe I woll forsake;   *renounce*
To Jesu Criste I wyll me take,   *commit myself*
60   To hym my sowle I yelde.   *submit*
In yowthe I may ryde and go;   *walk*
In elde I may noght do so:
   My lymes wyll wex unwelde.   *become feeble*
Lorde, yf it thy wyll be,
65 In yowthe sende me poverté,
   And welthe in myne elde.'

---

33 *With tunge als I yow neven* T.   36 *Undir the kynge of heven* T.   38 He
paid no heed to God at all.   44 take his recreation.   50 forgotten what you
once were.   52 sends you this greeting.   53 must endure sorrow.

Awey that fowle toke his flyghte;
Alone he lette that drurye knyghte; *left, sorrowful*
 Full sone he wente his wey;   *promptly*
70 And whenne he that fowle had lore, *lost (sight of)*
His steede that was so lyghte byfore, *fast*
 Dede under hym ley.
His hawkes and his howndes bothe
Ronne to wode as they were wrothe, *wild*
75 And eche on taketh here weye. *goes its own*
What wondur was thowgh hym were wo?
On fote byhoveth hym to go: *he must*
 To peyne turned his pleye. *anguish, joy*

And as he by the wode wente
80 A lytyll knave was to hym sente, *(servant) boy*
 Come rennynge hym ayeyne. *running, towards*
Worse tydynges he hym tolde:
'Syr, brent be thy byggynges bolde, *burnt, dwellings*
 Thy menne be manye slayne.
85 Ther is noght lefte on lyve   *alive*
But thy children and thy wyfe,
 Withouten any delayne.' *concealment (?)*
He seyde, 'If they on lyve be,
My wyfe and my children thre,
90 Yet were I nevur so fayne.'

Forth he wente hymself alone;
His herdemen he mette eche one,
 He seyde, 'What eyleth yowe?' *is wrong with*
'Owre fees ben fro us revedde, *cattle, stolen*
95 There is nothynge y-levedde, *left*
 Nowghte on stede to thy plowe.' *horse*

The[y] wepte and yaf hem yll; *were distressed*
The knyghte badde they schold be styll:
 'I wyte nowght yow this wo.
100 For God bothe yeveth and taketh *gives*
And at his wyll ryches maketh,
 And pore men also.'

---

74 Ronne: Wente T. *75 Ilkone a dyverse waye* T. *84 menne: bestes* T.
87 The sothe es noghte to layne (hide) T. *90 In spite of everything, I should
never have been happier.* *93 With a full drery swoghe* (sigh) T. *96 stede:
stotte* (ox) T. *97 They: The* L. *99 I do not hold you responsible for this
sorrow; woghe* (harm) T. *102 And yitt may send ynoghe* T.

A dolfull syghte thenne ganne he se:
His wyfe and his chylderen thre
105   Owte of the fyre were fledde,
As naked as they were borne,
There they stode hym byforne;   *before*
    Were browghte out of here bedde.

Yette chaunged nothyng his ble   *expression*
110 Tyll he sawe his wyfe and children thre
    That erste were comely cladde;   *before, fairly*
The lady badde her children be blythe: *cheerful*
'For yette I se your fadur on lyve—
    For nothynge be ye dradde.'   *afraid*

115 They wepte and yafe hem ylle;   *were distressed*
Her fader badde they scholde be stylle
    And wepe nowghte so sore.   *bitterly*
'All the sorow that we ben inne
Hit is for owre wykked synne:
120   Worthy we be well more.   *deserve*

And we full evell kan wyrke
Owre frendes of us wyll yrke: *tire*
    Of londe I rede we fare.
Of myselfe have I no thowghte,
125 But that I may yeve my menn noghte,
    For hem is all my kare.'   *them*

He toke his mantell of ryche pall
And ovur his wyfe he lette hit fall
    With a drewrye mode.   *sorrowfully*
130 His ryche sirkote then toke he   *gave*
To his pore chyldren thre
    That naked byfore hym stode.
'Do ye schull aftur my rede,
To seke God wher he was quykke and dede,   *alive*
135   That for us shedde his blode.
For Jesu Criste that is so fre,
Hym to seche wher it be: *search for*
    He sende us our lyves fode.'

107 Stode togedir undir a thorne T. *110 To* (until) *he sawe tham so nakede bee* T. *116* ordered them to be quiet. *121* If we are not able to labour well. *123* My advice is that we should leave the country. *133* You must act according to my counsel. *137 That whoso sekes hym with herte fre* T.

With his knyfe he share   *cut*
140 A crosse on his sholder bare,
    In storye as clerkes seye.   *scholars tell*
They that wer here frendes byfore
They wepte and syked sore: *were grieved*
    Her songe was 'wellawaye'.
145 The knyghte and the lady hende
    Toke here leve at her frende,   *of their*
    And forth they wente her waye.
For hem wepte both olde and yynge
For that doolfull partynge,
150 Forsothe as I you seye.

For thay bare with hem nothynge   *took*
That longed to here spendynge,
    Nother golde nor fee;
But forto begge here mete
155 Where they myghte ony gete,
    For love of seynt charyté.
Thorow two kynges londes they gan pas,
As Cristes owen wyll was,
    They and here children thre.
160 Suche sorwe as they wer inne,
    That wer wonte forto wynne,
    Grette dole hit was to se.   *sorrow*

Sex deyes were come and gone,
Mete ne drynke hadde they none,
165 For hongur they wepte sore.
They kome by a watur kene,   *turbulent river*
Therovur they wolde fayn have bene,   *gladly*
    Thenne was her kare the more.   *sorrow, greater*

---

144 was of lamentation.   *147 And made thaire ffondynge* (departing) *daye* T.
150 And sythen thay went thaire waye T.   *152* That would enable them to
buy anything.   *161* That were accustomed to be successful (?); *wonte to
wele and wyn* (prosperity and joy) T.   *163–8* A complete stanza in TEA:
see Commentary.

His eldeste sone he toke there
170 And ovur the water he hym bere,   *carried*
   And sette hym by a brome.   *broom (plant)*
He seyde, 'Leve sone, sytte her styll,   *dear*
Whyle I fette thy brodur the tyll   *fetch, to*
   And pley de with a blome.'   *thee, flower*
175 The knyghte was both good and hende
And ovur the watur he ganne wende;
   His othur sone he nome.   *took*
He bare hym ovur the watur wylde;
A lyon fette his eldeste chylde   *snatched away*
180   Or he to londe come.   *before*

With carefull herte and sykynge sore,
His myddleste sone he lafte thore,   *left*
   And wente wepynge aweye.
Ther come a lybarte and fette that other,   *leopard*
185 And bare hym to wode to his brothe[r],
   As I you seye in faye.   *truth*
The knyghte seyde his lady tyll,
'Take we gladly Goddes wyll,   *accept*
   Hertyly I yow praye.'   *earnestly, implore*
190 The lady wepte and hadde grette care;
She hadde almoste herselfe forfare,   *killed*
   On londe ther she ley.

He toke his lady that was hym dere
And ovur the watur he hyre bere,
195   His yonge sone also.
In that foreste forth thenne wente he
Tyll they come to the Grekys see;   *sea*
   Forther they myghte not go.
On the londe as they stode,
200 They sey kome selynge on the flode   *sea*
   Thre hondreth shyppes and mo.   *more*
And on the londe as the[y] seete   *were sitting*
They loked down into the deepe:
   The shypes they sey glyde so.

185 brother: brothe L.   *192* As she lay prostrate there; followed by an extra
stanza in TEA: see Commentary.   *193–228* have different stanza-limits in
TEA: see Commentary.   *196 he: thay three* T.   *198 Thare thay sawe
stormes bloo* (dark) T.   *202 they: the* L.

205 The topcastell drawen on hyghe: *set aloft*
    All the[m] thowght rede golde they syghe, *seemed, saw*
      So it glistered as they gan glyde.
    An hethen kynge was therinne,
    Come Cristendome forto wynne,   *conquer*
210   To walke so ferre and wyde.
    The kynge thought he wolde londe
    By that forest at the havenne ende, *harbour*
      A lytyll ther bysyde.
    The shypes hoved in the stronde; *anchored, beach*
215   His meyné drowen faste to londe, *quickly*
      And yerne gan they ryde.

    Syr Isumbras loked hym bysyde;
    He sawe moche folke passe and ryde,
      Mo thenne I kan nemenn.   *name*
220 The knyghte seyde to his lady fre,
    'Lord God, what may al this be?'
      With so lowde a stevenn.   *voice*
    'In this foreste have we gone,
    Mete nor drynke [ne] have [we] none,
225   Not these dayes sevenn;
    Go we to hym and aske somme mete,
    If we may any gete,
      For Cristes love of hevenn.'

    To the galye ganne they w[ynn]e;   *go*
230 (An hethen kynge was therinne):
      So wonderlye was wroghte.   *made*
    He bede of hem somme lyves fode, *asked*
    For his love that dyed on rode,
      And with his blode us bowghte.
235 Whenne the kynge herde hym so crye,
    He seyde he was some Cristen spie,
      And asked what they sowghte.
    He commanded to bete hym aweye; *drive*
    For they leved not on his laye, *believed, religion*
240   Of hym they schulde have noghte.

---

206 *them: the* L. 208 *and* 230 *An hethen kynge: The sowdane* T. 210 To
overrun it (?); *Thare wakkyns woo full wyde* T. 211 *londe: lende* (stay) E.
215 *His followers quickly made their way to land.* 219 *nemenn: neven* T.
224 *ne, we:* omitted L. 229 *wynne: wende* L. 237 *That thaire schippes had
soghte* T.

Thenne seyde a knyghte to the kynge,
'Syr, it is a rewfull thynge,   *pitiful*
    The yondur manne to se;
He is moche and he is stronge,
245 Sholdres brode and armes longe,
    A fayre manne to se.
Bones thenn hath he grete,
Eyen greye and wonthur stepe: *remarkably, staring*
    A knyghte hym semeth to be.
250 His lady is wyte as wales bone,
Here lere bryghte to se upon,   *face*
    So fayre as blosme on tre.'

The kynge grete thole thenne thowghte;
He commaunded hem ayeyne be browghte,   *back*
255   He myghte hem se with syghte.
When he syghe hem he rewed sore,   *took pity*
So feyre as they bothe wore,
    If they were cladde aryghte.
He seyde to hem, 'Leveth on my laye   *properly*
                                                             believe
260 And lete your fals goddes awaye,   *renounce*
    And be with me in fyghte;   *side*
Of golde schalt thou nevur have nede:
If thou be dowghty manne in dede,   *(your) actions*
    Thow shalt be doobbed knyghte.'   *made*

265 Stylle stode sir Isumbras   *silent*
And thowghte an hethen kyng he was:
    'Syr,' he sey[de], 'nay.
Schall I nevur more
Ayeyns Cristen werre,
270   Nor forsake my laye.
We pray the of som lyves fode,
For his love that dyed on rode,   *cross*
    And lette us go our weye.'
The kynge behelde his lady there;
275 Hym thowghte an angell that she were,
    Komen out of hevenne that day.

251 Hir lyre es als the see fome T.   *253* The king was very sorrowful then.
262 you will never be short.   *267 seyde: sey* L.   *268* never at any time to
come.   *265–82* are two complete stanzas in TEA: see Commentary.   *271*
food to keep us alive.

He seyde, 'Wylt thou thy wyfe sell me?
I wyll yefe for here golde and fe,   *give*
  And ryche robes sevenne;
280 She shall be crowned qwene of my lond,
And every man bowe to her hond,
  Shall no man bysette here steven.'   *ignore (?), commands*

The knyghte answered and seyde, 'Nay,
My wyfe I wyll not selle away,
285 But thou me for here wyll sloo.   *unless, kill*
I wedded her with Goddes laye
To kepe here to my endynge daye,
  For wele or for woo.'
Reed gold in a mantell they tolde   *counted out*
290 And aftur togedur the mantell they folde,
  His wyfe they toke hym fro.
On the londe they dede hym caste
And beten hym and his rybbes braste,   *broke*
  And made his flessh full blo.   *black and blue*

295 His yonge sone on the londe satte;
He syghe men his fader bette;
  He wepte and was full wo.
He seyde, 'Dere God, wo is me,
That evur I shall this daye se:
300   What is me beste to do?'

The kynge, with his owene honde,
Crownede her qwene of his londe,
  And sente here ovur the see;
With ryche karykkes that wer stronge   *ships*
305 He sente her into his londe,
  Qwene ther sholde she be.
Sone whenne the knyghte myghte stonde,   *as soon as*
He toke his yonge sone by the honde
  And forth thenne wente he.
310 By thenne were the schyppes yare   *ready*
With that lady forth to fare,   *journey*
  Ovur that salte see.

---

281 will acknowledge her as their lady. *282 bysette: withstande* T. *286
with: in* T. *290 And till hymselfen thay gan it falde* T. *297* followed by
six extra lines in TEA: see Commentary. *301–6* placed after *307–12* T.
303 ovur the see: to his conntre T.

Whenne the shyppes were yare,
The lady wepte and made grette care,
315   And kneled byfore the kynge;
And seyde, 'Syr kynge, I praye the,
One boone that thou graunte me,
  Withoute any dwellynge.   *delay*
Or I passe ovur the see,
320 Lette my lorde speke with me
  A worde of pryvy thynge.'
The knyghte was kalled ayeyne;   *back*
The lady therof was full fayne:
  Her tokenynge was a rynge.   *token*

325 Grete dole it was to se hem mete,
With kyssynge and with clyppynge swete,   *embracing*
  To shyppe whenne she sholde go.   *had to*
She seyde, 'Dere God, wo is me,
That I were not drowned in the see,
330   Or we sholde parte in two.
But in what londe that I am inne,
Fonde the thyder forto wynne:
  The hethen kynge shall ye slo;
And by crowned kynge of that londe,
335 And evury manne bowe to your honde;
  So shall ye kevere your wo.'   *put an end to*

Mete and drynke she dede hym yeve,
That he myghte be sevennyghte lyfe,   *for a week*
  His yonge sone and he.
340 The lady was both meke and mylde;
She kyssed her lorde and her chylde,
  And swonedde tymes thre.
Sayles they drewen up of good hewe;   *colour*
The wynde was gode and ovur hem blewe,
345   With that lady fre.
The knyghte on the londe sette;
For his lady sore ganne he wepe,
  Whyles he myghte the sayles se.   *as long as*

---

318 Now at oure parttynge T.   *321* In private conversation.   *331–2* Strive
to reach whatever country I may be in.   *344 The wynde tham sonne owte of
haven blewe* T.   *347 ganne ... wepe: grett* T.

He toke his yonge sone by the hond
350 And forth he wa[l]keth in that lond
    Amonge the holtes hore.   *grey woods*
They sette hem down undur a tre;
Nothur of hem myght othur se,
    So hadde dey wepte sore.   *they*
355 Here mete thenne forth they drowgh   *took out*
And whenne they hadde eten ynowgh,
    His yonge sone sykedde sore.   *sighed*
In here mantell of skarlette rede
Amonge her gold they putte her brede
360 And forth with hem it bere.

Tyll they come to an hyll an hyghe,
Ther they thowghte all nyghte to lye;   *intended, sleep*
    No fordur they myghte drygh.   *endure (to go)*
On the morn whenne it was daye
365 A gryffyn bare the golde awaye,
    For the rede cloth that he syghe.
The knyghte was both hende and fre
And folowed hym to the Grekes See,
    Therovur the gryffyn he flyghe.
370 Therwhyles ther come an unykorne;   *meanwhile*
His yonge sone awey hath borne,
    Sich sorowe the knyghte gan dryghe.

For evur he was in wele and wo,
But nevur half as he was tho:
375   He sette hym down on a stone.
He seyde, 'Dere Godde, wo is me,
I have loste my wyfe and children thre,
    And am myselfe alone.
I am as kerefull a manne   *sorrowful*
380 As any with tonge telle can,
    To God I make my mone.   *complaint*
God, as thou werest hevenn crowne,
Wysse me the wey to som towne,
    For all amysse have I gone.'   *astray*

350 walketh: wakketh L (cf. variants of *210*); *And when the knyght myghte up stande* T (placed before *349*). *361 to a banke* (hillside) *full drye* T. *365 gryffyn: egyll* E; *angelle* A. *367 The sory knyght uppe sterte hee* A. *373 For evur: Ofte* T. *383 Direct me to some settlement.*

385 And as he wente by a lowe,   *hill*
    Smythes faste herde he blowe,   *ironsmiths*
      A grete fyre sawe he glowe.
    He beede hem of som mete for charité: *asked*
    The[y] seyde, 'Com swynke as don we—   *labour*
390 We have none othur plowghe.'
    The knyghte answered ageyn:
    'For mete wolde I swynke fayn:'
      Full faste he bere and drowghe.   *carried, pulled*
    They yafe hym mete and drynke anon
395 And tawghte hym to bere stone   *ore*
      Out of a fowll depe slowghe.   *bog*

    There the knyghte bare stone
    Tyll twelve monthes wer come and gone:
      He wroghte his body mykyll wo.
400 Tyll he kowthe wyrke a fyre,   *keep up*
    Thenne toke he mannes hyre,   *wages*
      And wroghte more thenne two.
    In myche sorowe and care,
    Sevenn yer he was smythes man ther,
405   And monethes mo also.
    By thenne he cowthe armour dyghte,
    All that fell for a knyghte,
      To batell whenn he sholde go.

    And all that sevenn yere so longe
410 The hethen kynge with batell stronge   *forces*
    Stryden Cristendome full wyde.   *ravaged*
    A Cristen kynge he suwed so longe   *pursued*
    Till he hadde purveyed hym batell st[ron]ge,
      With hym to abyde.
415 A day of batell ther was sette   *fixed*
    That the Cristen and the hethen mette
      A lytell ther bysyde.   *near at hand*
    Thenne syr Isumbras thydur he thoghte: *determined to go*
    On a hors that koles browghte   *carried*
420 Thyderwarde gan he ryde.   *towards there*

---

389 They: The L. *390* no other means of earning a livelihood. *395
yrne-ston* (iron-ore) E. *399* He severely strained his body. *405 And blewe
thaire belyes* (bellows) *bloo* T. *406–7* knew how to make all the armour that
a knight should have. *412 The Crysten kynges hase fledde so lange* T.
413–14 had assembled forces strong enough to face (the sultan); *he: thay* T;
stronge: sturoge L.

Tyll he come on a hyll so hye,
The Cristen and the hethen he sye: *saw*
  Two kynges thydur were browghte.
They batelled hom on a lowe;
425 Trumpes herde he ther blowe,
  And wepenes he seygh ther well wroght.
The knyghte was hende and fre.
And sette hym down on his knee,   *went*
  And to Jesu he besowghte   *implored*
430 To yeve hym grace in that felde
The hethen kynge forto yelde,   *repay*
  That in bales hadde hym browghte.   *to disaster*

The knyghte was hende and good:
He styrte up with herty mode,   *sprang, boldly*
435   And blessed [hym], sothe to sayn;   *crossed himself*
And sprange forth as spark of flynte:
Ther was no man withstode his dynte   *endured*
  Tyll his sory hors was sleyn.
Whenn he was to grownde browghte,
440 An erle out of the batell hym sowghte,   *took (?)*
  And ledde [hym] to an hygh mownteyne;
And all changed the knyghtes wede;   *armour*
He horsedde hym on a full good stede,
  And sone he wente ayeyne.   *promptly, returned*

445 Whenne he was on that gode steede,
He spronge forth as sparke on glede,   *from ember*
  And thowghte to smyte sore.   *strove*
Hit was seene ther his stede yode;   *where, went*
The knyghte slewe all that byfor hym stode,
450   Bothe lesse and more.

Till he come to the hyghe mountayn;
The hethenn kynge then hath he sleyn
  And all that with hym were.
All that day leste the fyghte,   *lasted*
455 And syr Isumbras, that nobyll knyghte,
  Wanne that batell there.

---

424 They took up their battle positions on a hill. *434 herty: hardy* T.
435 hym: for L; *And thryse he gonne hym sayne* (cross) T. *439 was ...
browghte: sought* A. *440 sowghte: brought* A. *441 hym: omitted* L.

Whenne the hethen kynge was sleyn,
The Cristen kynge was full fayn,
   And seyde, 'Where is he?
460 Where is that nobull knyghte,
That in this batell was so wyghte: *valiant*
   I kanne hym nowher se.'

Knyghtes and sqwyeres up hym sowghte;   *searched out*
Byfore the kynge he was browghte,
465 With wondes evell i-dyghte.   *seriously wounded*
The kynge asked what was his name:
'Syr,' he seyd, 'I am a smythes manne;
   Byholde and thou may se with syghthe.'
The kynge answered ayen thanne:
470 'I trowe nevur smythes manne   *swear that*
   In werre were so wyghte.'
He bad yeve hym mete and drynke   *give*
And all that his herte wold aftur thynke, *might desire*
   Kever yif that he myghte.   *recover*
475 In a nonrye they hym leved   *convent, left*
To hele the wondes on his hedde
   That he kawghte in fyghte.   *received*
Then sware the kyng that was so fre,
If that he myghte kevered be,   *restored to health*
480 He shulde be dubbed knyghte.

The nonnes of hym were full feyne
For he hadde the sowdan sleyne
   And mony hethen houndes.
And of his peynes they gan rewe,
485 And every day dyghte hym newe,
   Forto hele his woundes.

They yafe hym mete and drynke inowe,
And heled his wondes as I tell youw,
   Withinne a lytyll stounde.   *time*
490 Sir Isumbras bythowghte hym thare *determined*
That he wolde ther dwelle no mare,
   Whenne he were hole and sounde.

459 Thay made tham gamen and glee T. *463 up: hafe* T. *465 A full sare*
wondide man was hee T. *468 What es your will with me* T. *475-7 after*
478-80 T. *484 And his sufferings moved them to pity. 485 put fresh*
dressings on his wounds. 487 inowe: also A. *488 as I tell youw: that wer*
bloo A.

	He hym purveyde scryppe and pyke	*wallet, staff*
	And dyghte hym a palmere lyke,	*dressed*
495	Ageyn that he wolde wende.	
	He toke leve at the pryores	*of*
	And at the nonnes more and lesse,	
	For he was curteys and hende.	
	Thenne forth wente he	
500	Tyll he come to the Grekes See,	
	As Criste hym thydur gan sende.	
	A shyppe he fonde redy there	
	Ovur the see forto fare,	*cross*
	And to a crosse gan he wende.	

He hym purveyde scryppe and pyke   *wallet, staff*
And dyghte hym a palmere lyke,   *dressed*
495 Ageyn that he wolde wende.
He toke leve at the pryores   *of*
And at the nonnes more and lesse,
  For he was curteys and hende.
Thenne forth wente he
500 Tyll he come to the Grekes See,
  As Criste hym thydur gan sende.
A shyppe he fonde redy there
Ovur the see forto fare,   *cross*
  And to a crosse gan he wende.

505 Whenne he to the crosse was come,
With drwry bones he up nome,   *got up*
  To Jesu he bysowghte of mede.   *support*
And sevenn yer he was palmere thare,
With scrippe and pyke in sorowe and care,
510 In story as we rede.

In that clothynge he wente all day,
In that same all nyghte he lay,
  Ryghte in his pore wedes.
Of that penaunce wolde [he] not yrke,   *grow tired*
515 Forto fulfylle Goddes werke,
  And lette all his evell dedys.   *give up*

All a cyté he hadde thorow gone,
Mete ne drynke hadde [he] none;
  Nor no hows to harborow inne.   *lodge*
520 Bysyde the borow of Jerusalem   *city*
He rested hym by a welle streme,
  And sore he wepte for pyne.   *anguish*
Hit was abowte hygh mydnyghte;
To hym come an angell bryghte,
525 And browghte hym brede and wyne,
And seyde, 'Palmere, wellcome thou be:
Hevenne kynge thus greteth the,   *salutes*
  And foryeveth the synnes thyne.

---

495 So that he might set out. *504 In Acris gun thay lende* T; *In a karyc*
(ship) E. *506 drwry: wery* T. *507 Into that haythen stede* T. *514 and*
518 he: omitted L. *516 And to mende hi[s] are* (previous) *mysdede* T.
517 cyté: syde of a cunntre T.

And wele the greteth hevenne kynge,
530 And yeveth the his blessynge,
  He byddeth the turne ayeyne.'   *commands, return*
The knyghte was bothe hende and fre;
He sette hym down on his kne,   *went*
  And wepte, so was he fayne.

535 Yette wyste he nevur what to do,
But forto lyve in care and wo;
  In sore pyne he yode.   *anguish*
All a londe he hadde gone thorow   *a whole*
Tyll he come to a ryche borowe:
540 A ryche castell therin stode.
He herde telle therin was a ryche qwene,
She was bothe bryghte and shene,   *fair*
  Of here grette lose yede.
Every day she yafe at here yate   *gave, gate*
545 To menne that stode therate   *before it*
  A floreyne fayre and goode.
Syr Isumbras thowghte, if he myghte any gete,
Hit wolde hym helpe to clode and fede,
  And to other lyves fode.
550 He dede hym to the castell yate;   *made his way*
Pore men he fonde therate,
  And fele menne ther stode.   *many*

Everych she yaf a floreyne;
Syr Isumbras was fayn of hysen,   *his*
555 For he bymente hym sore.   *lamented*
Eche day she toke in fyftene and mo
Of seke men that myghte not go,   *walk*
  And of hem that poreste wore.

529–94 correspond to six complete stanzas in TEA: see Commentary. *535 what to do: whedirwarde to gonne* T. *536 For had he no[w]e no wonnynge wone* T. *538 All a londe: Sevenn kynges landes* T. *543* She was greatly praised. *554 Sir Ysambrace was never so fayne* T.

She toke in syr Isumbras;
560 For a pore palmere he was,
      She rewed hym most of all.   *pitied*
The ryche qwene in golde seete;
Menne her served to honde and feete,
      In ryche robes of palle.
565 A cloth in the flore was leyde;
'The pore palmere,' the stewarde seyde,
      'Shall sytte above you all.'
Mete and drynke ther was forth browghte,
The palmere sette and ete ryght nowghte,   *sat*
570 But loked abowte the halle.   *around*
He syghe myche game and gle—
For he was wonte therin to be,
      Theres he lette down falle.   *tears*
The lady of hym grette doole thowghte,
575 For he sette and ete ryght nowght,
      Thenne she a knyghte gan calle:

Fech me a schayer and a coyschenn   *chair, cushion*
And make this palmere to sytte therin
      That he me telle may
580 What maner aventours he hath seyn
In dyvers londes ther he has bene,   *various*
      By many dyvers way.
Ryghte soone a cheyere was forth fette;
The pore palmere therin was sette:
585 He tolde here of his leye.   *faith*
Goode tales he her tolde;
The lady asked what she wolde,
      In longynge as they satte aye.

'For my lordes sowle Y wyll yeve the,
590 And for his love if he on lyfe be,
      Evurmore cloth and mete;
And a chambur fayer and fre,
And a page forto serve the,
      Withinne my castell yate.'

562 golde: haulle T.   *567* In a higher place than any of you.   *572 Because*
he had (once) been accustomed to such surroundings; *And thoghte what he*
was wonnt to be T.   *582 dyvers: wilfull* T.

595 Now is syr Isumbras lafte thare:
     I wote he is wele of his care,
         But yette he morneth by wode and wall.   *forest, stream*
     He was so myche and so hye,   *great, exalted*
     All they of hym hadde envye,
600   So stronge he was ovur all.   *pre-eminently*
     But of the Sarezenes he yafe no more
     Thenne twenty menne do of a boore
         Whenne he is down fall.
     A turnement they gan hym bede   *proclaim*
605 And horsed hym on a croked steede,
         And mony he made down falle.

     Whenne they come into the felde
     Was non so dowghty unthur schelde
         That durste mete his stede.
610 And somme he yafe such a rowte   *blow*
     That bothe her eyghen styrte oute,   *started*
         And many he made to bleede.

     The ryche qwene satte and lowe;   *laughed*
     She thoghte the palmere was stronge ynow,
615   And worthy forto fynde.   *provide for*
     Nowe it byfell upon a daye,
     The knyghte wente forth forto pleye,
         As hit was evur his kynde.   *custom*
     And in a gryffen neste on hyghe,
620 A rede clothe therin he seghe,
         Wavynge with the wynde;
     And to the neste he ganne wynne;   *go*
     His skarlette mantell he fonde therinne,
         Hys golde allso ther he gan fynde.
625 And whenne he syghe ther that golde,
     He thowghte his wyfe therfore was solde;
         His sorowe he hadde in mynde.   *remembered*
     To his chamber he gan hit bere,
     Unthur his bedde he putte hit there,
630   He wente awey wepynge.

595 He duellid there full many a yere T. *596 Till that he was bothe hale and
fere* (sound) T. *597 And served in that haulle* T. *599 Alle had wondir that
hym see* T. *607–42* have different stanza-limits in TEA: see Commentary.
610 rowte: clowte T. *611 styrte oute: stode one strowte* (protruded) T.
615 fynde: fede T.

Thawgh he were nevur so mylde of mode,
Whenne he to his chaumbur yode,   *after*
   He syked all that daye;   *grieved*
And so he dede at nyghte also,
635 Whenne he myghte no forther go,
   In chamber ther he laye.
Ther he lyved and ledde hys lyfe,
And in the castell it sprong full ryfe,
   And to the qwene menne seye:
640 'This palmere hath don somme traytourré,   *treason*
Of your golde or of your fee,
   By nyghte or by daye.'

So it byfell upon a daye
The knyghte wennte hym forth to playe,
645   And his sorowe to mene.   *lament*
Sqwyeres breke up his chambur dore
And fonde the golde in the flore
   And shewed it to the qwene.
Whenne she it syghe in syghte,
650 Thenne swowened that lady bryghte,
   For that syghte that she hadde seene.
She kyssed the golde and seyde, 'Allas,
This hadde my lorde syr Isumbras,
   That my lorde was wonte to beene.   *was once*

655 Jesu Criste, hevenne kynge,
Sende me somme tokenynge   *sign*
   Of my trewe fere,   *husband*
That I myghte wyte somme gladnes
Of my lorde syr Isumbras,
660   In what londe that he were.

Where is the palmere?' then seyde she:
'Hastely make hym come speke with me,
   For aftur hym me longeth sore.'
And when he was come to the hall
665 To counseyll then she dede hym call,
   And askede hym ryghth thore:

---

631 *mylde: glad* A.   638 the news spread everywhere.   639 *seye: seyde* L.
645 *sorowe: myrthis* T.   649 *in: in that* L.   655–717 correspond to only
three stanzas in TEA: see Commentary.   658 learn some good news.

'Tell me palmere, if thou kanne,   *are able*
Wherevur thou this golde wanne:'   *acquired*
   Thenne was his sorowe grete.
670 With karefull herte and hevy chere,
He yaf the lady an answere,
   And on knees hym sette.
The firste tale that he tolde,
He seyde his wife was therfore solde,   *for it*
675   And hymself all to-beete.   *badly beaten*
'I have lorne my wyfe and children thre;   *lost*
My skarlet mantell was born fro me,
   And in a neste I hit fette.'   *found*

'Say me, palmere or thou go,   *tell, before*
680 Was ther any token betwene you two,
   Whenne ye departed atwynne?'   *separated*
The palmere answered thus:
'A rynge was broken betwyx us,
   That no man shulde it kenne.'

685 The lady toke up a grete sykynge,
And seyde, 'Lette me se that rynge,
   If that thou trewe be.'
'Loo, madame, have it here,
I have born it this fourtene yere,
690   I shewde hit non but the.'

She toke forth a purse so clene;   *bright*
The halle shone therof bydene,
   So wele it was i-wroughte.   *fashioned*
That othur party therinne was—   *half*
695 Nowe was this a wonthur kace,   *marvellous chance*
   So mony londis as he hadde sowghte.

She layde togydur the partyes tweyne,   *put, two*
Hole it wax, the sothe to seyne,   *became, truly*
   Ryghte amonge hem alle.
700 'Blessed be God of his swete grace,
Nowe have I my lord, syr Isumbras,
   Here all in myn halle.'   *entirely*

---

667 *Was thou ever gentyll man* T.   669 *His sorowe than wexe the mare* T.
684 In such a way that no-one should know of it.   685 began to sigh
bitterly.   692 It illuminated the (entire) hall.   696 After he had searched
(for her) in so many countries.

  The lady that was so fayre of face,
  Swonedde thryes in that place,
705 For fayne she hadde her lorde bolde.   *joy*
  Grete joye it was to se hem mete,
  With clyppynge and with kyssynge swete,   *embracing*
   In armes forto folde.
  Eche on of othur was so fayne
710 That no lengur wolde they leyne,   *keep silent*
   But to knyghtes they hit tolde.
  A ryche feste they gon bede   *proclaim*
  And ryche and pore therto yede,
   Erles and barouns bolde.

715 Now is syr Isumbras ryghte   *indeed*
  Crowned kynge, that hardy knyghte,   *bold*
   Of many ryche londes thare.
  Now is this kynge syr Isumbras
  In more welthe then evur he was,
720 And rekovereth hath all his care.

  Cristendome he lette crye;
  He sende abowte ferre and nye   *to all parts*
   To hem that hethen were.
  All the Sarezens were of on assente
725 Syr Isumbras forto have shente,
   And all [that] with hym were.
  A daye of batell ther was sette
  That Cristen and hedhen shulde mete: *heathen*
   Two hethenne kynges were there.
730 Whenne he was horsed on a steede   *mounted*
  The folke hym fayled at his nede: *let him down*
   All that with hym were.

714 Hadun robys mony folde E. *717* followed by an extra stanza in TEA: see Commentary. *718–26* and *727–32* each a complete stanza in TEA: see Commentary. *720 Of haythen landes thare* T. *721* He had Christianity proclaimed the official religion. *724–6* decided unanimously to destroy sir Isumbras and all his followers. *726 that:* omitted L.

Whenne he shulde to the batell gone,
His folke wente fro hym echone,
735   And thenne he syked sore.
  A doolfull worde thenne ganne he seye
To his lady: 'Now have good daye,   *farewell*
   For now and evurmore.'
She seyde, 'Lord God that I ne were dyghte   *equipped*
740 In armour as I were a knyghte,   *as if*
   For with you wyll I fare.   *go*
If Jesu wolde us grace sende
That we myghte togydur ende,   *die*
   Lyve wolde I no more.'

745 He halpe his lady that she was dyghte
In armour as she were a knyghte,
   And forth wente with spere and shelde.
Ayeyn thrytty dowsande and mo: *thousand*
Ther come no Cristen but they two,
750   Whenne they mette in the felde.   *joined battle*

And whenne they shulde asseyld be   *attacked*
Ther come rydynge knyghtes thre
   On bestes that were so wylde:
That on upon a lybarde, that othur on a unykorn;
755 The thrydde on a lyoune come byforn,   *advanced*
   And that was her eldest childe.   *their*

The beste[s] were both wylde and wode;   *ferocious*
The childeren slowgh all that byfore hem stode: *killed*
   Grete joye it was to see.
760 They slowgh hethen kynges two
And othur Sarezens mony mo:
   Thrytty thowsand and thre.
Syr Isumbras thanked hem yare   *promptly*
And prayde hem with hym to fare,
765   All thre that nyght with hym to be.
The chyldren answered, that wer so hende: *courteous*
'The grace of God us hydur dede sende;
   Thyne owen sones be we.'

733 Sir Ysambrace was than full waa T.   *734 Every one of his men deserted him; He kyssede his lady and wolde furthe gaa* T.   *757 bestes: beste* L; *In angells wede were thay alle clede* T.   *758 An angelle tham to the batelle lede* T. *766 Thay ansuerde als the angelle tham kende* (instructed) T.

Ofte was he welle and wo,
770 But nevur so well as he was tho: *joyful*
    On knees he hym sette,
And seyde, 'Jesu Criste, hevenne kynge,
Graunte us all thy blessynge,
    That thus our bales has bette.'

775 A ryche borow stode ther bysyde;   *city, nearby*
Thyder thenne gon they ryde,
    And his sones with hym ganne lede;
And in a chambur fayre and bryghte,
Ther he dede hem newe dyghte,
780   And chaunged all here wede.
And aftur, thre kynges londes gon thei wynne,
And cristened all that were therinne,
    In story as we rede;
Each of his sones he yafe a londe .   *gave*
785 And crowned hem kynges with his honde,
    Or they fro hym yede.

Whenne eche of hem a kynge was,
They thanked God of his grace
    That browghte hem out of care.
790 They lyved and dyed in gode entente,   *devoutly*
Her sowles I wote to hevenn wente,
    Whenne they dede ware.

Thus ended syr Isumbras,
That an hardy knyghte was,
795   In sorowe allthowgh he wore.
Jesu Criste, hevenne kynge,
Graunte us all thy blessynge,
    F[o]r now and evurmore.

769 in joy and sorrow. *774* has put an end to our misfortunes; followed by
six extra lines in T: see Commentary. *780* followed by three extra lines in
T: see Commentary. *783* followed by three extra lines in T: see Commentary. *786 Whareso that thay solde fare* T. *797* [ ] not now visible.

Sir Gowther

[God that art of myghtis most,
Fader and Sone and Holy Gost,
 That bought man on rode so dere;   *redeemed, cross*
Shilde us from the fowle fende   *protect, devil*
5 That is about mannys sowle to shende   *bring to ruin*
 All tymes of the yere.
Symtyme the fende hadde postee   *once, the power*
Forto dele with ladies free   *have intercourse*
 In liknesse of here fere;   *shape, husband*
10 So that he begat Merlyng and mo
And wrought ladies so mikil wo   *caused, much*
 That ferly it is to here.   *astonishing*

A selcowgh thyng that is to here: *strange*
A fende to nye]ght wemen nere,   *lie with*
15 And makyd hom with chyld,
Tho kynde of men wher thei hit tane   *nature, assumed*
(For of homselfe had thei never nan,   *in themselves*
 Be meydon Maré mylde).   *virgin, gracious*
Therof seyus clerkus, Y wotte how,
20 That schall not be rehersyd now,
 As Cryst fro schame me schyld.
Bot Y schall tell yow of a warlocke greytt,   *powerful demon*
What sorow at his modur hart he seyt,   *brought to*
 With his warcus wylde.   *deeds*

25 Jesu Cryst, that barne blythe,   *gracious child*
Gyff hom joy that lovus to lythe   *hear*
 Of ferlys that befell.   *marvels*
A la[y] of Breyten long Y soght   *studied*
And owt therof a tale have Y broght,   *composed*
30 That lufly is to tell.   *delightful*
Ther wonde a duke in Estryke,   *lived, Austria*
He weddyt a ladé, non hur lyke,   *peerless*
 For comly undur kell;   *fair(ness), robe*
To th[e lyly was likened that lady clere];   *bright*
35 Hur rod rey[de as blosmes on brere],
 That ylke der[e] damsell.   *excellent*

1–14 [ ] missing in A, supplied from B. *19–20* I know, but will not repeat here the views of scholars on this matter. *25* Of that baron y-born unblithe B. *28* lay: law A. *34–5* [ ] missing in A, supplied from B; *35* Her complexion as red as wild roses. *36* [ ] not now visible.

When he had weddyd that meydyn schene,   *fair*
And sche duches, withowt wene,   *doubt*
   A mangeré con thei make.   *feast, 'did' hold*
40 Knyghtus of honowr tho furst dey
Justyd gently hom to pley,
   For that lady sake.
Tho duke hymselfe wan stedys ten   *horses*
And bare don full doghty men,   *felled*
45   And mony a cron con crake.   *skull, split*

When this turment was y-ses,   *tournament, over*
Tho ryche duke and tho duches   *noble*
   Lad hor lyfe with wyn.
Ten yer and sumdele mare,   *somewhat more*
50 He chylde non geyt ne sche non bare: *begot, bore*
   Ther joy began to tyne.   *(come to an) end*
To is ladé sone con he seyn,
'Y tro thou be sum baryn,   *believe, barren*
   Hit is gud that we twyn;   *part*
55 Y do bot wast my tyme on the,
Eireles mon owre londys bee—'
   For gretyng he con not blyn.   *weeping, finish*

Tho ladé sykud and made yll chere,
That all feylyd hur whyte lere,
60   For schu conseyvyd noght,
Scho preyd to God and Maré mylde
Schuld gyffe hur grace to have a chyld,
   On what maner scho ne roghth.
In hur orchard, apon a day,
65 Ho meyt a mon, tho sothe to say,   *she*
   That hur of luffe besoghth;
As lyke hur lorde as he myght be—
He leyd hur down undur a tre,
   With hur is wyll he wroghtth   *his, did*

---

41 Took their sport in jousting nobly; followed by three extra lines in B: see Commentary. *48* Lived happily together. *56* Our lands will remain without an heir. *58–9* The lady sighed and was so unhappy that her face lost its brightness; *falwyd* (grew pale) B. *63* She did not care how. *66* Who asked her to lie with him. *68* Undernethe a chestayn tree B.

70 When he had is wylle all don,
    A felturd fende he start up son,   *shaggy, leaped*
      And stode and hur beheld.
    He seyd, 'Y have geyton a chylde on the
    That in is yothe full wylde schall bee
75   And weppons wyghtly weld.'   *powerfully manage*
    Sche blessyd hur and fro hym ran;   *crossed herself*
    Into hur chambur fast ho wan,   *made her way*
      That was so bygly byld;   *strongly built*
    Scho seyd to hur lord, that ladé myld,
80 'Tonyght we mon geyt a chyld,   *will*
      That schall owre londus weld.   *rule over*

    An agell com fro hevon bryght
    And told me so this same nyght:
      I hope was Godus sond.   *believe, messenger*
85 Then wyll that stynt all owr stryfe—' *bring to an end*
    Be tho lappe he laght his wyfe
      And seyd, 'Dame, we schall fonde.'   *try*
    At evon to beyd thei hom ches,   *bed, went*
    Tho ryche duke and tho duches
90   And wold no lengur wonde.   *refrain*
    He pleyd hym with that ladé hende,
    And ei yode scho bownden with tho fende,
      To God wold losse hur bonde.   *until*

    This chyld within hur was non odur
95 Bot eyvon Marlyon halfe brodur,
      For won fynd gatte hom bothe.   *begot*
    Thei servyd never of odyr thyng
    But forto temp[t]e wemen yong:
      To deyle with hom was wothe.
100 Ylke a day scho grette fast
    And was delyverid at tho last
      Of won that coth do skathe.   *could, evil*
    Tho duke hym gard to kyrke beyre,
    Crystond hym and cald hym Gwother,
105   That sythyn wax breme [and brathe]. *later, fierce, unruly*

86 He caught his wife by the fold of her robe. *91* He took his pleasure
with that gracious lady. *92* And all the time she was carrying the devil's
child. *97* They had no other concern. *98 tempte: tempe* A. *99* It was
a sin to have intercourse with them. *100* she became more obviously
pregnant. *103* had him taken to the church. *105 and brathe* B: *as barre*
(boar) A.

  The duke comford that duches heynde   *gracious*
  And aftur melche wemen he sende,   *wet nurses*
    Tho best in that cuntre,
  That was full gud knyghttys wyffys:
110 He sowkyd hom so thei lost ther lyvys,
    Sone had he sleyn three.
  The duke gard prycke aftur sex;
  Tho chyld was yong and fast he wex—   *grew*
    Hende, harkons yee.   *listen*
115 Be twelfe monethys was gon
  Nyne norsus had he slon   *killed*
    Of ladys feyr and fre.

  Knyghtus of that cuntre geydyrd hom samun   *gathered together*
  And seyd to tho duke hit was no gamun   *joke*
120   To lose hor wyffus soo.
  Thei badde hym orden for is son:
  'He geytys no more is olde won,
    Norsus now no moo.'
  His modur fell a fowle unhappe;   *suffered, misfortune*
125 Apon a day bad hym tho pappe,
  He snaffulld to hit soo,   *worried at*
  He rofe tho hed fro tho brest;   *tore, nipple*
  Scho fell backeward and cald a prest,
    To chambur fled hym froo.

130 Lechus helud that ladé yare;   *promptly*
  Wemen durst gyffe hym souke no mare,
    That yong chyld Gowther,
  Bot fed hym up with rych fode
  And that full mych, as hym behovyd,   *was needful to*
135   Full safly mey Y sweyre.
  Be that he was fyftene yere of eld,   *age*
  He made a wepon that he schuld weld
    (No nodur mon myght hit beyr):   *carry*
  A fachon bothe of styll and yron;
140 Wytte yow wyll he wex full styron   *fierce*
  And fell folke con he feyr.   *many, terrify*

112 had six more found hastily; *The duk sent after other sex* B.   *121* They told him to make (other) arrangements.   *122–3* He will no longer have nurses, as he has been used to do.   *125* One day she gave him her breast. *126 And he arighte* (treated) *hire soo* B.   *134 behovyd* for **behode*.   *139* A curved sword made of iron and steel.

In a twelmond more he wex   *year*
Then odur chyldur in seyvon or sex;
   Hym semyd full well to ryde.
145 He was so wekyd in all kyn wyse   *ways*
Tho duke hym myght not chastyse,
   Bot made hym knyght that tyde,
With cold brade bronde: *broad sword*
Ther was non in that londe
150   That dynt of hym durst byde.   *blow, endure*
For sorro tho duke fell don ded;
His modur was so wo of red
   Hur care scho myght not hyde.

Mor sorro for hym sche myght have non,
155 Bot to a castyll of lyme and ston,
   Frely then scho fled.
Scho made hit strong and held hur thare;
Hor men myght tell of sorro and care,
   Evyll thei wer bested.
160 For wher he meyt hom be tho way,   *wherever*
'Evyll heyle,' myght thei say,   *alas*
   'That ever modur h[i]m fed.'
For with his fachon he wold hom slo,
And gurde hor horssus backus in too: *smite*
165   All seche perellys thei dred.

Now is he duke of greyt renown   *notoriety*
And men of holy kyrke dynggus down,   *church, beats*
   Wher he myght hom mete.
Masse ne matens wold he non here
170 Nor no prechyng of no frere,
   That dar I heyly hette.   *solemnly swear*
[Erly and] late, lowde and styll,
He wold wyrke is fadur wyll
   Wher he stod or sete.
175 Hontyng lufde he aldurbest,   *best of all*
Parke, wodd and wylde forest,
   Bothe be weyus and strete.

144 He seemed ready to manage a horse. *148 He gaf him his best swerd in honde* B. *152* His mother's lot was so sorrowful. *154 Mor sorro: Dowrey* B. *156 Frely: Fast* B. *157* She fortified it and kept within it. *158–9* Her men had reason to lament, as they were in a dangerous situation. *162 him* B: *hom* A. *172 Erly and* B: *For* A; At all times and in all ways.

	He went to honte apon a day;	
	He see a nonry be tho way	
180	And thedur con he ryde.	*towards it*
	The pryorys and hur covent	
	With presescion ageyn hym went	*to meet*
	Full hastely that tyde.	*time*
	Thei wer full ferd of his body,	*frightened, him*
185	For he and is men bothe leyn hom by:	*lay with*
	Tho sothe why schuld Y hyde?	
	And sythyn he spard hom in hor kyrke	*shut up*
	And brend hom up—thus con he werke;	
	Then went his name full wyde.	

	All that ever on Cryst con lefe,	*believe*
190	Yong and old, he con hom greve	
	In all that he myght doo.	
	Meydyns' maryage wolde he spyll	*ruin*
	And take wyffus ageyn hor wyll,	
195	And sley hor husbondus too.	
	And make frerus to leype at kraggus	*over cliffs*
	And persons forto heng on knaggus,	*hooks*
	And odur prestys sloo.	
	To bren armettys was is dyssyre:	*hermits*
200	A powre wedow to seyt on fyre,	
	And werke hom mykyll woo.	*do*

	An olde erle of that cuntre	
	Unto tho duke then rydys hee,	
	And seyd, 'Syr, why dose thou soo?	
205	We howpe thou come never of Cryston stryn,	
	Bot art sum fendys son, we weyn,	*imagine*
	That werkus hus this woo;	
	Thou dose never gud, bot ey tho ylle:	*always, evil*
	We hope thou be full syb tho deyll'—	
210	Syr Gowther wex then throo.	*angry*
	Hee seyd, 'Syr, and thou ly on mee,	*if*
	Hongud and drawon schall thou bee,	
	And never qwycke heythyn goo.'	

---

188 this is how he behaved.   *189* his (evil) reputation spread everywhere.
198 *Thus wonderly wold he doo* B.   *205* We do not think you were begotten by a Christian.   *209* We believe that you are close kin to the devil.   *213* And will never leave this place alive; *Or tha[t] thow fro me go* B.

He gard to putte tho erle in hold,
215 And to his modur castyll he wold,   *set off*
      As fast as he myght ryde.
He seyd, 'Dame, tell me in hye,   *haste*
Who was my fadur, withowt lye,
      Or this schall thoro the glyde.   *pierce you*
220 He sette his fachon to hur hart:
      'Have done yf thou lufe thi qwart!'   *health*
      Ho onswarde hym that tyde:
'My lord,' scho seyd, 'that dyed last.'   *recently*
'Y hope,' he seyd, 'thou lyus full fast.'   *very greatly*
225   Tho teyrus he lett don glyde.   *flow*

'Son, sython Y schall tho sothe say: *since, must*
In owre orcharde apon a day,
      A fende gat the thare;
As lyke my lorde as he myght be,
230 Undurneyth a cheston tre.'
      Then weppyd thei bothe full sare.   *bitterly*
'Go schryfe the, modur, and do tho best,   *confess*
For Y wyll to Rome or that Y rest,
      To lerne anodur lare.'
235 This thoght come on hym sodenly:
      'Lorde, mercy', con he cry
      To God that Maré bare.

To save hym fro is fadur tho fynde,
He preyd to God and Maré hynde,
240   That most is of posté;
To bryng is sowle to tho blys
That he boght to all his   *for*
      Apon tho rode tre.   *cross*
Sythyn he went hym hom ageyn
245 And seyd to tho erle withowt leyn,   *openly*
      'Tho sothe tale tolde thou mee.   *truth*
Y wyll to Rome to tho apostyll,   *pope*
That he mey schryfe me and asoyll:
      Kepe thou my castyll free.'   *watch over*

214 He had the earl imprisoned.   234 a different way of life.   248 So that
he may hear my confession and give me absolution.

250 This old erle laft he theyr
    Forto be is stydfast heyre;   *reliable successor*
      Syr Gwother forthe con glyde.   *go*
    Toward Rome he radly ranne,   *quickly*
    Wold he nowdur hors ne man
255   With hym to ren ne ryde.
    His fauchon con he with hym take,
    He laft hit not for weyle ne wrake,
      Hyt hong ei be his syde.   *always*
    Toward Rome cety con hee seche;   *journey*
260 Or he come to tho powpe speche,
      Full long he con abyde.   *wait*

    As sone has he the pope con see
    He knelys adown apon is kne
      And heylst hym full sone.   *saluted*
265 He preyd hym with mylde devocyon   *humble piety*
    Bothe of schryfte and absolycion;
      He granttyd hym is bone.   *request*
    'Whethon art thou and of what cuntre?'   *from where*
    'Duke of Estryke, lorde,' quod hee,
270   'Be tru God in trone.
    Ther was Y geyton with a feynde
    And borne of a duches hende;
      My fadur hase frenchypus f[one].'   *few friends*

    'Y wyll gladly, be my fey;
275 Art thou crystond?' He seyd, 'Yey,
      My name it is Gwother.'
    'Now Y lowve God thou art commun hedur,   *praise*
    For ellus Y most a traveld thedur,   *otherwise*
      Apon the forto weyre;
280 For thou hast holy kyrke dystryed—'
    'Nay, holy fadur, be thou noght agrevyd: *angry*
    Y schall the truly swere
    At thi byddyng beyn to be   *command, obedient*
    And hald tho penans that thou leys to me,   *perform, impose*
285   And never Cryston deyre.'   *harm*

251 To kepe his londes lesse and mare B.   *255 Him was lever* (preferable) *to ryn than ryde* B.   *257 He would not leave it behind for good or evil fortune.*   *260 Before he could have audience with the pope.*   *273 fone: few* A; *I trowe my good dayes been done* B.   *279 And that ful lothe me were* B.   *281 agrevyd: anoyed* B.

'Lye down thi fachon then the fro;   *lay*
Thou schallt be screvon or Y goo   *confessed*
    And asoyly[d] or Y blyn.'   *absolved, leave off*
'Nay, holy fadur,' seyd Gwother,
290 'This bous me nedus with mee beyr:
    My frendys ar full thyn.'   *few*
'Wherser thou travellys be northe or soth,   *wheresoever*
Thou eyt no meyt bot that thou revus of howndus mothe, *snatch*
    Cum thy body within;
295 Ne no worde speke for evyll ne gud,
Or thou reydé tokyn have fro God   *before, sign*
    That forgyfyn is thi syn.'

He knelyd down befor tho pope stole,   *throne*
And solemly he con hym asoyle,
300   Tho sarten sothe to sey.   *absolute*
Meyte in Rome gatte he non,   *food*
Bot of a dog mothe a bon,
    And wyghttly went is wey.   *quickly*
He went owt of that ceté
305 Into anodur far cuntre:
    Tho testamentys thus thei sey.   *authorities*
He seyt hym down undur a hyll;
A greyhownde broght hym meyt untyll   *to*
    Or evon yche a dey.   *evening*

310 Thre neghthtys ther he ley;
Tho grwhownd, ylke a dey,   *every*
    A whyte lofe he hym broght.
On tho fort day come hym non;   *fourth*
Up he start and forthe con gon,
315   And lovyd God in his thoght.   *praised*
Besyde ther was a casstell,   *nearby*
Therin an emperowr con dwell,
    And thedurwarde he soght.
He seyt hym down withowt the yate,   *outside*
320 And durst not entur in theratte,
    [Th]of he wer well wroght.

288 [ ] not now visible.   290 I am bound to take this with me.   294 *This penaunce shalt thow gynne* B.   295 *for evyll ne gud: even ne odde* B.   298 *pope stole: worthy appostell* B.   317 *The emperour of Almayn* B.   318 he made his way towards it.   321 *Thof: Of* A; *Though him were woo yn thowght* B.

Tho weytus blu apon tho wall,
Knyghttus geydert into tho hall,   *assembled in*
  Tho lord buskyd to his saytte.   *hurried, seat*
325 Syr Gwother up and in con gwon;
At tho dor uschear fond he non,
  Ne porter at tho yatte,
Bot gwosse prystely thoro tho pres,
Unto tho hye bord he chesse,   *went*
330 Therundur he made is seytt.   *under it*
Tho styward come with yarde in honde;
To geyt hym thethyn fast con he fonde
  And throly hym con threyt   *fiercely, threaten*

To beyt hym bot he wende awey;   *unless*
335 'What is that?' tho emperour con sey.
  'My lord,' he seyd, 'a mon,
And that tho feyryst that ever Y sye;
Cum loke on hym, it is no lye—'
  And thedur wyghtly he wan.   *quickly, went*
340 Won word of hym he myght not geyt;
Thei lette hym sytt and gafe hym meyt:
  'Full lytyll gud he can;
And yett may happon thoro sum chans
That it wer gyffon hym in penans,'
345 Tho lord thus onsward than.

When tho emperowr was seyt and servyd
And knyghttus had is breyd karvyd,
  He send tho domp mon parte.   *share*
He lette hit stond and wold ryght non;   *not touch it*
350 Ther come a spanyell with a bon,
  In his mothe he hit bare.
Syr Gwother hit fro hym droghe   *pulled (away)*
And gredely on hit he gnofe,   *gnawed*
  He wold nowdur curlu ne tartte.
355 Boddely sustynans wold he non
Bot what so he fro tho howndus wan,   *took*
  Yf it wer gnaffyd or mard.   *chewed, spoiled*

322 The guards on the wall sounded their trumpets. *324 They wysshe and went to mete* B. 328 But makes his way quickly through the crowd. 332 He tried hard to drive him away from there. 342 He has very little sense. *351 hit bare: that lart* B.

     Tho emperowre and tho emperys
     And knyghttys and ladys at tho des   *dais*
360   Seyt and hym behelld.
     Thei gaffe tho hondus meyt ynoghe;   *plenty of*
     Tho dompe duke to hom he droghe: *moved over*
      That was is best beld.   *support*
     Among tho howndys thus was he fed,
365   At evon to a lytyll chambur led
      And hyllyd undur teld;   *hidden, curtains*
     At none come into tho hall—
     Hob hor fole, thei con hym call;   *their*
      To God he hym con yelde.   *submit*

370 Bot now this ylke emperowre
     Had a doghtur whyte as flowre,
      Was too soo dompe as hee;   *twice*
     Scho wold have spokyn and myght noght;
     That meydon was worthely wroght,   *nobly formed*
375   Bothe feyr, curteys and free.
     A messynger come apon a dey,
     Tyll her fadur con he sey,
      'My lord wele gretys the:
     Tho sawdyn that is of mykyll myght
380 Wyll wer apon the dey and nyghtt   *make war*
      And bren thi bowrus free,

     And sley thi men bot thou hym sende   *unless*
     Thi doghttur that is so feyr and heynde
      That he mey hur wedde.'
385 Tho emperowr seyd, 'Y have bot won,
     And that is dompe as any ston,
      Feyrur thar non be feyd;
     And Y wyll not, be Cryst wonde,   *wounds*
     Gyffe hor to no hethon hownde:
390   Then wer my bale bredde.
     Yeit mey God, thoro is myght,
     Ageyn to geyt hur spech ryght'—
      Tho messynger ageyn hym spedde.   *hastened back*

---

374 Therefore ful ofte she sighed (*: ne myght*) B.   *381* And burn down your
splendid apartments.   *387* No-one will ever bring up one more beautiful.
390 I should then bring disaster upon myself.   *391 Yett may she sum good
halowe* (shrine) *seche* B.   *392 Thorow grace of God to have speche* B.

To tho sadyn and told hym soo;
395 Then wakynd ey more wo and wo;
    He toke is oste and come nere.   *army, closer*
Tho emperowr doghtty undur schyld
With anodur kepped hym in tho fyld,   *engaged*
    Eydur had batell sere.
400 Syr Gwother went to a chambur smart   *promptly*
And preyd to God in his hart,
    On rode that boghtt hym dere,
Schuld sende hym armus, schyld and speyr,
And hors to helpe is lord in weyr,
405   That wyll susstand hym thare.   *well, supported*

He had no ner is preyr made,   *sooner (?)*
Bot hors and armur bothe he hade,
    Stode at his chambur dor;
His armur, is steid was blacke color;
410 He leypus on hors, that stythe in stowr,
    That stalworthe was and store.   *strong, powerful*
His scheld apon his schuldur hong;
He toke his speyre was large and long
And spard nodur myre ne more.   *bog, heath*
415 Forthe at tho yatus on hors he went,
Non hym knew bot that meydyn gent,
    And aftur hur fadur he fore.   *rode*

Tho emperour had a batell kene;   *army*
Tho sawden anodur, withowt wene,
420   Assemuld as was hor kast.
Bot fro syr Gwother comun were,   *once*
Mony a crone con he stere,   *head, damage*
    And hew apon full fast.
He gard stedus forto stakur   *stagger*
425 And knyghttus hartys forto flakur,   *falter*
    When blod and brenus con brast; *brains, burst out*
And mony a heython hed of-smott,   *cut off*
And owt of hor sadyls, wylle Y wott,   *well, know*
    Thei tombull at tho last.

---

395 This resulted in ever-increasing sorrow. *399* Each had a number of battalions. *406* He ne had so sone that i-thought (:y-brought) B. *414* And, whatever the ground, did not slacken speed; *myre: lesse* B. *420* Drawn up in accordance with their practice. *422* *And many stowte shildes down he bere* B. *426* and brenus: thorow brenyys (mail-shirts) B.

430 He putte tho sawden to tho flyghth
      And made tho chasse to it was nyghth,   *until*
        And sluye tho Sarsyns kene;
      Sython rode befor tho emperowr;
      Non hym knew bot that bryghtt in bowr,   *fair (lady)*
435   Tho dompe meydon schene.
      To chambur he went, dysharnest hym sone;   *unarmed*
      His hors, is armur awey wer done: *vanished*
        He ne wyst wher hit myght bene.
      In hall he fond his lorde at meyt,
440 He seytt hym down and made is seytt,
        Too small raches betwene.   *hunting dogs*

      Tho meydon toke too gruhowndus fyn
      And waschyd hor mowthus cleyn with wyn,
        And putte a lofe in tho ton,   *one*
445 And in tho todur flesch full gud;   *other*
      He raft bothe owt with eyggur mode,   *snatched, violently*
        That doghthy of body and bon.
      He seytt, made hym wyll at es,
      Sythyn to chambur con he ches,   *go*
450   In that worthely won.   *noble dwelling*
      On the morne cum a messengere
      Fro tho sawdyn with store chere,   *forbidding*
        To tho emperowr sone he come.

      He seyd, 'Syr, Y bryng yow a lettur;
455 My lord is comun, wyll take hym bettur;   *acquit*
        Yesturdey ye slogh his men.
      Todey he is comun into tho feyld
      Wyth knyghtys that beyrus speyr and schyld,
        Thowsandus mo then ten' . . . .
460 God sende Syr Gwother thro is myghth
      A reyd hors and armur bryghth,
        He fo[lw]yd thro frythe and fen.   *wood, marsh*

---

431 *Sir Gowghter so moch of myght* B.   440 *Undur the hegh bord he made his
sete* B.   447 That supremely valiant warrior; *Ful wel was him bygone* B.
455 *wyll take hym: to assay the* B.   459 followed by three lines in B: see
Commentary.   462 *folwyd: fowlyd* A.

When bothe batels wer areyd,
Truly as tho romandys seyd,   *French tale*
465 Syr Gwother rode betwene.
Mony a sturdy gard he stombull,
Toppe over teyle hor horssus to tombull,
    Forto wytte wythowt wene.
He hewde in sondur helme and schelde,   *in two*
470 He feld tho baner in tho feld
    That schon so bryght and schene.
He leyd apon tho Sarsyns blake   *struck*
And gard hor basnettus in too crake: *helmets*
    He kyd that he was kene.   *showed*

475 'A, lord God!' seyd tho emperowre,
'What knyght is yondur so styffe in stowr,   *bold, battle*
    And all areyd in red
Bothe his armur and his sted?
Mony a hethon he gars to bled
480   And dynggus hom to tho deyd.
And hedur come to helpe me
Anodur in blacke yesturdey had we,
    That styrd hym wyll in this styd;   *exerted, place*
Dyscomfytt the sawden and mony a Sersyn,   *defeated*
485 So wyll yondur do, as Y wene,
    His dyntus ar heyvé as leyde;   *lead*

His fochon is full styffe of stele;   *sword*
Loke he warus his dyntus full wele
    And wastus of hom never won.'
490 Tho emperowr pryckus into tho pres,   *gallops*
Tho doghtty knyght wyth hym he ches
    And byrkons hom flesche and bon.   *belabours them*
Tho sawdyn to a forest fled
And his ost with hym he led
495   That laft wer onslon.   *alive*
Syr Gwother turnyd is brydyll bryght
And rode befor is lorde full ryghtt: *directly*
    To chambur then he [is gon].

---

463 When both lines of battle had been drawn up.   *468* *That hardy were
and kene* B.   *473* *basnettus in too: backes forto* B.   *478* *sted: stedyd* A.
480 And strikes them down dead.   *488* See how efficiently he strikes his
blows.   *498* *is gon: hym cheys* A.

When his armur of wer don   removed
500 His hors and hit awey wer son,
    That he wyst not whare.
When he come into tho hall
He fond tho emperour and is men all
    To meyt was gwon full yare.   promptly
505 Among tho howndus down he hym seytt,
Tho meydon forthe tho greyhondus feytt   fetched
    And leytt as noghtt ware;
Fedde Hob tho fole, forsothe to sey,
Lyke as sche dyd tho forme dey;   first
510   To chambur sython con fare.

Tho emperour thonkud God of hevun,
That schope tho nyght and tho deyus seyvun,   created
    That he had soo sped.   prospered
Dyscomfyd tho sawdyn thwys   twice
515 And slen is men most of prys,
    Save thos that with hym fled.
'Anturus knyghtus come us too,
Aydur dey won of thoo:
    Y ne wyst wher thei wer bred;
520 Tho ton in reyd, tho todur in blacke,
Had eydur of hom byn to lacke,   absent
    Full evyll we had ben steyd.'

They pypud and trompud in tho hall,
Knyghtus and ladys dancyd all
525   Befor that mynstralsy.   musicians
Syr Gwother in his chambur ley;
He lyst nowdur dance ne pley,
    For he was full wery.
Bryssud for strokus that he had laghtth   bruised, received
530 When he in tho batell faghtth
    Amonghe that carefull cry.
He had no thoght bot of is syn
And how he myght is soule wyn   bring
    To tho blys that God con hym by.

---

507 And behaved as if nothing had happened. *510* Afterwards she went to
her room. *517–18* On each of the two days a stranger knight came to our
help. *522* We would have been in a very dangerous situation. *523* There
was music of pipes and trumpets. *534* God purchased for him; *To blysse
above the skye* B.

535 Thes lordys to bed con hom bown   *got ready*
    And knyghttys and ladys of renown,   *excellent*
      Thus this romans told.
    On tho morne come a messynger
    And seyd to tho emperour, 'Now is wer:
540   Thi care mey be full cold.   *bitter*
    My lord is comun with his powyr,
    Bot yf thou gyff hym thi doghttur dere
    He wyll hampur the in hold;   *besiege, castle*
    And byrkon the bothe blod and bon   *thrash*
545 And leyve on lyfe noght won   *alive*
      Of all thi barons bold.'

    'Y count hym noght,' quod tho emperour;
    'Y schall gare sembull as styff in stour   *bring together*
      And meyt hym yf Y mey.'   *fight*
550 Tho doghtty men that to hym dyd long   *were his*
    Anon wer armyd old and yong,
      Be undur of tho dey.   *noon*
    Thei leype on hors, toke schyld and speyr,
    Then tho gud knyght Gwotheyr
555   To God in hart con prey,
    Schulde sende hym hors and armur tyte;   *quickly*
    Sone he had bothe, mylke whyte,
      And rod aftur in gud arey.   *proper manner*

    Hys to commyngus tho dompe meydon had sene,   *two*
560 And to tho thryd went, with[owt] wene:
      No mon hit knew bot God.
    For he fard nodur with brag ne bost   *pomp, ostentation*
    Bot preystely pryckys aftur tho ost,   *quickly*
    And foloud on hor trowd.   *path*
565 Tho emperour was in tho voward,   *vanguard*
    And Gowther rode befor is lord;
      Of knyghttys was he odde.   *supreme*
    Tho berons wer to tho dethe dongon,   *struck*
    And barons bryght in sladus slongon,   *valleys*
570   With strokus greyt and lowd.

---

539 Fro the sowdan with sterne chere B.   *543 Or dere hir love shall be sold* B.
547 He does not worry me.   *560 withowt: with* A; *And his thyrdde wendyng,*
withowten wene B.   *561 She prayd for him full radde* B.   *569 And hire baners*
to the erth he slong B.   *570 His strokes fil full sadde* B.

Tho sawdyn bare [in] sabull blacke
Thre lyons rampand withowt lacke,   *peerless*
   All of silver [shene];
Won was corvon with golys redde,   *adorned*
575 Anodur with gold in that steyd,   *there*
   Tho thryde with aser, Y wene;   *azure*
And his helmyt full rychely frett   *inlaid*
With charbuckolus stonus suryly sett   *rubies, firmly*
   And dyamondus betwene;
580 And his batell wele areyd,
And his baner brodly dyspleyd—   *unfurled*
   Sone aftur tyde hom tene.   *befell, harm*

Tho gud knyght syr Gowtheyr
He styrd hym styfly in his geyr,
585   Ther levyd non doghttear, Y wene.   *more valiant*
Ylke a dyntte that he smotte
Thro-owt steyll helmus it boott: *cut*
   He felld bothe hors and mon,
And made hom tombull to tho gronde;
590 Tho fote men on tho feld con stonde
   And thenward radly ranne.
Tho sawdyn for tho emperourus doghttur
Gard Cryston and hethon to dye in slaghttur: *be massacred*
   That tyme hym burd wele ban.

595 B[e] whyle syr Gwother freschely faghtte;   *at (all) times*
Mony a doghtté hors is deythe ther kaghtte   *received*
   That he myghtte over-reche.   *overtake*
All that he with his fawchon hytte
Thei fell to tho ground and rosse not yette,
600   Nor lokyd aftur no leyche.
Bot he wold not, for yre ne tene,   *any threat*
No worde speyke, withowt wene,
   For dowtte of Godus wre[ch]e.   *vengeance*
Yf all he hongurt, noght he dyd eytte,   *even though*
605 Bot what he myght fro tho howndus geytte:
   He dyd as tho pwope con hym teche.   *instruct*

---

571 in B: *a* A.   *573 All, shene* B: *That all, schone* A.   *574 corvon: crowned*
B.   *584* In his armour he fought strenuously.   *590–1* The foot-soldiers
who were on the field fled from it as fast as they could.   *594* He had good
reason to curse that day.   *595 Be: Bo* A.   *600* And were past all healing.
603 wreche B: *wreke* A.

Syr Gwother, that stythe in stowre,   *bold*
Rydys ey with tho emperour
  And weyrus hym fro wothe.   *protects, harm*
610 Ther was no Sarsyn so mykull of strenthe
That durst come within is speyre lenthe: *reach of*
  So doghtty wer thei bothe.
With his fachon large and long
Syche dyntus on them he dong,   *struck*
615   Hor lyfus myghtte the[m] lothe.   *be painful to*
All that ever abode that becur
Of hor deythus meghtt be secur,   *sure*
  He styrd his hondus so rathe.

That dey he tent noght bot is fyght;   *paid attention to*
620 Tho emperour faght with all his myght,
  Bot radly was he takon,   *soon*
And with tho sawdyn awey was led;
Tho dompe duke gard hym ley a wed—
  Stroke of his hed anon,
625 Rescowyd is lord, broght hym ageyn,   *back*
Lovyd [h]e God—in hart was full feyn—   *praised, glad*
  That formod bothe blod and bon.   *created*
Ther come a Sarsyn with a speyre,
Thro tho scholdur smott Gotheyr;
630   Then made the dompe meydon mon;   *cry out*

For sorro fell owt of hur toure
Tho doghtur of tho emperour,
  To whyte withowt wene.   *know*
A doghtty sqwyer in hur bare,
635 Of all too deyus hoo styrd no mare   *fully two, moved*
  Then ho deyd had ben.   *than if she*
Tho lord come hom, to meyt was seytt,
And tho doghtty knyght, withowt leytt,   *delay*
  That had in tho batell byn
640 To chambur he went, dyd of is geyre,   *armour*
This gud knyght, syr Gwothere,
  Then myssyd he that meydon schene.

608 All the time rides at the side of. *612 doghtty: doghttely* A. *615 them: the* A. *616* All those who stood their ground in that onslaught. *618* He struck blows so fast. *621 takon: tanne* B. *623–4* made him leave a pledge: the head which he quickly struck off. *626 he: be* A. *633 And brak full negh hir necke (: had be dede)* B.

Emong tho howndus is meyt he wan;   *took*
Tho emperour was a drury man   *sorrowful*
645   For his doghttur gent.   *gracious*
He gard erlys and barons go to Rome
Aftur tho pope, and he come sone
        To hur enterment;   *burial*
And cardynals to tho beryng
650 To assoyle that swett thyng: *creature*
        Syche grace God hur sentt
That scho raxeld hur and rase   *stretched, got up*
And spake wordus that wyse was   *intelligent*
        To syr Gwother varement.   *truly*

655 Ho seyd, 'My lord of heyvon gretys the well
And forgyffeus the thi syn yche a dell   *every part*
        And grantys the tho blys,
And byddus the speyke on hardely,   *without fear*
Eyte and drynke and make mery,
660   Thou schallt be won of his.'   *his elect*
Scho seyd to hur fadur, 'This is he,
That faght for yow deys thre,
        In strong batell, ywys.'
Tho pope had schryvon syr Gother;
665 He lovyd God and Maré ther,   *praised*
        And radly hym con kys.

And seyd, 'Now art thou Goddus chyld;
The thar not dowt tho warlocke wyld: *need, devil*
        Ther waryd mot he bee.'
670 Thro tho pope and tho emperour asent,   *consent*
Ther he weyd that meydyn gent,
        That curtesse was and fre,
And scho a lady gud and ffeyr,
Of all hur fadur londus eyr:
675   Beyttur thurte non bee.   *need*
Tho pope toke his leyfe to weynde,   *go*
With tham he laft his blessyng [hend];
        Ageyn to Rome went hee.

---

665 *Byknew him whan he theder come* (∴ *Gowghter at Rome*) B.   669 May he
be accursed.   677 *hend* B: omitted A.

When this mangeyré was broght to ende   *feasting*
680 Syr Gwother con to Estryke wende
    And gaffe tho old erle all;
Made [h]ym duke of that cuntre
And lett hym wed his modur fre,
    That ladé gent and small.   *slender*
685 And ther he made an abbey
And gaff therto rent for ey:
    'And here lye Y schall.'
And putte therin monkus blake
And rede and syng for Godys sake,
690   And closyd hit with gud wall.   *surrounded*

All yf tho pope had hym schryvyn   *even though*
And God is synnus clene forgevon,
    Yett was his hart full sare;   *grieved*
That ever he schuld so yll wyrke   *act so badly*
695 To bren tho nunus in hor kyrke,
    And made hor plasse so bare.   *destitute*
For hom gard he make that abbey
And a covent therin for ey
    That mekull cowde of lare;
700 For them unto tho wordus end,   *world's*
For hor soulus that he had brend,   *burned*
    And all that Cryston ware.

And then he went hym hom ageyn,
And be that he come in Allmeyn;
705   His fadur tho emperour was deyd.
And he lord and emperowr,
Of all Cryston knyghttus tho flowre,   *most excellent*
    And with tho Sarsyns dredde.
What mon so bydus hym for Godys loffe doo,   *asks*
710 He was ey redy bown thertoo,   *perfectly ready*
    And stod pore folke in styd;
And ryche men in hor ryght,
And halpe holy kyrke in all is myght:
    Thus toke he bettur reyd.   *followed, counsel*

682 hym: kym A. *686* And endowed it with lands in perpetuity. *689* To celebrate mass in God's honour. *699* Who were well instructed in theology. *704* And by the time that. *711* And was the support of poor men. *712 And: And maynteyned* B.

715 Furst he reynod mony a yere,
    An emperour of greyt power,
       And whysylé con he wake;
    And when he dyed tho sothe to sey,
    Was beryd at tho same abbey
720   That hymselfe gart make;
    And he is a varré corsent parfett,   *true saint*
    And with Cryston pepull wele belovyd;
       God hase done for his sake
Myrrakull, for he [w]as hym hold,   *faithful to*
725 Ther he lyse in schryne of gold,
       That suffurd for Goddus sake.

    Whoso sechys hym with hart fre,   *prays to*
    Of hor bale bote mey bee: *suffering, remedy*
       For so God hase hym hyght.   *promised*
730 Thes wordus of hym thar no mon wast,   *need*
    For he is inspyryd with tho Holy Gost,
       That was tho cursod knyght.
    For he garus tho blynd to see   *makes*
    And tho dompe to speyke, pardé,   *indeed*
735   And makus tho crokyd ryght;
    And gyffus to tho mad hor wytte
    And mony odur meracullus yette,
       Thoro tho grace of God allmyght.

    Thus syr Gwother coverys is care,
740 That fyrst was ryche and sython bare,   *destitute*
    And effte was ryche ageyn;   *afterwards*
    And geyton with a felteryd feynd,
    Grace he had to make that eynd
       That God was of hym feyn.
745 This is wreton in parchemeyn,   *manuscript*
    A story bothe gud and fyn
       Owt off a la[y] of Breytyn.
    Jesu Cryst, Goddys son,
    Gyff us myght with hym to won,   *dwell*
750   That lord that is most of meyn.   *might*

717 And ruled over his lands wisely.   *724 was: has* A.   *726 And hatt* (is called) *seynt Gotlake* B.   *739* is brought out of his sorrow.   *747 lay* B: *law* A.

Sir Amadace

Thenne the knyght and the stuard fre — *noble*
Thay casten there houe hit best myghte be, — *considered, how*
   Bothe be ferre and nere.
The stuard sayd, 'Sir, ye awe wele more — *owe*
5 Thenne ye may of your londus rere, — *from, raise*
   In faythe this sevyn yere.
Quoso may best, furste ye mun pray,
'Abyde yo till anothir day'— — *wait*
   And parte your cowrte in sere, — *split up*
10 And putte away full mony of your men, — *get rid of*
And hald butte on quere ye hald ten, — *keep only, where*
   Thagh thay be nevyr so dere.'

Thenne sir Amadace sayd, 'I myghte lung spare,
Or all these godus qwitte ware, — *before, paid for*
15   And have noghte to spend;
Sithun duell here, quere I was borne, — *and then*
Bothe in hething and in scorne— — *contempt*
   And I am so wele kennit. — *known*
And men full fast wold waré me — *curse*
20 That of thayre godus hade bynn so fre, — *extravagant*
   That I have hade in honde. — *my possession*
Or I schuld hold men in awe or threte, — *fear*
That thay myghte noghte hor awne gud gete; — *property, recover*
   Thenne made I a full fowle ende.

25 Butte anothir rede I wulle me toe, — *course, follow*
Wurche anothir way then soe, — *act, this*
   Bettur sayd soro thenne sene. — *than*
Butte, gode stuard, as thou art me lefe, — *dear*
Lette nevyr mon wete my grete mischefe, — *know, misfortune*
30   Butte hele hit us betwene. — *keep it secret*
For sevyn yere wedsette my lond, — *mortgage*
To the godus that I am awand — *until, owing*
   Be quytte holly bidene. — *repaid, altogether*
For oute of the cuntray I wille weynde, — *go*
35 Quil I have gold, silvyr to spende, — *until*
   And be owte of dette full clene.

The beginning missing in both copies; A has *Thoffe Y owe syche too* (twice as much) before 1. *3* From all points of view. *7* You must first of all ask the creditor best able to do so. *8 And take of hym a lengur day* (get him to give you more time) A. *13* I would have to economize for a long time. *21 To gyffe me and to sende* A. *27 sayd: hyd* A. *32 godus: deyttus* A.

Yette wulle I furst, or I fare,   *leave*
Be wele more riall then I was are,   *magnificent, before*
    Therfore ordan thou schall;   *see to it*
40 For I wulle gif full ryche giftus
Bothe to squiers and to knyghtis;
    To pore men dele a dole.   *give, share*
Suche mon myghte wete that I were wo,
That full fayn wold hit were suche toe;
45   That myghte notte bete my bale.   *remedy, suffering*
So curtase a mon was nevyr non borne
That schuld scape withoute a scorne
    Be iche mon had told his tale.'

Thanne sir Amadase, as I yo say,
50 Hase ordanut him opon [a] day
    Of the cuntray in a stownnde.   *(certain) time*
Yette he gafe ful riche giftus,
Bothe to squiers and to knyghtis,
    Stedus, haukes, and hownndes.
55 Sethun afturward, as I yo say,   *then*
Hase ordanut him opon [a] day,
    And furthe thenne conne he founde.   *go*
Be that he toke his leve to wynde,   *go*
He lafte no more in his cofurs to spende,
60   But evyn fourty pownnde.   *only just*

Thenne sir Amadace, as I yo say,
Rode furthe opon his way,
    Als fast as evyr he myghte.
Thro-owte a forest, by one cité,
65 Ther stode a chapell of stone and tre,   *wood*
    And therinne se h[e] a lighte;
Comawnndut his knave forto fare,   *boy*
To wete quat lighte that were thare: *find out*
    'And tithing bring me ryghte.'   *directly*
70 The knave did as his maistur him bade,
Butte suche a stinke in the chapell he hade,
    That dwelle ther he ne myghte.

43–4 find out about my sufferings who would be glad if they were twice as
great.   47–8 Who would not be derisively spoken of at some time or other.
50 Has arranged to leave; *a* omitted I; *Buskyd hym* A.   51 *On his way to
founde* A.   56 *a* omitted I; *He buskyd hym on his jornay* A.   57 *Hastely in
that stonde* A.   66 *he: ho* I.

He stopput his nase with his hude;
Nerre the chapell dur he yode,   *closer, went*
75   Anturs forto lere.
And as he loket in atte the glasse   *through*
To wete quat mervail that ther wasse,
    So see he stonde a bere.   *bier*
Candils ther were brennyng toe,   *burning, two*
80 A woman sittyng, and no moe:
    Lord, carefull wasse hur chere!   *sorrowful, face*
Tithingis there conne he non frayn,
Butte to his lord he wente agayn: *back*
    Told him quat he see thare.

85 And sayd, 'Sir, atte yondur chapell have I bene,
A selcothe sighte ther have I sene;   *strange*
    My herte is hevy as lede.
Ther stondus a bere and canduls toe;
Ther sittus a woman, and no moe:
90   Lord, carefull is hur rede!   *lot*
Seche a stinke as I had thare,
Sertis thenne had I nevyr are,
    Noquere in no stid.   *nowhere, place*
For this palfray that I on ryde,
95 Ther myghte I no lengur abide: *stay*
    I traue I have keghte my dede.'

Thenne Sir Amace commawnndut his squier to fare,
To witte quat woman that there ware;   *find out*
    'And tithingis bring thou me.'   *news (of it)*
100 As he loket in atte the walle,
As the knave sayd, he fund withalle;   *found, too*
    Him thoghte hit grete peté.
Butte in his nace smote suche a smelle   *nose, struck*
That there myghte he no lengur duelle,   *stay*
105   But sone agayn gose he.
He sayd, 'Gud Lord, nowe with your leve,
I pray yo take hit noghte on greve,
    For ye may notte wete for me.'

75 To find out what strange things were going on.   *81 carefull: sympull*
(wretched) A.   *82* He was not able to ask the reason for it there.   *96* I
believe that it will prove fatal to me.   *107–8* I beg you not to be angry with
me, because I cannot tell you (what you want to know).

He sayd, 'Sir, ther stondus a bere and candils toe,
110 A woman sittyng, and no moe:
  Lord, carefull is hur chere!
Sore ho sikes and hondus wringus,   *she sighs*
And evyr ho crius on hevyn kyng,   *constantly asks*
  How lung ho schall be thare.   *must remain*
115 Ho says, 'Dere God'—quat may that be,
The grete soro that ho opon him se,
  Stingcand opon his bere?   *stinking*
Ho says ho will notte leve him allone
Till ho fall dede downe to the stone,   *(paved) floor*
120 For his life was hur full dere.'

Thenne sir Amadace smote his palfray with his spur
And rode unto the chapell dur,
  And hastelé doune he lighte.   *dismounted*
As his menne sayd, so con him thinke: *seem to him*
125 That he nevyr are hade suche a stynke,
  And inne thenne wente that knyghte.
He sayd, 'Dame, God rest with the;'   *be*
Ho sayd, 'Sir, welcum most ye be;'
  A salit him anon ryghte.
130 He sayd, 'Dame, quy sittus thou here,
Kepand this dede cors opon this bere,   *watching over*
  Thus onyli upon a nyghte?'   *alone at*

Ho sayd, 'Sir, nedelongis most I sitte him by; *of necessity*
Hifath, ther will him non mon butte I,   *indeed*
135 For he wasse my wedutte fere.'   *husband*
Thenne sir Amadace sayd, 'Me likes full ille; *upsets greatly*
Ye ar bothe in plyit to spille,
  He lise so lung on bere.
Quat a mon in his lyve wasse he?'   *sort of man*
140 'Sir, a marchand of this cité,
  Hade riche rentus to rere.
And eviryche yere thre hundrythe pownde
Of redy monay and of rownnde,
  And for dette yette lise he here.'   *nevertheless*

---

129 She greeted him at once; *A: And* A. 133 *Syr Y schall yow tell forwhy*
A. 137 in danger of ruin. 138 He has been lying so long unburied; *so:*
or (too) A. 141 He had a considerable income; *to rere: be* (every) *yere* A.

145 Thenne sir Amadace sayd, 'For the rode,   *cross*
 On quat maner spendutte he his gud,
  That thusgate is away?'
'Sir, on gentilmen and officers,
On grete lordus that was his perus: *companions*
150 Wold giffe hom giftus gay.   *splendid*
Riche festus wold he make,
And pore men, for Goddus sake,
  He fed hom evyriche day.
Quil he hade any gud to take,
155 He wernut no mon, for Goddus sake,   *refused*
  That wolnotte onus say nay.

Yette he didde as a fole:
He cladde mo men agaynus a Yole
  Thenne did a nobull knyghte;
160 For his mete he wold not spare,
Burdes in the halle were nevyr bare,   *tables*
  With clothes richeli dighte.   *covered*
Giffe I sayd he did noghte wele,   *if*
He sayd God send hit everyche dele,   *bit*
165 And sette my wurdus atte lighte.
Bi thenne he toke so mycul opon his name
That I dar notte telle yo, lord, for schame,
  The godus now that he aghte.   *owed*

And thenne come dethe, wo hym be,   *accursed*
170 And partutt my lord and me;   *separated*
  Lafte me in all th[is] care.
Quen my neghteburs herd telle that he seke lay,
Thay come to me as thay best may,
  Thair gud aschet thai thare.   *demanded*
175 All that evyr was his and myne,
Hors and naute, shepe and sqwyne,   *cattle*
  Away thay drafe and bare.   *drove, carried*
My dowary to my lyve I sold,
And all the peneys to hom told: *money, paid*
180 Lord, yette aghte he wele mare!

147 For it to vanish in this way. *154* As long as there was any money at
his disposal. *156* Who will never deny (us) anything. *158* At Christmas
he provided more men with clothing. *165* And paid no heed to what I
said. *171 this: the* I. *173 Thei com yerne with greyt afray* A. *178 to my*
lyve: and odur thyng A.

Quen I hade quytte all that I myghte gete,   *paid*
Yette aghte he thritté pownnde bi grete,   *owed, altogether*
    Holly till a stydde;
Till a marchand of this cité,   *to*
185 Was fer oute in anothir cuntre,   *abroad*
    Come home quen he was dede.
And quenne he herd telle of my febull fare,   *wretched condition*
He come to me as breme as bare: *fierce, boar*
    This corse the erthe forbede,
190 And sayd hownndus schuld his bodi todraw,   *pull apart*
Then on the fild his bonus tognaue—   *chew up*
    Thus carefull is my rede.

And this sexten weke I have setyn here,
Kepand this dede cors opon this bere,
195   With candils brennand bryghte.
And so schall I evyrmore do
Till dethe cum and take me to,
    Bi Mary most of myghte!'   *powerful*
Thenne sir Amadace franut hur the marchandis name   *asked*
200 That hade done hur all that schame;
    Ho told him anon ryghte.   *at once*
He sayd, 'God that is bote of all bale,
Dame, cumford the (and so he schale),
    And, dame, have thou gud nyghte.'

205 Thenne sir Amadace on his palfray lepe;
Unnethe he myghte forgoe to wepe,
    For his dedus him sore forthoghte;
Sayd, 'Yondur mon that lise yondur chapell withinne
He myghte full wele be of my kynne,
210   For ryghte so have I wroghte.'   *just, done*
Thenne he told his sometour quat the marchand heght,
And sayd, '[I] will sowpe with him tonyghte,
    Be God that me dere boghte!
Go loke thou dighte oure soper syne,   *afterwards*
215 Gode ryalle metis and fyne,
    And spicis thenne spare thou noghte.'

183 To a single place. 189 Denied burial to this body. 204 followed by
a ffitte in margin 205–40 very different in A: see Commentary. 206 He could
hardly keep from weeping. 207 For he bitterly regretted his (past) actions.
211 told the driver of his pack horse. 212 *I* omitted I.

And sone quen the sometour herd,   *as soon as*
To the marchandus howse he ferd   *went*
 And ordanut for that knyghte.   *made preparations*
220 Thenne sir Amadace come riding thoe,   *then*
But in his hert was him full woe,
 And hasteli downn he lighte.
Sithun intylle a chambur the knyghte yede *afterwards, into*
And kest opon him othir wede,
225 With torches brennyng bryghte.
He cummawnndutte his squier forto goe
To pray the marchand and his wife allsoe   *beg*
 To soupe with him that nyghte.

Thenne the squier weyndut upon his way   *went*
230 And to the marchand conne he say:
 His ernde told he thenne.   *errand*
He squere, 'Be Jesu, Maré sone,
That lordus wille hit schall be done:'
 Of cumford was that man.   *was pleased*
235 Thenne thayre soper was nere dighte;
Burdes were hovyn hee on highte;
 [The] marchand [the] dees began.
Sir Amadace sate and made gud chere
Butte on the dede cors that lay on bere
240 Ful mycull his thoghte was on.   *very much*

Sir Amadace sayd, 'Tonyghte as I come bi the strete,
I see a sighte I thenke on yete:
 That sittus me nowe fulle sore.   *afflicts, grievously*
In a chapell beside a way
245 A dede cors opon a bere lay,
 A womon all mysfare.'   *very unfortunate*
'Ye,' the marchand sayd, 'God gif him a sore grace, *evil fortune*
And all suche waisters as he wasse,
 For he sittus me nowe sare;
250 For he lise there with my thritti pownnde
Of redy monay and of rownnde,
 Of hitte gete I nevyr more.'

224 And changed his clothing. 235 Then their supper was nearly ready.
236 Tables were quickly set up. 237 sat at the head of the table; *the . . . the*
omitted I. 249 *That make men wondur bare* A. 252 I shall never see it
again.

Thenne sir Amadace sayd, 'Take the till a bettur rede;
Thenke that Gode forgave his dede: death
255 Grette merit thou may have.
Thenke how God ordant for the   decreed
Bettur grace then evyr had he:
    Lette the cors go inne his grave.'
Thenne he squere, 'Be Jesu, Maré sun,   swore
260 That body schall nevyr in the erthe come,
My silvyr tille that I have;
Till ho be dede as wele as he,
That hownndus schall, that I may se,
    On filde thayre bonus tognaue.'

265 Quen sir Amadace herd that he hade squorne,
He cald his stuard him beforne;
    Of kyndenesse that knyghte con kithe,   display
And bede, 'Go foche me thritti pownnde   fetch
Of redy monay and of rownnde,
270   Hastely and belyve.'   promptly
The stuard thoghte hit was agaynus skille,
Butte he most nede do his maistur wille:
    Now listun and ye may lithe.   hear
Ther sir Amadace payd him thritti pownnd of monay fyne,
275 And thenne sir Amadace asket to wyne,
    And prayd the marchand be blythe.   cheerful

Then sir Amadace asket, 'Awe he the any mare?'
'Nay, sir,' he sayd, 'wele most ye fare.
    For thus muche he me aghte.'
280 Thenne sir Amadace sayd, 'As furthe as ten pounde will take,
I schall lette do for his sake,   have done
    Querthroghe he have his righte.
I schall for him gere rede and singe,   have mass sung
Bringe his bodi to Cristun beriinge,
285   That schall thou see wythe sighte.
Go pray all the religius of this cité   ecclesiastics
To-morne that thay wold dyne with me,
    And loke thayre mete be dyghte.'   got ready

253 Follow a better course of action. 271 contrary to common sense.
275 asket to: *cummandyt tho* A. 278 may you have good fortune. 279 *I
have that ye me hyght* A. 280 As far as ten pounds will stretch. 282 What
is right and proper for him.

Howe erly quen the day con spring,	*when, dawn*
290 Then holli all the bellus con ring	*altogether*
That in the cité was.	
Religius men evirichon	
Toward this dede cors are thay gone,	
With mony a riche burias.	*citizen*
295 Thritty prustus that day con sing,	
And thenne sir Amadace offurt a ring	
Atte evyriche mas.	
Quen the servise was all done,	
He prayd hom to ete with him atte none,	
300 Holli more and lasse.	*great, small*

Thenne the marchand wente tille one pillere;	
Mony a mon droghe him nere	*went up to*
To wete quat he wold say.	
He sayd, 'Sirs, there hase byn here	
305 A ded cors opon a bere—	
Ye wotte querfore hit lay;	
And hase comun a full riall knyghte,	*generous*
Of all the godes the cors me heghte,	*promised*
Hase made me redi pay.	*prompt payment*
310 Unto his cofurs he hase sente,	
And gevyn ten pownnde to his termente,	*for, burial*
Wythe riche ringus today.	

Hit is on his nome that I say:	*behalf*
He prays yo holly to mete today,	*all of you*
315 All that ther bene here.'	
Thay did as the marchand bade;	
Mete and drinke ynughe thay hade,	
With licius drinke and clere.	*delicious*
And sir Amadace wold noghte sitte downe,	
320 Butte to serve the pore folke he was full bowne,	
For thay lay his hert nere.	
And quen thay hade etun withinne that halle,	
Thenne sir Amadace toke leve atte alle,	*of*
Unsemand with full glad chere.	

---

289 *Howe erly: At morne* A. 291 *That soole forto plese* A. 306 You know
why it was lying there. 321 were dear to his heart. 324 *Unsemand:*
Semyng (dissimulating) A.

325 Quen sir Amadace hade etun,
  To sadull his horse was noghte foryetun:
   Thay broghte hym his palfray.
  Thenne his sometour [m]on before was dyghte,
  Ther as that lord schuld leng all nyghte,   *where, lodge*
330   And hade nothing to pay.
  Quat wundur were hit thaghe him were wo,
  Quen all his godus were spendutte him fro,
   The sothe gif I schuld say?   *if*
  Thenne sir Amadace kidde he was gentilman borne; *showed that*
335 He come the grattust maystur beforne,
   Toke leve, and wente his way.

  Qwen he was gone on this kin wise,   *this way*
  Thenne iche mon sayd thayre devise,   *gave, opinion*
   Quen he wasse passutte the yate.   *had*
340 Sum sayd, 'This gud full lighteli he wan, *easily, obtained*
  That thusgate spendutte hit on this man, *in this way*
   So lightely lete hit scape.'   *go*
  Sum sayd, 'In gud tyme were he borne
  That hade a peny him biforne,'
345   That knew full litulle his state.   *circumstances*
  Lo how thay demun the gentill knyghte! *condemn*
  Quen he hade spendut all that he myghte—
   Butte the trauthe full litull thay wote.

  Quen he come sex mile the cité fro,
350 A crosse partut the way atoe;
   Thenne speke sir Amadace.
  To his stuard he sayd full rathe,   *promptly*
  His sometour and his palfray mon bothe,
   And all ther evyr was.
355 Sayd, 'Gode sirs, take noghte on greve,
  For ye most noue take your leve,
   For yourselvun knauyn the cace.   *situation*
  For I may lede no mon in londe,
  Butte I hade gold, silvyr to spend,   *without having*
360   Nevyr noquere in no place.'

326 they did not forget to. *328* was sent ahead to prepare; *mon: non* I.
335 He went up to the most powerful lord present. *343–4* That man is
fortunate who keeps hold of his money. *350* marked the parting of the
ways. *355* don't be annoyed. *358* For I cannot maintain a retinue; *londe:
londe leyde* A. *359 Bot Y myght tham clothe and feyde* A.

Now the hardust hertut men that there ware
For to wepe thai myght notte spare   *refrain*
  Quen thay herd him say so.
He sayd, 'Gode sirs, have ye no care,
365 For ye mone have maysturs evyrqware,
  As wele wurthi ye ar soe.
Yette God may me sende of his sele   *mercy*
That I may kevyr of this fulle wele,   *recover from*
  And cum owte of this wo.
370 A mery mon yette may ye se me,   *still*
And be full dere welcum to me,   *others*
  Bothe ye and mony moe.'

Quen all his men wos partutte him fro,   *were*
The knyghte lafte still in all the woe,   *remained*
375   Bi himselvun allone.
Throghe the forest his way lay righte;   *straight*
Of his palfray doune he lighte,
  Mournand and made grete mone.   *grieving, lamentation*
Quen he thoghte on his londus brode,   *remembered*
380 His castels hee, his townus made,   *high, (well) built*
  That were away evyrichon,   *gone*
That he had sette and layd to wedde,   *mortgaged*
And was owte of the cuntray for pourté fledde,   *poverty*
  Thenne the knyghte wexe wille of wone.   *grew perplexed*

385 The[n]ne bespeke sir Amadace,   *said*
'A m[o]n that litul gode hase,
  Men sittus ryghte noghte him bye;
For I hade thre hundrythe pownnde of rente,
I spendut two in that entente:
390   Of suche forloke was I.   *foresight*
Evyr quyll I suche housold hold,   *as long as*
For a grete lord was I tellut,   *accounted*
  Muche holdun uppe thereby.   *esteemed*
Nowe may wise men sitte atte home,   *stay (comfortably)*
395 Quen folus may walke full wille of wone,
  And Christ wotte, so may hi.'

365 For you may find (other) service anywhere. *366* As you well deserve
to do. *372* followed by an extra stanza in A: see Commentary. *385–420* very
different in A: see Commentary. *385, 386* [ ] not now visible. *387* Is considered of very small importance. *389 that entente: lyghtte atent* (frivolously)
A. *395* must wander at random.

He sayd, 'Jesu, as thou deet on the rode   *died*
And for me sched thi precius blode,
  And all this word thou wanne;   *world, conquered*
400 Thou lette me nevyr come in that syghte
Ther I have bene knauen for a knyghte,
  Butte if I may avoue hit thanne.
And gif me grace to somun all tho   *recall*
That wilsumly ar wente me fro,   *in bewilderment*
405   And all that me gode ons hase done.   *once*
Or ellus, Lord, I aske the rede,   *as my lot*
Hastely that I were dede:
  Lord, wele were me thanne.   *happy, I*

For all for wonting of my witte,   *lack, common sense*
410 Fowle of the lond am I putte;   *shamefully*
  Of my frindes I have made foes;
For kyndenes of my gud wille
I am in poynte myselfe to spille:'
  Thus flote syr Amadace.   *reproached himself*
415 He sayd, 'Jesu as thou deut on tre,
Summe of thi sokur send thou me,   *help*
  Spedely in this place.   *promptly*
For summe of thi sokur and thou me send,   *if*
And yette I schuld ful gladely spende
420   On all that mestur hase.'   *need*

Now thro the forest as he ferd,
He wende that no mon hade him herd,   *supposed*
  For he seghe non in sighte.
So come a mon ryding him bye,
425 And speke on him fulle hastely,   *to*
  Therof he was afryghte.
Milke quyte was his stede,
And so was all his othir wede;
  Hade conciens of a knyghte.   *emblem*
430 Now thoghe sir Amadace wasse in mournyng broghte,
His curtasé foryete he noghte;
  He saylut him anon ryghte.   *greeted*

400-2 Let me never be seen in any place where I was known as a knight,
unless I am then in a position to admit the fact.   413 I have brought myself
to the verge of ruin.   417 *in this* repeated in I.

Quod the quite knyghte, 'Quat mon is this,
That all this mowrnyng makes thus   *lamentation*
435   With so simpull chere?   *so wretchedly*
Thenne syr Amadace sayd, 'Nay!'
The quite knyghte bede the[n], 'Do way:
  For that quile have I bene here.
Thowe schild noghte mowrne no suche wise,   *way*
440 For God may bothe mon falle and rise,   *abase, exalt*
  For his helpe is evyrmore nere.
For gud his butte a lante lone,
Sumtyme men [have] hit, sumtyme none:
  Thou hast full mony a pere.

445 Now thenke on him that deut on rode,
That for us sched his precius blode,
  For the and monkynd alle.
For a mon that geves him to gode thewis,   *practises virtue(s)*
Authir to gentilmen or to schrewis,   *with, scoundrels*
450   On summe side wille hit falle,
A mon that hase allway byne kynde,
Sum curtas mon yette may he fynde,
  That mekill may stonde in stalle;
Repente the noghte that thou hase done,
455 For he that schope bothe sunne and mone,   *created*
  Full wele may pay for alle.'   *easily*

Quod the quite knyghte, 'Wold thou luffe him aure all thing *above*
That wold the owte of thi mournyng bringe,
  And kevyr the owte of kare?   *bring*
460 For here beside duellus a rialle king,   *near at hand*
And hase a doghtur fayre and yinge;   *young*
  He luffis nothing mare.
And thou art one of the semelist knyghte   *most handsome*
That evyr yette I see with syghte,
465   That any armes bare.
That mun no mon hur wedde ne weld,   *have (as his)*
Butte he that furst is inne the fild,
  And best thenne justus thare.

437 The white knight told him to stop; *then: the* I. *438* Because I was here all the time (you were complaining). *442* wealth is merely a transient gift. *443* have: omitted I. *444* There are very many like you. *448 geves: gevees* I. *450* It will eventually come about that. *453* Who will help him greatly. *467* supreme in tournament.

And thou schalt cum thedur als gay   *gaily dressed*
470 Als any erliche mon may,   *earthly*
   Of thi sute schall be non.
Thou schall have for thi giftus gevand,
Grete lordus to thi honde,
   And loke thou spare righte non[e].   *deny*
475 Thou say the menne that come with the,
That thay were drounet on the see,
   With wild waturs slone.   *raging, killed*
Loke that thou be large of fey[c]e,   *rewards*
Tille thou have wonun gode congre[c]e,   *retinue*
480   And I schall pay ichone.'   *every one*

He sayd, 'That thou be fre of wage,
And I schall pay for thi costage,   *expenses*
   Ten thowsand gif thou ladde.
Ther schall thou wynne full mekille honowre,   *obtain*
485 Fild and frithe, towne and towre,   *forest, castle*
   That lady schall thou wedde.
And sithun I schall come ayayne to the,   *return*
Qwen thou hase tome thi frindus to see,   *leisure*
   In stid quere thou art stadde.   *wherever, lodged*
490 Butte a forwart make I with the or that thou goe,   *agreement*
That evyn to part betwene us toe   *exactly, divide*
   The godus thou hase wonun and spedde.'

Thenne bespeke sir Amadace,   *spoke out*
'And thou have myghte thrughe Goddus grace   *if, power*
495   So to cumford me,
Thou schalt fynde me true and lele   *faithful*
And evyn, lord, forto dele,
   Betwix the and me.'
'Farewele,' he sayd, 'sir Amadace!
500 And thou schall wurche thrughe Goddus grace,   *act*
   And hit schall be with the.'
Sir Amadace sayd, 'Have gode day,
And thou schall fynde me, and I may,
   Als true as any mon may be.'

---

471 You will have no followers. 472–3 your gifts will attract great lords
into your service. 474 none: nono I. 478, 479 feyce, congrece: feyte,
congrete I. 483 Even if you had ten thousand followers. 492 Whatever
goods you have acquired by fortune. 495 me: to me I. 503 if I have
anything to do with it. 504 a ffitte in margin.

505 Now als sir Amadace welke bi the se sonde,   *walked*
    The broken schippus he ther fonde,
        Hit were mervayl to say.   *astonishing, relate*
    He fond wrekun amung the stones
    Knyghtes in menevere for the nones,
510   Stedes quite and gray;
    With all kynne maner of richus
    That any mon myghte devise,   *imagine*
        Castun uppe with waturs lay.
    Kistes and cofurs bothe ther stode,   *chests*
515 Was fulle of gold precius and gode,
        No mon bare noghte away.

    Thenne sir Amadace he him cladde,
    And that was in a gold webbe,   *cloth*
        A bettur myghte none be.
520 And the stede that he on rode,
    Wasse the best that evyr mon hade,
        In justing forto see.
    Ther he wanne fulle mecul honoure,   *possessions*
    Fild and frithe, toune and towre,
525   Castell and riche cité.
    Aure that gud he hovet full ryghte:
    That see the king and his doghtur bryghte,
        The justing furthe schild be.

    The kinge sayd to his doghtur bryghte,
530 'Lo, yond hoves a rialle knyghte!'   *stands*
        A messyngere he ches   *takes*
    (His aune squier) and knyghtes thre,
    And bede, 'Go loke quat yone may be,   *commanded*
        And telle me quo hit is.
535 And his gud hitte schull be tente,   *taken care of*
    Holly to his cummawnndemente,
        Certan withowtun lesse.   *truly, lie*
    Go we to his comyng all togethir,   *to meet him*
    And say that he is welcum hethir,
540   And he be comun o pese.'   *in*

505 walked along the shore. 509 (The bodies of) knights in fur-trimmed
robes, indeed. 516 None of it had been pillaged. 526 He tarried for a
long while over those riches. 528 Who was to be the prize in the tournament (?); *The turnament that for schuld bee* A. 532 squier: *styward* A.
536 Just as he would have it; *cummawnndemente: one hande* A.

As the messingerus welke bi the see sonde,
Thay toke sir Amadace bi the quite honde,
    And tithinges conne him fraynne:
And sayd, 'Oure lord, the king, hase send us hethir
545 To wete youre comyng all togethir,
    And ye wold us sayn.
He says yore gud hitte schall be tente,
Holly atte yaure commawnndemente,
    Sertan is noghte to layne.
550 Quatsever ye wille with the kingus men do,
Yo thar butte commawnnde hom therto,   *need only*
    And have servandis fulle bayne.'   *obedient*

And sir Amadace sayd, 'I wasse a prince of mekil pride, *power*
And here I hade thoghte to ryde,   *intended*
555   Forsothe atte this journay.   *tournament*
I was vetaylet with wyne and flowre,   *had provisions of*
Hors, stedus and armoure,
    Knyghtus of gode aray.   *well equipped*
Stithe stormes me oredrofe,   *overtook*
560 Mi nobull schippe hit all torofe,   *split*
    Tho sothe youreselvun may say.
To spende I have enughe plenté,
Butte all the men that come with me,
    Forsothe thai byne away.'

565 Then sir Amadace, that wasse so stithe on stede,   *bold*
To the castelle yates thay conne him lede,
    And told the king all the cace.   *details*
The king sayd, 'Thou art welcum here;
I rede the be of full gud chere: *urge you*
570   Thonke Jesu of his grace.
Seche a storme as thou was inne,
That thou myghte any socur wynne,
    A full fayre happe hit wase.
I see nevyr man that sete in sete,
575 So muche of my lufve myghte gete,
    As thou thiselvun hase.'

543 And asked him to tell them about himself. *549* Truly, without keeping
anything back. *564* Indeed, they are here no longer. *571–3* The storm
that you were in was so violent that you are very lucky to have gained shelter
(from it). *574 Yette harde Y never no mon speyke* A. *576 I not what hit
wasse* A.

Thenne the king for sir Amadace sake
A rialle cri thenne gerutte he make,   *proclamation, did*
   Thro-oute in that cité.
580 To all that ther wold servyse have,
Knyghte, squiere, yoman and knave—
   Iche mon in thayre degre,
That wold duelle with sir Amadace,   *be*
Hade lost his men in a cace,   *by chance*
585   And drownet hom on the se:
He wold gif hom toe so muche, or ellus more,   *twice*
As any lord wold evyr orqware,   *elsewhere*
   And thay wold with him be.

Quen gentilmen herd that cry,
590 Thay come to him fulle hastely,
   With him forto be.
Be then the justing wase all cryed,
There was no lord ther besyde
   Had halfe as mony men os he.
595 Ther he wanne so myculle honoure,
Fild and frithe, towne and toure,
   Castell and riche cité;
A hundrithe stedis he wan and moe,
And gave the king the ton halve of thoe,
600   Butte the othir til his felo keput he.   *for, companion*

Quen the justing was all done,
To unarme hom thay wente anone,
   Hastely and belyve;   *very quickly*
Then sayd the king anon ryghte,
605 And bede, 'Gromersy, gentull knyghte!'   *hearty thanks*
   Ofte and fele sithe.   *many times*
Then the kingus doghtur that wasse gente,   *gracious*
Unlasutte the knyghte, to mete thay wente;   *unarmed*
   All were thay gladde and blithe.
610 Quen aythir of othir hade a sighte,
Suche a lufve betuene hom lighte,
   That partut nevyr thayre lyve.

579 In all parts of. *582* Every man according to his rank. *587 Then any*
lord that ever thei with wore A. *592* By the time that the tournament had
been fully proclaimed. *600 the: ther* I. *601–12* very different in A: see Commentary. *610–12* When each of them caught sight of the other, a love sprang
up between them that remained perfect throughout their lives.

Quen thay hade etun, I undurstonde,   *am told*
The king toke sir Amadace bi the quite honde,
615   And to him conne he say:
'Sir,' he sayd, 'withoutun lesse,   *lie*
I have a doghtur that myn ayre ho isse,
And ho be to yaure pay,
And ye be a mon that will wedde a wife,
620   I vouche hur safe, be my life,   *bestow*
On yo that fayre may.
Here a gifte schall I yo gife,
Halfe my kyndome quiles I life;   *as long as*
Take all aftur my daye.'   *all of it, death*

625   Thus is sir Amadace kevyrt of his wo,   *recovered*
That God lene grace that we were so l   *grant*
A riall fest gerut he make.
Ther weddut he that lady brighte;
The maungery last a faurtenyghte,   *feast, lasted*
630   With schaftes forto schake.
Othir halfe yere thay lifd in gomun,   *the next, joy*
A fayre knave child hade thay somun,   *together*
Grete myrthes con thay make.
Listuns now, lordinges, of anters grete,   *remarkable happenings*
635   Quyll on a day before the mete,   *meal*
This felau come to the yate.

He come in als gay gere,   *brilliant array*
Ryghte as he an angell were,
Cladde he was in quite.
640   Unto the porter speke he thoe,   *then*
Sayd, 'To thi lord myn ernde thou go,   *errand*
Hasteli and als tite.   *at once*
And if he frayne oghte aftur me,
F[ro] quethun I come, or quat cuntre,   *whence*
645   Say him my sute is quite.   *tell*
And say we have togethir bene;
I hope ful wele he have me sene: *am quite sure*
He wille hitte nevyr denyte.'   *deny*

618 If she is pleasing to you; *In hall scho eytte today* A.   624 followed by
an extra stanza in A: see Commentary.   630 Attended with jousting.   631
Othir halfe yere: Thre yer A.   634 *Now of anodur thyng wylle we speyke* A.
635 *Quyll on: Apon* A.   643 asks any questions about me.   644 *Fro: For* I.

Thenne the porter wente into the halle;
650 Alsone his lord he metes withalle,   *at once*
    He sailles him as he conne: *goes up to*
Sayd, 'Lord, here is comun the fayrist knyghte
That evyr yette I see with syghte,
    Sethen I was market mon.   *created*
655 Milke quite is his stede,
And so is all his other wede,
    That he hase opon.
He says ye have togethir bene;
I hope full well ye have him sene,   *believe*
660   Butte with him is comun no mon.'

'Is he comun, myn owun true fere?
To me is he bothe lefe and dere;   *precious*
    So aghte him wele to be.
Butte, all my men, I yo cummawnnde,
665 To serve him wele to fote and honde,   *in all ways*
    Ryghte as ye wold do me.'   *just*
Then sir Amadace ayaynns him wente,   *up to*
And allso did that ladi gente,
    That was so bryghte of ble.   *face*
670 And did wele that hur aghte to do,
All that hur lord lufd wurschipput ho,   *honoured*
    All suche wemen wele myghte be.

Quo schuld his stede to stabulle have?   *take*
Knyghte, squier, yoman ne knave,
675   Nauthir with him he broghte.   *none of these*
Thenne sir Amadace wold have takynn his stede,
And to the halle himselvun lede,
    Butte so wold he noghte.
He sayd, 'Sertan, the sothe to telle,
680 I will nauthir ete, drinke, ne duelle,
    Be God that me dere boghte.
Butte take and dele hit evun in toe,   *divide, exactly*
Gif me my parte and lette me goe,
    Gif I be wurthi oghte.'

660 *Now mey ye ken hym sone* A.   661 *he sayd* added above line after *comun*.
663 And so indeed should he be.   670 And carefully performed all her
duties.   672 May all such women prosper!   677 And escorted the knight
himself into the hall.   684 If you value me at all.

685 Thenne speke sir Amadace so fre,
     'For Goddus luffe lette suche wurdus be!
          Thay grevun my herte full sore.   *afflict*
     For we myghte noghte this faurtenyghte
     Owre rich londus dele and dighte,
690   Thay liun so wide-quare.
     Butte lette us leng togethir here,   *remain*
     Righte as we brethir were,
          As all thin one hit ware.
     And othir gates noghte part will wee,   *otherwise*
695 Butte atte thi will, sir, all schall bee: *disposal*
          Goddes forbote, sir, thou hit spare!'

     He sayd, 'Broke wele thi londus brode,   *enjoy*
     Thi castels hee, thi townus made,   *(well) built*
          Of hom kepe I righte none;
700 Allso thi wuddus, thi waturs clere,
     Thi frithis, thi for[e]stus, fer and nere,
          Thi ringus with riche stone;
     Allso thi silvyr, thi gold rede,
     For hit may stonde me in no stidde,
705   I squere, bi sayn Johne!   *swear*
     But, be my faythe, withowtun stryve,   *dispute*
     Half thi child and halfe thi wyve,
          And thay schall with me gone.'

     'Alas!' sayd sir Amadace than,
710 'That evyr I this woman wan,   *married*
          Or any wordes gode.   *(had), worldly*
     For his lufe that deet on tre,
     Quatsever ye will, do with me,
          For him that deet on rode.
715 Ye, take all th[at] evyr I have,
     Wythe thi that ye hur life save:'   *as long as*
          Thenne the knyghte wele undurstode,
     And squere, 'Be God, that me dere boghte,
     Othir of thi thinge then kepe I noghte,
720   Off all thi wordes gode!'

---

686 stop talking in that way!   *688–90* Because it would take more than a
fortnight to settle the division of our noble lands: they are so extensive.   *696* God forbid, sir, that you should not make use of them.   *699* I don't
want any of them.   *701* [ ] not now visible.   *704* cannot do me any good.
715 that: ther I.

Butte thenke on thi covenand that thou made,   *remember, agreement*
In the wode, quen thou mestur hade,   *need*
    How fayre thou hettus me thare!'
Sir Amadace sayd, 'I wotte, hit was soe,
725 But my lady forto sloe,
    Me thinke grete synne hit ware.'
Then the lady undurstode anon
The wurd that was betwene hom,
    And grevyt hur nevyr the more.
730 Then sayd: 'For his luffe that deut on tre,
Loke yore covandus holdun be: *are kept*
    Goddes forbotte ye me spare!'

Thenne bespeke that ladi brighte,   *fair*
Sayd, 'Ye schalle him hold that ye have highte, *must, promised*
735   Be God and Sayn Drightine!   *Holy Lord*
For his lufe that deet on tre,
Loke yaure covandus holdun be,
    Yore forward was full fyne.   *absolute*
Sithun Crist will that hit be so,   *since*
740 Take and parte me evun in toe;   *divide*
    Thou wan me and I am thine.
Goddus forbotte that ye hade wyvut,
That I schuld yo a lure makette,
    Yore wurschip in londe to tyne!'

745 Still ho stode, withoutun lette,   *indeed*
Nawthir changet chere ne grette   *grew pale, wept*
    That lady myld and dere;   *gentle*
Bede, 'Foche me my yung sun beforne,   *bring to me*
For he was of my bodi borne,
750   And lay my herte fulle nere.'
'Now,' quod the quite knyghte thare,
'Quethur of hom luffus thou mare?'   *which*
    He sayd, 'My wife so dere!'
'Sithun thou luffus hur the more,
755 Thou schalt parte hur evyn before,   *first*
    Hur quite sidus in sere.'   *apart*

723 What gracious promises you made me there. *727–8* realized then
what they were talking about. *729* And was none the more distressed for it.
730 ladi added above the line after *Then*. *742–4* God forbid that your wife
should be a source of loss to you, (making you) forfeit your honour among
men. *748 me* added above line after *sun*. *750* And was very dear to my
heart.

Thenne quen sir Amadace see
That no bettur hitte myghte bee,
   He ferd as he were wode.   *behaved, mad*
760 Thenne all the mene in that halle
Doune on squonyng ther con thay falle,
   Before thayre lord thay stode.
The burd was broghte that schuld hur on dele;
Ho kissutte hur lord sithis fele,   *many times*
765   And sithun therto ho yode.
Ho layd hur downe mekely enughe,
A clothe then aure hur enyn thay droghe;   *over, eyes*
   That lady was myld of mode.

Thenne the quite knyghte: 'I will do the no unskille:
770 Thou schalt dele hit atte thi wille,
   The godus that here now is.'
Thenne speke sir Amadace so fre,   *noble*
Sayd, 'Atte your wille, lord, all schalle be—
   And so I hope hit is.'   *believe*
775 Then sir Amadace a squrd uppe hente;   *lifted up*
To strike the ladi was his entente,   *intention*
   And thenne the quite knyghte be[de], 'Sese!'
He toke uppe the ladi and the litulle knave,
And to sir Amadace ther he hom gave,
780   And sayd, 'Now is tyme of pees!'

He sayd, 'I con notte wite the gif thou were woe,
Suche a ladi forto slo,
   Thi wurschip thus wold save.
Yette I was largely as gladde   *fully*
785 Quen thou gafe all that evyr thou hade,   *possessed*
   My bones forto grave.   *bury*
In a chapelle quere I lay to hownndus mete,   *as food for*
Thou payut furst thritty pownnd be grete,   *in full*
   Sethun all that thou myghtus have.
790 Ther I besoghte God schuld kevyr the of thi care,   *prayed*
That for me hade made the so bare,   *destitute*
   Mi wurschip in lond to save.'

758 That there was no help for it. *763* They brought the table on which
she must be cut in two. *765* And then she went over to it. *769* I will not
act unreasonably towards you. *770* divide as pleases you. *777 bede: be* I;
seyd A. *783* Who was so concerned to save your honour. *789* And then
everything that you possessed.

'Farewele now,' he sayd, 'myne awne true fere!   *companion*
For my lenging is no lengur her,   *place*
795   With tunge s[o] I the telle.   *as*
Butte loke thou lufe this lady as thi lyve,   *see to it*
That thus mekely, withouten stryve,   *dispute*
   Thi forwardus wold fulfille.'   *keep*
Thenne he wente oute of that toune;
800 He glode away as dew in towne,
   And thay abode ther stille.
Thay knelutte downe opon thayre kne
And thonket God and Mary fre,
   And so thay hade gud skille.   *reason*

805 Thenne sir Amadace and his wive,
With joy and blis thay ladde thayre live,
   Unto thayre ending daye.   *dying*
Ther is ladis now in lond fulle foe   *few*
That wold have servut hor lord soe,
810   Butte sum wold have sayd nay.   *refused*
Botte quoso serves God truly
And his modur Mary fre,
   This dar I savely say: *swear*
Gif hom sumtyme like fulle ille,
815 Yette God wille graunte hom alle hor wille,
   Tille hevyn the redy waye.   *direct*

Then sir Amadace send his messingerus,
All the londus ferre and nere,
   Unto his awne cuntre.
820 Till alle that evyr his lond withheld,   *had possession*
Frithe or forest, towne or filde,
   With tresur owte boghte he.
His stuard and othir that with him were,
He send aftur hom, as ye may here,   *for*
825   And gafe hom gold and fee.
And thay ther with him forto leng,   *remain*
Evyrmore tille thayre lyvus ende,
   With myrthe and solempnité.   *joy, pomp*

---

795 so: sum I.   *799 Ther west no mon wher he become* A.   *800 in towne* for
*of downe (hill)?; *in son* (sun) A.   *809* acted in this way towards their husbands.
814 Even though they may sometimes be distressed.

     Thenne sone aftur the kinge deet, atte Goddus wille,   *as was*
830 And thay abode thare stille;
     As ye schall undurstond.   *must realize*
     Thenne was he lord of toure and towne,
     And all thay comun to his somoune;
     All the grete lordus of the londe.
835 Thenne sir Amadace, as I yo say,
     Was crownette kinge opon a day,
     Wyth gold so clure schinand.   *brightly*
     Jesu Criste in Trinité,
     Blesse and glade this cumpany,
840 And ore us halde his hande.   *over*

Commentary

THE SEGE OF MELAYNE

55–60 This is the point at which *Melayne* comes closest to the romances of piety and suffering: in *Isumbras* 277 ff., the hero and his wife are likewise threatened by a sultan whose demands the former is in no position to resist, and the family is dispersed as a result. In *Melayne* however—where the main emphasis is on a quite different set of characters—we hear no more of the wife and children.

165 For the sake of rhyme Herrtage emended *undirtake* to *undirnome*, but this is unsatisfactory: the word could hardly be a present form of ME. *undernime(n)*, and the latter verb does not, in any case, seem to have been used, like *undertake(n)* in the sense of 'pledge' or 'lay', that is necessary here.

169 Ganelon is the arch-traitor of the *chansons de geste*, and in the *Roland* he is an impressive and complex figure, possessing great soldierly virtues, but driven to betray the French through his hatred for Roland. This complexity is not usually carried over to the English Charlemagne romances in which he appears, except for the Ashmole *Sir Ferumbras*. Here (as in *Melayne*) he is delighted by the news of Roland's difficulties, and advises Charles against taking the field himself (4019–46), but on the other hand he later refuses to leave Charlemagne in the lurch when he is hard pressed (4753–8), agrees without hesitation to perform a very dangerous mission (5287–90), and subsequently defends himself so manfully as to win Oliver's praise (5395–8). The vital difference, however, is that these diverse elements in his character are never brought into plausible and meaningful focus, as in the *Roland*.

193–204 On this occasion Charles (at first) resists Ganelon's advice: contrast 659–67.

265–70 Catastrophes on this scale are hardly to be found in any romances but the heroic. In the first part of the Middle English *Sowdone of Babylone* (which in its second half tells very much the same story as *Ferumbras*), we have a disastrous sortie of a Christian army from Rome under the leadership of the Pope (who, as a militant cleric, serves as a kind of anti-type to Turpin, in that he is totally unsuccessful in battle and his life is ignominiously spared by Ferumbras (547–74)).

415–17 Triplets instead of couplets occur quite often in the Thornton text of *Isumbras*: see, for example, the notes to lines 717 and 718–26 in that romance.

423 If this line is kept without alteration then 424 must mean 'do not respect any other Christian images'. But it would be more natural to insert *ne* before *sett* and take the line as meaning 'do not respect the gods of any other religion'.

491–3   The sultan Garcy is also an important figure in the romance of *Roland and Otuel* which follows *Melayne* almost immediately in MS. Additional 31042. The romance begins with Garcy's despatch to Charlemagne of his champion Otuel (55–60), and ends with his capture by this same champion, now converted to Christianity (1565–75). See also the note to 1600.

548–65   The extreme oddness of this passage is discussed in the Introduction (p. xiii). Compare the more violent scene in the tail-rhyme *King of Tars* in which the sultan avenges himself on his gods for their failure to answer his prayers:

He hent a staf with grete hete	*anger*
And stirt anon his godes to bete,	
And drough hem alle adoun;	*pulled*
And leyd on til he gan to swete	
And yaf hem strokes gode and gret,	
Bothe Jovine and Plotoun;	
And alder-best he bete afin	*most completely*
Jubiter and Apolin,	
And brac hem arm and croun.	
And Tervagaunt that was her brother,	
He no lete never a lime with other,	*limb*
No of his god Mahoun. (A 646–57)	

Turpin does not actually do violence to the statue of Mary, but he does throw down the symbols of his ecclesiastical office in 542–3. He reverts to a more orthodox treatment of the Virgin in 1041–2 (perhaps because Charles is here the real object of his exhortations and suspicions).

569 ff.   As Trounce pointed out, the conflict of king and archbishop is also a central theme in the tail-rhyme *Athelston*. He regarded the theme as essentially English, inspired by actual struggles between church and state, and not derived—like so much else in *Athelston* no less than *Melayne*—from the *chansons de geste*. The more detailed similarities between the two romances he explained as the product of direct borrowing from *Melayne* into *Athelston* (*Athelston*, pp. 6–8, 12–13, 31–8). This is the beginning of the quarrel of the two men in that romance:

Thanne the kyng wax wroth as wynde,	*angry*
A wodere man myghte no man fynde	*more frenzied*
Than he began to bee;	
He swoor othis be sunne and mone:	
'They schole be drawen and hongyd or none—	
With eyen thou schalt see.	

> Lay doun thy cros and thy staff,
> Thy mytyr and thy ryng that I the gaff;
>   Out off my land thou flee!
> Hyye the faste out off my syght;   *hasten*
> Wher I the mete, thy deth is dyght;   *doom, sealed*
>   Non othir then schal it bee.'
>
> Thenne bespak that erchebysschop,   *replied*
> Oure gostly fadyr undyr God,   *spiritual*
>   Smertly to the kyng:
> 'Weel I wot that thou me gaff
> Bothe the cros and the staff,
>   The mytyr and eke the ryng;
> My bysschopryche thou reves me,   *take away from*
> And Crystyndom forbede I the:
>   Preest schal ther non syngge;   *celebrate mass*
> Neyther maydynchyld ne knave
> Crystyndom schal ther non have;
>   To care I schal the brynge.   (453–76)

827–74 In its description of elaborate ceremony and splendid gifts this passage is more courtly in tone than any of the scenes at the court of Charlemagne. But it also serves to point the moral inferiority of the heathen: the *sexty maydyns* that seem at first to be only one lavish gift among others cause Garcy's men to sin in a way that Charles's do not: what references there are in *Melayne* to the womenfolk of the Christians are extremely respectable. All this contrasts markedly with the beginning of the English *Song of Roland*, where the French troops are debauched, before battle, by a troop of maidens brought back by Ganelon from his meeting with the Saracens (1–4, 28–9, 72–6).

881–910 In this passage the character of Turpin is less extreme and idiosyncratic than is usual in *Melayne*; as in some comparable passages in the *Roland*, his function here is essentially that of a priest, though still a very militant one (*Roland* 1124–38, 1515–23).

1031–42 Thanks to Turpin's intervention, Darnadowse is unable to get very far in his attempt to convert Charles. But in the tail-rhyme *Roland and Vernagu* a comparable—but much longer—period of rest in the middle of a decisive single combat turns into quite an elaborate scene of theological exposition. But here the advantage is all on the side of the Christian (Roland); his opponent (Vernagu) is quite unable to refute any of the doctrines that he puts forward, and can only say that the outcome of their fighting—which is then resumed—will alone prove which of their religions is superior (671–790).

1064–6 This act of courtesy is not paralleled by anything in Charles's behaviour; indeed, the Christian monarch cuts a rather poor figure throughout the combat, even though he is finally victorious. And in the climactic fight with Baligant in the *Roland* he had needed no prompting from Turpin to reject any conciliatory offer from the heathen (3595–9).

1078   *Blende* could here be emended either to *blande* or to *splitte*; the first possibility, however, would lead to the production of stanzas of nine and fifteen lines, respectively.

1304   The emendation of *browe* to *browne* is rather tempting in view of the fact that *schelde* and *browne/brawne* occur in conjunction in descriptions of wild boars in Middle English, standing for the hard skin and tough flesh (of the shoulders) of the beast: see *Sir Gawain and the Green Knight* 1611. The phrase *als breme als bare* is of course sufficiently commonplace in descriptions of warriors in the romances (*Melayne* 946, for example); what is suggested here would be much rarer, but apt enough for this particular piece of characterization.

1344–5   Here Turpin seems to be telescoping allusions to two quite distinct passages of fighting: see 1106 and 1302.

1363   MS. Additional 13042 has been rebound in such a way that the original collation can no longer be determined, and it is therefore impossible to decide whether only one leaf has been lost here and after 1600. But whatever the length of the missing portion here, it must—as Herrtage remarks (p. 44)—have told how Charles, hard pressed by the Saracen reinforcements mentioned in 1358–63, tries to find a baron who will ride through the enemy lines for help.

1403   *Banarett* has been emended to *banerer* because the first would imply that sir Barnarde either was not only a knight already, but one of especial rank and dignity, or had already been knighted 'for valiant deeds done in the king's presence on the field of battle' (O.E.D.). In either case, the word would be at odds with its immediate context.

1559   This nephew of the sultan is presumably to be identified with the Tretigon of 1358.

1600   We can of course do no more than speculate as to how *Melayne* finished, but the total victory of the French can hardly have been deferred for much longer. *Roland and Otuel* is of no help in settling the matter, since in spite of its setting in Lombardy (in its second half) and the part which Garcy plays in it, it contains no detailed reference back to *Melayne*. It seems likely, indeed, that the two romances had not originally been linked in any really meaningful way (in contrast to *Roland and Vernagu* and *Otuel and Roland*), but were simply brought (almost) together in the present manuscript collection because of the minor points of contact noted above. This view is supported by the fact that the compiler of this collection is shown by his arrangement of its first four items—religious pieces, all of quite diverse provenance—to have been concerned to find as meaningful a grouping as possible for his material: see F. A. Foster, *The Northern Passion* (EETS 147), p. 13.

EMARÉ

1–18 Most popular romances begin with a pious invocation, but very few carry it to such lengths as the present example.

23 As Rickert pointed out, it is unlikely that the author meant the name Emaré to have the force of OF. *esmarie* ('troubled', 'afflicted'), since if it had, there would have been no very sharp contrast with the name of Egaré (OF. *esgarée*, 'outcast') which she adopts in 360, after being cast out by her father. She suggests that OF. *esmerée* ('refined', 'excellent') may have been the word that the author had in mind (p. xxix).

40–1 One of the most frequently-recurring rhymes in the poem; it is also found, with only minor variations, at 64–5, 379–80 and 724–5.

52–4 In some versions of the story, notably Beaumanoir's *La Manekine*, it is this wife who, by her death-bed wish, really pushes the king towards an incestuous marriage. She insists that he must only marry if the barons refuse to recognize their child (a daughter) as heir to the throne; if this happens, and he does take another wife, she must be one who exactly resembles his first (128–44). After long searching it is found that the only woman who fulfils this condition is the daughter herself.

78 The exact kind of 'sport' implied by *playnge* here is ambiguous; it could be sexual.

83–168 The splendid cloth that is described in this passage is one of most interesting and controversial features of the romance. To Rickert, the description seemed so out of scale with the modest proportions of *Emaré* as a whole, that she suggested that it had been taken over more-or-less verbatim from a narrative poem on a much larger scale (p. 38). More recently, an attempt has been made by H. Schelp in his *Exemplarische Romanzen* to give a predominantly moral sense to the passage (pp. 105–13); his views are summarized by Dieter Mehl in his *Middle English Romances*:

> 'the robe is an inseparable attribute, like her outward beauty ... [and] is in many ways symbolic of her inner perfections. The portraits of famous lovers can be seen as an allegorical representation of faith ... the precious stones, in particular, illustrate the virtues of the lady.' (p. 139)

But we cannot overlook the fact that this cloth (which is in any case adorned with representations of wholly secular lovers) comes into the story just after the emperor has lost his wife and turned his thoughts to *playnge*; what is more, on two of the later occasions on which the heroine wears it as her robe, the man who sees her in it at once expresses his determination to marry her (247-9, 451-3). This makes it likely that one of its functions, at least, was to stand for the sexual attraction exerted by the lady; as French and Hale put it:

> 'Though here rationalized, the cloth is a love-charm—originally given to the fairy Emaré by supernatural well-wishers.' (*Middle English Metrical Romances*, p. 428)

See also the note which follows, and that to 1030.

121-56 Rickert compared some of the details in this description with their counterparts in the account of the robe worn by the heroine of *Mai und Beaflor*, a story of the same general type as *Emaré* (pp. xxx-xxxi). Rather more striking parallels can be found in the description of the cloth in which the heroine of *Galeran de Bretagne* is wrapped, when she is abandoned soon after birth (509-51). For on this, too, pairs of lovers are represented: Paris and Helen and (as in *Emaré*) Floris and Blancheflor. This second couple is an apt choice in both stories, though for different reasons: in *Galeran*, because the lovers there are very young, and their courtship is idyllic; in *Emaré*, because their love works itself out against an oriental setting. The other two pairs of lovers in our romance are traditionally very different both from each other and from Floris and Blancheflor. Amadas—who is quite distinct from the hero of the tail-rhyme romance bearing that name—is the social inferior of Ydoine, and has to undergo a long and painful courtship before he can win her; Tristan and Isolde are the supreme medieval exponents of tragic adulterous love. But in the description of *Emaré* none of the most strikingly individual features of these lovers is allowed to come through; they are essentially decorative motifs, multiplied so that the power of love among men may be the more heavily stressed. The lack of any precise realization is, of course, made still more noticeable by the repetition of the same phrases at 89-96 and 137-44, and 124-6 and 148-50.

247-9 The stages of the father's infatuation are rather oddly set out. The first hint of it is in 188-9, which in any other story would be taken as a sign of fatherly affection, quite without any sinister overtones. In 223-8, on the other hand, his intentions are made perfectly clear, but he does not actually confide his love to her until 247-9, after she has put on the dazzling robe for the first time.

268 The adjective here, which contrasts markedly with everything else we are told about the vessel, bears witness to the author's (or scribe's) love of stressing the excellence of all the properties of the romance.

280-300 The sudden repentance of the emperor is a narrative effect typical of the tail-rhyme style, where reversals of emotional and mental states were always apt to be both immediate and absolute. In *La Manekine* the same change of heart, while not described at much greater length than in *Emaré*, is still made to appear much more gradual (6697–714).

303 *Comely unthur kelle* is a phrase conventionally applied to women in the romances; the noun is usually glossed as 'headdress', but it could also stand for 'cloak', 'garment' or 'shroud', and it is this second group that is suggested by the examples in *Emaré*. The importance that is placed, throughout the story, on the heroine's robe suggests that this phrase, like the very similar *worthy unthur wede* and *goodly unthur gore* that are applied to her in 612 and 938, is given more meaning than would normally be the case.

415 In itself the line might be allowed to stand unaltered, with *ray* interpreted as 'striped cloth', but the occurrence of the phrase *ryche ray(e)* in 430 and 451 makes the emendation seem reasonable.

441 This line seems to be a clumsy and conventional substitute for an original *She semed non erthely may*: compare *She semed non erthely wommon* (245) and *She semed non erdly thyng* (396), both of which occur in a very similar narrative context.

445 *Unhende*, which normally means no more than 'discourteous' or 'rough' when applied to persons, seems a rather weak word to characterize the mother-in-law here and at 534 and 794: compare the vigorous reactions to the chief villains of the tail-rhyme romances of *Athelston* (*He was a devyl of helle* (156)) and *Amis and Amiloun* (*So wicked and schrewed was his wüf* (1561)). Although we cannot wholly rule out the possibility of a stronger meaning for the adjective (since the related noun is recorded in the sense of 'trouble' or 'mischief'), it seems likely that we have here a further example of the deliberately low-keyed style of our poem.

481–95 Rickert suggests that these wars against the heathen may be a distorted reflection of 'the last great Saracenic attempt upon Europe' in 1212, when the king of Castile (here the king of France) had sent to other Christian countries, and particularly France (here Galicia) for help against the invaders (p. 41). The opening of the passage here suggests that the author is going to develop subject-matter of a familiarly 'heroic' cast, but this does not in fact happen. The king's rôle in this story is purely that of husband to Emaré, and it is significant that when we see him next it is not in battle as a soldier, but as the recipient of the garbled letter (545–73).

504 This birthmark could have been functional in a romance-story like that of *Havelok*, where the young hero is never brought up by his parents at all, but nothing is made of it, because Segramowre remains with his mother throughout. See also the note to *Isumbras* 140.

540 Compare the description of Gowther's diabolical father as *a felturd fende* (71).

631–3 The lady's 'explanation' of her rejection by the king is unexpected in the context of this romance, but is central to the story of Griselda, familiar from Chaucer's *Clerk's Tale* (see especially *Canterbury Tales*, E 463–83).

667–8 This is one of the few moments at which the heroine departs from her normally passive acceptance of misfortune: compare the point at which Griselda herself turns (however mildly) on her persecutor of a husband (*Canterbury Tales*, E 1037–43).

685–7 In most versions of the common story, in which the lady is cast adrift at sea, she in the end finds shelter at the house of a Roman senator: see, for example, Chaucer's *Man of Law's Tale* (*Canterbury Tales*, B 967–80). But the substitution of a merchant for the senator here makes very little difference, since he is a quite colourless character, with no trace of the gross vitality of Clement in *Octavian*.

733–41 Segramowre, likewise, seems rather devitalized when set against his counterpart in *Octavian* (Florent); here, as at other points in *Emaré*, vividness is sacrificed to the celebration of well-bred courtesy.

799–804 The softening of the sentence originally passed upon the mother is typical of the mood of this romance; in the other versions of the story she is more often than not killed once her perfidy has been made known (compare *Octavian* 1768–82).

820–2 The king's wish to do penance is rather unexpected, as he had never, even in his thoughts, been guilty of his wife's 'death', but it enhances the parallelism between his situation and that of his father-in-law. In the *Man of Law's Tale*, it is remorse at having slain his mother that brings him to Rome as a penitent (*Canterbury Tales*, B 988–94).

1030 Of all the other Breton lays in Middle English which have survived, the closest to *Emaré* in its general tone and in some of its detail is the *Lay le Freine*, a close (but defective) translation of the *lai* of Marie de France that was subsequently expanded to produce the romance of *Galeran de Bretagne* (see the note to 121–56). The heroine, Freine, is separated from her twin sister soon after birth, and abandoned, so that it will not be supposed that her mother was an adulteress (see the note to *Octavian* 112–14). Once grown up, she is taken away by a young nobleman as his mistress, but after a time his vassals persuade him to reject her (like Griselda) and make a respectable marriage. But the bride-to-be proves to be none other than the heroine's twin sister; Freine's identity is discovered after she displays the elaborate cloth in which she was wrapped as a baby and which—like *Emaré*—she has kept with her through all her wanderings.

OCTAVIAN

64–84 The barrenness of the wife is also stressed at the same point in *Gowther* (49–57); in *Octavian* her proposed remedy is more considered and orthodox, but the barrenness itself is still made to lead on to tragedy through the contrivings of the mother-in-law.

96 Romance hyperbole: contrast 1246, where T gives a less extravagant variant of a similar detail in C.

112–14 In the other romance versions, the empress gives as a reason for her conviction the popular belief that twins could only be conceived by a woman who had had intercourse with two men (FO 118–24; SO 127–32). This same belief is found in *Lay le Freine* (69–72) and *Chevelere Assigne* (28–31).

132 is followed in T by three extra lines which reaffirm the profit-motive and make the change of speaker quite unambiguous:

> Than said that lady to that knave:
> 'Hye the faste thi golde to hafe—   *hasten*
> Thou schall be rewarde this nyghte.'

160–8 A very similar dream is narrated at the same point in FO (250–6) and SO (195–200), although in both of these it is an eagle and not a dragon that carries off the child. It foreshadows the later scene in which the lady's twins are actually taken from her; the animals directly responsible here are an ape and a lioness, but the second of these is itself seized by a creature that is in FO described, first as a dragon (587) and then—as in the English versions—as a griffin (FO 601; NO 350; SO 447).

169–80 As given in C, a perplexing stanza. 169 and 179 appear to contradict each other, and 171, although just possible, is certainly unexpected. T offers more plausible variants of 169 and 171: *Therewith the lady bygan to wake* (stirred in her sleep, but didn't necessarily rouse completely) and *And scho syghede full sare*. It also gives a quite different version of 175–80:

> The lady blyschede up in the bedde,   *looked*
> Scho saw the clothes all byblede;
>   Full mekyll was hir care.
> Scho bygan to skryke and crye   *shriek*
> And sythen in swonynge forto ly,   *after that*
>   Hirselfe scho wolde forfare.

But this, while following on more naturally from 172–4, is less convincing as an introduction to 181 than is the variant of C.

211–28 The motif of the king's rash judgment is not found in the other romance versions; it may have been suggested by a moment further on in FO in which king Dagonbert gives Octavian some (unsolicited) advice concerning the punishment of his treacherous mother (1671–6).

241–3 are omitted in T, which has three extra lines after 252:

> The emperoure graunted hir righte so;
> Ilke a man than was full woo,
>> That were that day in the felde.

331 In stories of this kind the kidnapping animals are usually four-footed predators (see *Isumbras* 179, 184, 370), but the ape is a very natural substitute. One is shown holding a swaddled child in the right-hand supporter of the misericord in Manchester cathedral showing apes robbing a sleeping pedlar: see G. L. Remnant, *A Catalogue of Misericords in Great Britain*, Oxford, 1969, p. 82 and plate 9b.

336 is directly followed in both FO and SO by the further adventures of the child carried off by the ape; the lioness does not appear until later.

341–2 The lioness has the same intention in FO 560–1, and carries it out after the fight with the griffin (FO 616–18). In the Thornton variant of 346–8, the explanation of her behaviour is given:

> Bot for it was a kynge-sone, iwysse,   *truly*
> The lyones moghte do it no mys,   *harm*
>> Bot forthe therwith scho yede.

The same idea appears in SO 481–4.

382 A very sudden transition that is softened in the variant of T: *The lady that was leved allone.*

397–402 These lines bring the lady unexpectedly close to the penitent heroes of *Isumbras* and *Gowther*.

502–4 Such immediate recognition of the lady when she comes to land is not to be paralleled in *Emaré* (at 360 and 704), but is a feature of both *Sir Eglamour* (949–51) and *Torrent of Portyngale* (2059–64).

613–18 sound more logical and (less repetitive) in T:

> Clement saide to his wyfe tho:
> 'Sen the childe es getyn so,   *since*
>> In the hethen thede,
> And now es it to this land broghte,
> I pray the dame that thou greve the noghte,
>> And riche sall be thi mede.'

641–2 In FO, Clement decides on this first occasion that his own son is to become a money changer, and Florent, a butcher (976–99). In T, 641 reads: *He sett his ownn son to the lore.*

649–60 In T the tail-lines of this stanza are quite different, and on the whole more conventional: *A semely syghte sawe he* (651); *That semly was to see* (654); *For that fowle so fre* (657); *Florent was blythe in ble* (660).

662–804 are missing in T.

675 begyfte does not seem to occur elsewhere in Middle English; the obvious emendation would be to *behyght(e)*, but this too raises difficulties, since the required sense of 'entrusted to' or 'granted' is not certainly attested for this verb.

754–6 At this point the wheel comes full circle; once again it is stressed that Florent cannot really be the son of the man who appears as his father—but this time, of course, the implications are wholly flattering to the boy.

769 Octavian is here reintroduced into the story, relatively unobtrusively, as one of the kings rallying to the defence of Christendom. FO, however, reminds the audience very explicitly of his part in earlier events, both at the moment of his reappearance (1579–90), and soon afterwards (when he tells the whole story of his wife's banishment to Dagonbert, to whose aid he has come: 1637–70).

787–92 In FO this request forms part of a much longer scene (1849–926); there, it is brought by the dwarf messenger who also brings a challenge to armed combat from the giant who is in love with this maiden. Borogh Larayn is modern Bourg-la-reine in the arrondissement of Sceaux.

804 To judge from what is left of the Thornton version of this part of the story, it would seem that two stanzas have been dropped from C after this line. All that are left of them in T are the last seven lines:

> 'Merveylle therof thynkes mee,
> If thou and alle thi men will blyn,   *leave off*
> I will undirtake to wynn
>   Paresche, that stronge ceté,
> Bot Mersabele than weedde I will.'
> Sayd the sowdane: 'I halde thertill   *will abide by*
>   With thi that it so bee.'   *provided that*

(The first speaker is clearly the giant.) The omission of the stanzas in C may have been deliberate, since there 805–7 give, for the first time, information about the giant that must have been contained in the seventeen lines of these stanzas, now lost from T; in T, 805–7 read:

> Arageous, appon that same daye
> To the Mount Martyn, ther the lady laye,
>   The waye he tuke full ryghte.

It may also be noted that the Thornton variant of 811–13 refers back to a
meeting between the giant and the sultan that is not mentioned in C:

> He sayse, 'Leman, kysse me belyve;   *quickly*
> Thy lorde me hase the graunte to wyefe,
> And Paresche I hafe hym hyghte.'   *promised*

808–10 contrast sharply with what FO tells us about the relationship of the
lady and the giant. In this version she seems quite favourably disposed
towards him at first (1817–22) and does not give way to her feelings for the
hero without a long struggle (2801–90).

852 is followed by two extra stanzas in T:

> When he had slayne the knyghtes fyve,
> Agayne to the walles gan he dryve,
>   And over the bretage gan lye;   *parapet*
> 'Kynge Dagaberde of Fraunce,' he sayde,
> 'Come thiselfe and fyghte a brayde,   *bout*
>   For thi curtasye!
> For I will with none other fyghte:
> Thi hevede I hafe my leman highte,
>   Scho salle me kysse with thi.   *for it*
> And if thou ne will noghte do so,
> Alle this ceté I will overgo:
>   Als dogges than sall thay dy!'
>
> Grete dole it was than, forto see
> The sorowe that was in that ceté,
>   Bothe with olde and yonge.
> For ther was nother kynge ne knyghte,
> That with that geaunt than durste fyghte:
>   He was so foulle a thynge.
> And ay iwhills Arageous with his staffe   *all that time*
> Many a grete bofete he gaffe,   *blow*
>   And the walles down gan he dynge;
> And than gane alle the pepille crye
> Unto God and to mylde Marye,
>   With sorowe and grete wepynge.

The second of them at least, contains detail that is also present in FO: the
unwillingness of the French to fight on after the giant's first victory (FO
2095–6) and his battering of the city wall (FO 2148–9). And some of the
detail of the first stanza is found in C 859–64: in Thornton, these lines read
very differently:

> 'Oure kynges hede hase he highte
> The sowdan dogheter that es so bryghte;
>   For scho solde kysse hym then.

There es no man dare with hym fyghte;
Forthi, my dere sone, hase he tyghte   *so, determined*
      This ceté to breke and brynne.'   *burn down*

873–6   At this point T reads:

'For had thou of hym a syghte,
For all this ceté [ne] wolde thou habyde,
Bot faste awaywarde wold thou ryde:
      He es so fowle a wyghte.'   *creature*

The version of C, in fact, brings forward a motif that is developed in yet
another pair of stanzas omitted here, but retained in T (after 876):

'A, ffadir,' he said, 'takes to none ille,   *don't be angry*
For with the geaunt fighte I wille,
      To luke if I dare byde,   *see, face (him)*
And bot I titter armede be,   *the sooner*
I sall noghte lett, so mote I the,   *prosper*
      That I ne salle to hym ryde.'
Clement saide, 'Sen thou willt fare,   *since*
I hafe armoures, swylke als thay are,   *such*
      I sall tham lene the this tyde;
Bot this seven yere sawe thay no sonne.'
'Fadir,' he sayd, 'alle es wonne!
      Ne gyffe I noghte a chide!'   *curse*

'Bot fadir,' he sayde, 'I yow praye
That we ne make no more delaye,
      Bot tyte that I ware dyghte;   *quickly*
For I wolde noghte for this ceté,
That another man before me
      Undirtuke that fyghte.'
'Nay, nay,' saise Clement, 'I undirtake
That ther will none swylke maystres make,
      Nother kynge ne knyghte!
Bot God, sone, sende the grace wirchip to wyn,
And late me never hafe perelle therin,
      To the dede if thou be dyghte!'

958–60 are omitted in T.

1003–14   The head is not given to the maiden in either FO or SO (Florent
does take it with him when he rides off to her tent in SO 1171, but then
temporarily seems to forget all about it). Instead, it is presented to the king
after he has got back to Paris (FO 2900–16) and is then is set up in a public

place (FO 2981–3, also SO 1189–90). The version of our text may have been suggested by the scene near the beginning of the story, where another head (that of the kitchen boy) is returned to its owner's supposed mistress (172–7).

1096 As the heroine's *confidante*, Olyvan is one of the more 'courtly' elements in the story; she is the counterpart of a whole group of maidens to whom Marsabile reveals her love for the hero in FO 3777–94. She has no real equivalent in SO, since there the messenger sent by the lady to Florent in 1219 is not characterized at all.

1119 In C this line is followed immediately by 1180; the authenticity of the sixty lines omitted is proved by the presence of motifs that are also in FO, notably Clement's manhandling of the minstrels (1147–52; FO 3070–125) and his hiding of the guests' cloaks (1156–75; FO 3163–204). It is not quite clear whether the omission of the passage in C was deliberate or not. The sense certainly flows on smoothly enough from 1119 to 1180, and the redactor could well have imagined that Clement's grossness had already been laboured quite heavily enough, without further examples of it being necessary. But it is hard to believe that the new 'stanza' which results would not have been provided with a convincing sequence of tail-rhymes (in place of the impossible *lorne: lees: was: was*, which now stands), if there had been deliberate reworking here, and on the whole it seems most likely that the C-scribe has here copied faithfully from an exemplar in which two whole columns of text, on the recto and verso of the same leaf, had been torn away. For this reason the extra stanzas of T have this time been incorporated into the principal text (just as the opening of the British Museum text of *Gowther* has been set at the head of our transcript of the Auchinleck copy). See the note to 1645–56 for a similar case of accidental omission in C (in which T, being wholly defective at this point, cannot be used to set things right).

1246 Here T is more cautious in its remuneration of Clement, but the *townys* of C may still have been the original reading: see the note to 96.

1334 C, with its account of a leg being used as a weapon, is distinctly more savage in tone than T (where a bench is used instead).

1480–2 Bucephalus, Alexander's steed, is also represented as horned, in the romance of *Kyng Alisaunder* (B 691–2); in *Octavian* the mention of the unicorn reminds us that such a beast figures as a war-horse at the end of *Isumbras* (754). A further complication is introduced in SO 1419, since the claim there that the horse fights *before hym and behynde* suggests that its horn may be movable like those of the yale of the bestiaries: see T. H. White, *A Book of Beasts*, pp. 54–5.

1503 T gives almost the same reading: *lyke an unfrely fere. Fere* is presumably 'travelling companion', or even 'pilgrim'. In FO, Clement dresses in a pilgrim's cloak at this point (4078); in SO, as a *palmer* (1358).

1591–608 An interesting attempt to explain away the successive defeats of the Christians and of their principal champion. In FO 4604–50, Florent is taken prisoner at the same time as Octavian, to whose defence he has come.

1642–4 These lines bring together, if a little clumsily, the two chief concerns of the younger Octavian: to help the Christians against the heathen, and to reconcile his mother with her husband (see 1704). This last is his *errande*, and he makes it known to the emperor in 1713 ff. In FO this is in fact his dominant motive, since he sets out to justify his mother before he has heard of the war in France (4904–16).

1645–56 Since the tail-rhyme is not carried through in this stanza and there is a gap in the sense after 1650 (in that there is no mention of the journey from Jerusalem to the French battlefield), it appears that some authentic material has been left out here, as it was after 1119. T is wholly defective around this point, but since the two columns of text which it completely lacks could not have contained much more than 84 lines, while the corresponding part of C numbers 77, only two half-stanzas can be lacking at the most. The corresponding part of SO is also quite short and lacking in precise geographical detail (1597–608); that of FO is, as usual, more circumstantial (4914–79).

1722 This line suggests that the younger Octavian is ready to do battle to demonstrate his mother's innocence of the crime of which she was once accused; compare the scene at the end of *Chevelere Assigne* in which a young hero fights with and defeats the calumniator of his mother (314–35).

1732–4 These lines, like the three inserted in T before 133, spoil the balance of the stanza but remove the awkwardness caused by the sudden shift of speaker. T, in the other hand, diminishes this awkwardness by inserting *scho said* in 1735, so that it is the metre, and not the stanza-pattern, which suffers.

1788–91 are represented by ten lines in T:

> His lady by his syde
> And his two sonnes also,
> And with tham many one mo,
>   Home than gan thay ryde.

> And thus endis Octovean,
> That in his tym was a doghety man,
>   With the grace of Mary free.
> Now, Jesu lorde, of heven kynge,
> Thou gyffe us alle thi dere blyssynge:
>   Amen, amen, par charyté.

SIR ISUMBRAS

1–30 This passage corresponds to two stanzas in TEA:

> Hynd in hall, yf ye wyll here   *gracious (lords)*
> Of elders that befor hus were,
>   That gud were at nede:
> Jesu Cryst, heven kyng,
> Grant us all thi blessyng,
>   And heven tyll owr mede.
> I wyll yow tell of a knyght
> That was bothe hardé and wyghth,
>   And duxti in every dede;   *valiant*
> His name was callyd syr Ysumbras,
> For seche a knyghth as he was,
>   Non levys now in lede.   *lives*
>
> He was mycull mon and stronge,
> With schulders brode and armus longe,
>   That semely was to se;
> So was he bothe fayr and fre
> That all hym loved that hym se,
>   So fayr a mon was he.
> He loved wyll gle-men in hall;   *minstrels*
> He gafe hem robys ryche of pall,
>   Bothe golde and fe.
> Of curtesnesse he was kyng,
> Of meytt and drynke no nythyng: *niggard*
>   On lyfe is non so free.   *E*

53 Here E reads *Wordly* (worldly) *welthe thou schalt forgo*; both variants are incorporated into T, which as a result here (as elsewhere) produces a stanza of thirteen lines instead of twelve.

140 For *sholder* E reads *chyldur*: perhaps the scribe thought that the cross could serve later as a token by which the long-lost children might be recognized: compare the deliberate (and elaborate) use of the ring as a token of this kind in L 324 and 679–702.

163–8 correspond to a complete stanza in TEA. This begins:

> Yitt in a wode thay were gone wylle   *astray*
> Towne ne myghte thay none wyn tille,
>   Als wery als thay were.

There follow lines closely resembling L 163–5; for L 166–8 we have:

> Nothynge sawe thay that come of corne
> Bot the floures of the thorne,
>> Upone these holtes hore.
> Thay entirde than to a water kene;   *turbulent*
> The bankes were full ferre bytwene,
>> And watirs breme als bare.   *T*   *fierce, boar*

181–92 are different in TEA. Between L 183 and 184 we find:

> Thus with sorowfull chere and drery mode,
> Agayne over the water he wode: *went*
>> To pyn tornes alle his playe.   *T*

To balance this, there is nothing corresponding to L 187–9.

192 is followed by an extra stanza in TEA:

> The knyghte mase dole and sorowe ynoghe;   *makes*
> Nerehand he hymselven sloghe,   *almost*
>> Are he come to the banke.   *before*
> And the lady grett and gafe hir ill;
> Nowther of tham myghte other still,   *console*
>> Thaire sorowe it was full ranke.   *severe*
> Thay sayd allas that thay were borne:
> 'Felle werdes es layde us byforne,   *a cruel fate*
>> That are were wele and w[l]anke.'   *proud*
> The knyghte bad scho sulde be still
> And gladly suffir Goddes will:
>> 'Us awe hym alle to thanke.'   *T*

193–228 correspond to three complete stanzas in TEA, but the limits of these are differently defined by the tail-rhymes: (a) begins with three extra lines placed before L 193:

> Lytell wonder thofe thei had care,
> For both ther childer lefte thei there,
>> Of the eldyste two,   *A*

and ends at L 201. (b) begins with three lines corresponding to L 202–4:

> As thei stode on the londe
> And lokud into tho stronde,
>> Schyppus se thei ryde,   *E*

and ends at L 213. (c) begins with L 214–15 (in slightly different form); L 216–18 are omitted.

265–82 correspond to two complete stanzas in TEA: (a) includes three extra lines between 270 and 271:

> Now in this foreste hafe we gane;
> Mete ne drynke we myghte gete nane,
>   This es the sevent daye,   *T*

and ends at 273. In (b) L 276 reads *That ware commen owte of heven*, and three extra lines are inserted between 278 and 279:

> 'Yaa more than thou kane neven:
> I sall the gyffe ten thowsand pownde
> Of florence that bene rede and rownde.'   *T*

295–300 are a complete stanza in TEA; the six extra lines are between 297 and 298:

> The lady grete and gafe hir ill;
> Unnethes thay myght halde hir still:
>   That scho [ne] hirselve walde slaa.
> Hir armes scho sprede and lowde gan crye,
> And ofte scho cryed one oure lady:
>   'Sall we departe in two?'   *T*

298–30 then read:

> 'Alasse schall I never blythe be:
> My weddyd lord schal parte fro me:
>   Now begynnys all my woo!'   *E*

325–36 are not found in TEA.

365   In other tail-rhyme romances that tell of the separation of a family a griffin figures more prominently than an eagle, but as the agent which carries off one of the hero's children, and not his money: *Eglamour* 841–3, *Torrent of Portyngale* 1870–2 and—less directly—*Octavian* 349–60. The Ashmole variant is still less likely: see the note to *Gowther* 82 for the part which angels might play in these romances.

385–408   Trounce notes the special interest of this passage, with its allusions to the craft of medieval ironsmiths (*Medium Ævum* 3 (1934), 37):

> The furnaces were kept constantly alight ('fyres thore bryne and glewe'); the work was always reckoned as severe ('thay bade hym swynk')—this detail being also dramatic since Isumbras' experiences are in the nature of trials; the iron-ore was extracted in Northampton-shire from long open workings extending to some sixteen feet in depth ('garte hym bere irynstone, Owte of a sory'—or 'depe' ... 'sloghe'). Having served his apprenticeship at the rough work (for a 'twelfmonth'), he is promoted 'smethyman', and then earned 'mannes ... hire'; he helps with the bellows ('And blewe thair belyes bloo'), and takes a hand at actual ironworking ('he had hymselfene dyghte All the atyre that felle to a knyghte').

409–56 E gives a very individual (and decidedly longer) account of these four stanzas, that emphasizes still further the heroic nature of Isumbras. He does not now suffer any hurt until the very end of the passage and needs no help from anyone else (since his horse is not here killed as in L 438); more positively, he is made to inspire the utmost terror in his opponents:

> Tho men that see hym with ene,
> Thei wende tho dele of hel he had bene: *devil*
> So wer thei of hym bayst. *E*   *dumbfounded*

In addition, his private feud with the sultan is emphasized much more, through additional short passages of prayer (after L 432) and direct insult (after L 438). See the note to 601–6 for a second patch of 'heroic' amplification in E.

529–94 correspond to six complete stanzas in TEA: (a) begins with three lines not in L:

> 'And weleecome,' he sais, 'syr Ysambrace:
> Forgeffen es the alle thi tryspase,
> Forsothe als I the sayne;' *T*

the stanza ends with a variant of L 537 (*Bot aye to walke in payne* (*T*)). (b) ends with three lines corresponding to L 547–9:

> 'Wyll wer me,' seyd tho knyght,
> 'Myght I gete that florayn bryght:
> Or ellus sum lyveys fo[de]. *E*

(c) has as its first tail-line *Full many fand scho there* (*T* = L 552), and ends at L 561: *Of hym thei rewyd sore* (*A*). (d) ends at L 573: *And terys lete he falle* (*T*). (e) has for L 576: *And till a knyghte gan saye* (*T*), and ends at L 585. (f) has for L 588: *The lengur that sche sette* (*E*), and ends with an extra three lines after L 594:

> He thankyd mych the lady fre
> And in hur cort there dwellyd he
> Tyl he had covert ys astate. *E*

559–94 One of the most powerful stock scenes in the tail-rhyme romances is that of the reunion of a husband and wife, or of two friends, where one of them is prosperous and the other reduced to beggary, and so altered by suffering that there is no immediate mutual recognition. Here, as in stanzas 280–1 of the tail-rhyme *Guy of Warwick*, it is a husband who is the suppliant; in lines 1861–2100 of *Amis and Amiloun*, it is one of two sworn brothers who (more deviously and at much greater length) fills this role.

601–6 are quite different in TEA:

> When knyghtis went to pute the ston,   *throw*
> Twelve fo[t]e befor them everychon
> He putte it as a balle;

> Therfor envye at hym thei hade;
> They justyd at hym with strokis sadde,   *weighty*
> And he overcom them alle. *A*

In E, 604–6 are elaborated as a lively passage of invective and lead to a rather more lengthy description of fighting with the Saracens (see the note to 409–56). T combines both of the main versions of these lines to produce a stanza of sixteen lines.

607–42 are differently split up by the tail-rhymes in TEA. (a) has three extra lines after L 612:

> And some he keste into a slake   *ravine*
> That bothe braste neke and bakke,
> And many flede for drede; *T*

the stanza ends at L 615, where the rhyme-word is here *fede*. (b) ends at L 627. (c) reads *Wepand he went away* (*E*) at L 630, and follows this with three extra lines:

> And ei when he tho gold se
> He wept for his chyldur thre,
> To pyne turnyd all is pley; *E*

L 634–6 and 640–2 are not represented.

625–42 In the legend of Pope Gregory, the hero also keeps hidden in his room a vital memento of his past life, and is so cast down whenever he looks at is that the suspicions of others are aroused, and his secret is discovered. Here, however, the object is a written account of his incestuous birth, that was left with him when he was abandoned as a baby. (Hartmann von Ave, *Gregorius*, 2277–487).

655–717 contain the most remarkable passage of amplification in the whole of L, being represented by only three stanzas in TEA: (a) begins with three lines corresponding to L 655–60:

> Than scho to the knyghtes tolde
> How scho was for that golde solde,
> And hir lorde was wondide sore, *T*

and ends with a variant of L 669: *His mowrnyng was tho more* (*E*). (b) begins with L 670–5, continues with a variant of L 676–8:

> And how his chylder fro hym was born,
> And how his gold fro hym was lorne,
> And how that he was threte, *A*

and ends with one of L 703–5:

> Than sche kyssyd his face,
> And sey[d], 'Welcom sir Isombrace,'
> For joy [that thei wer mett *E*]. *A*

(c) begins with L 706 and ends at L 717 (*Over tho barons bolde* (*E*)). It will be noted that the whole of the later history of the ring is thus peculiar to L (679–705).

717 is followed in TEA by an additional stanza:

> Ther was made a ryche feste
> Of grett men and honeste,
>> Forsothe full gret plenté.
> When he was kyng and bare the crone
> He send his sonde fro twone to twone
>> Overall in that cuntr[e].
> And cummanddud that yche baron bolde,
> Ryche and pore, yong and olde,
>> That thei Cryston schull [be];
> And all that wold not soo,
> He badde that men schuld them sloo;
> That nothyng for them schuld goo:
>> Nodur golde nor fee.   *E*

The additional (eleventh) line is also in T but omitted in A; both T and A lack the first three lines.

718–26 correspond to a complete stanza in TEA; 724–5 are represented by six lines in T:

> Bot thay turnede alle till ane assent,
> That schortly thereto thay ne wolde cons[e]nt,
>> Bot to a batelle ffare.
> Thay sayde and thay myghte hym hent   *capture*
> That he solde come to thaire parlement,
> And there be bothe hangede and brynt.

A is still more diffuse (eight lines) in this passage; E, obviously corrupt in a number of its readings.

727–32 correspond to another complete stanza in TEA:

> Dey of batell ther was sette;
> Many hethen ther wer mette
>> Syr Isombras to sloo.
> Many Sarysins gedered that tyde;
> They came theder ferr and wyde,
>> With hethen knyghtis twoo.
> Syr Isombras was full off care,
> He had no man with hym to fare:
>> All his myrthe was goo.

> The Saryzyns falyd hym at nede
> When he was horsyd on a stede,
>   All thei flede hym froo. *A*

745–50 The overwhelming odds suggest that, armour or no armour, the husband and wife will be martyred for their faith; in the related legend of St. Eustace this actually happens.

751–6 In keeping back until now all mention of the children and the animals that had carried them off, *Isumbras* contrasts sharply with *Eglamour*, *Torrent* and *Octavian*. The massacre of the heathen which follows is surely meant as miraculous; compare the scene in the French *Othevien* when a great host led by St. George suddenly appears to slaughter more than thirty thousand of the heathen (FO 4703–33).

774 is followed by an extra six lines in TEA:

> Sir Ysambrace and that lady free
> Kyssed alle thaire childir three;
>   Ilkane for joye thay grett.
> Mare joye myghte never no mane see
> Than men myghte one tham see,
>   In armes when thay were mett. *T*

775–83 A complete stanza in TEA, with three extra lines after 780:

> Riche metis wantted tham nane,
> Nowther of wylde nor of tame,
>   Nor no riche brede. *T*

784–98 A complete stanza in TEA, with three extra lines before 784:

> A ryche mon was syr Ysumbrase,
> Rychur then he ever before was,
>   And covert all his care; *E*

785–6 read:

> Durste na man agayne tham stande,
> Whareso that thay solde fare; *T*

787–9 and *793–5* are not represented.

SIR GOWTHER

10 The begetting of Merlin on a mortal woman by a devil is described at length in *Arthour and Merlin* (A 793–868).

41 is followed by B by three extra lines:

> Here shaftes gan thei shake.
> On the morow the lordes gente
> Made a riall tournement.

55–7 sound less ruthless in B:

> But ye myght a childe bere
> That myght my londes weld and were:
> She wept and myght not blynne.

61–3 The wife's prayer is certainly reckless: compare the more thoughtful reaction of her counterpart in *Octavian* 76–8. In *Arthour and Merlin* the young girl is defenceless against the devil because she omits to hallow the entrances to her room, as a hermit had told her to do (A 813–16, 839–42).

82 This strange perversion of the truth is also found in B; it has, however, a certain aptness in a story of this type, since angels figure quite often in other edifying romances to herald the will of God (see, for example, *Isumbras* 523–31). And, for all his early wickedness, it is to this will that Gowther must at last conform.

136–41 are omitted in B.

139 This *fachon* (a sword with a curved blade) is mentioned quite often in *Gowther* (in 163, 220, 256, 286, 487, 598 and 613). The effect of such strenuous repetition is to make it seem the outward and visible symbol of both his unbridled violence in his unregenerate days, and his militancy in his later career. His refusal to give it up at the Pope's bidding in 289–91 underlines its significance as symbol and talisman: it is an essential part of him, and must go with him on his new quest for forgiveness: compare the importance of the harp to the hero of *Sir Orfeo* (34 ff., 229, 265 ff., 342, 434 ff., 498, 524 ff.).

172–4 are quite different in B:

> And tho that wold not werk his will,
> Erly and late, lowde and still,
> Ful sore he wold hem bete.

184–6 are even more so here:

> Thei kneled down oppon here knee,
> And said, 'Leige lord, welcome be yee!'
> (Yn hert is nowght to hide).

202 An old man who stands up for truth and justice when nobody else will is a character found in some other tail-rhyme romances: see, for example, the *Erl of Tolous* (C 883–900), where he defends the honour of a lady who, like Octavian's wife, has been falsely accused of adultery with the naked boy found in her bed.

220–5 are more readily comprehensible in B:

> He set the poynt to here brest,
> And said, 'Dame, thow getest non other prest,
>> The sothe if thow hide!'
> She said, 'Sone, the duke that deyde last,
> That is owt of this world past,
>> He weddid me with pride.'

232 Repentance for past villainy is usually sudden in the tail-rhyme romances: compare the emperor's change of heart in *Emaré* 280–2.

238–43 are omitted in B.

292–3 are less glaringly hypermetric in B:

> 'Thow shalt walk north and sowthe,
> And gete thi mete owt of houndis mouth.'

333–6 The sense is not allowed to run on in B:

> And thret him to bete.
> 'What is that?' said the emperour.
> The steward said, with grete honowre,
>> 'My lord, it is a man.'

352–7 are very different in B:

> The domme man to him he raught,   *reached out*
> And that bone to him he cawght;
>> Thereon fast he tare;   *tore*
> For other sustinaunce he had nowght
> But such as he fro houndes cawght;
>> The more was his care.

The new tail-rhymes here and the fact that *lart* replaces *bare* in 351 means that the original stanza now falls into two halves; in A, on the other hand, it splits into one part of three lines (tail-rhyme *bare*) and one of nine (tail-rhymes *parte: tartte: mard*). Perhaps the original sequence of tail-rhymes had been **share: bare: tare: care*, with the first word replaced by *parte* in the common source of A and B, and the other three variously treated in our two texts.

375 is in B followed by six extra lines:

> To him she was a ful good frend,
> And mete to houndes for his love wold send,
>> Ful ofte and grete plenté.
> Ether of hem loved other right,
> But to other no word thei speke ne myght:
>> That was the more peté.

These introduce a sentimental note that, although in one sense a natural development from the relationship of the two characters, still jars at this point; in addition, this insertion turns B's equivalent of 376–81 into a self-contained stanza of six lines:

> Than in on morow come a masynger
> To the emperour with sterne chere,
>   And said to him ful right:
> 'Syr, my lord wel greteth the,
> That is Sowdan of Percé,
>   Man most of myght.'

409 ff. We have here a version of the popular romance motif of the Three Days' Tournament, in which the hero fights incognito on three successive days in different suits of armour. The colours of these last are arranged in directly contrary sequence in *Ipomedon* (i.e. move from white to red to black), presumably because the vital point there is the increasing power and ferocity of the young hero in battle. In *Gowther*, on the other hand, the crucial issue is the expiation of sin, and for this white is an obvious terminal symbol. The same sequence of colours is found in *Richard Cœur de Lion*, where they apply to the suits of armour worn by the hero in the Salisbury tournament, and here their symbolic force is reinforced by the details given of the crests and other insignia of the king on the consecutive days. With the black armour go a raven and a bell (symbols of voyaging and of Holy Church); with the red, a hound (standing for the coming destruction of the heathen); with the white, a dove and a red cross (for the Holy Spirit and the Crusade): *Richard* 267–82, 331–42, 386–96.

418–20 read in B:

> The sowdan that was so sterne and stowte
> Ful fast in the fild he prikyd abowte;
>   To sembill his men he cast.

442–5 This considerate action seems a reward for Gowther's exploits in the day's fighting, and, by softening the harshness of his penance, marks the beginning of forgiveness.

459 is followed by three extra (but obviously corrupt) lines in B:

> 'On the he wil avenied be.'
> 'Hors and armour,' than said he,
>   'Hastly had we thenne.'

493–8 are omitted in B.

502–4 read better in B:

> The emperour wyssh and went to mete,
> And with him other lordes grete
>   That at the bataile were.

511–22 are omitted in B.

526–31   A realistic touch, elaborated at much greater length in the romance of *Robert le Diable*, where the wounds are so severe that the hero cannot play his usual part of court fool, on returning from the first day's fighting; the emperor believes that he has been badly knocked about by his men, while he had been away at the war (2049 ff.).

559–70   As Breul pointed out, the tail-rhymes of this stanza seem more than usually corrupt in A, and are not much better in the very different account given by B. But the B-reading of 566 is interesting, since the *bard* which it has in place of A's *lord*, nonsensical in itself, could be a miscopying of original *ward (*b* and *w* are certainly confused in the B-scribe's rendering of *hob as *how* at 508). If we accept the emendation to *ward*, then Gowther, like the emperor, would be represented as the commander of one of the main divisions of the Christian army: compare the division of the French army in *Melayne* into *vawarde* (267), *medillwarde* (274, 283) and *rerewarde* (346, 351).

608–19 are omitted in B, and 607 and 620 are rephrased to form the first couplet of a stanza:

> Thus did sir Gowghter, the gentil knyght,
> But the emperour that was so sterne in fight . . .

655–60   This astonishing, 'out-of-character' speech of the heroine's is thoroughly typical of the style of this romance. In *Isumbras*, where the same kind of information is given by an angel (523–31), the reunion of the hero and heroine can be presented in much warmer and more human terms (667–711).

721–3 and *727–32* are omitted in B.

733–6 read as follows in B:

> He make[th] blynd men forto se,
> Wode men to have here wit, pardé,
>   Crokyd here crucches forsake.

737–44 are omitted in B.

748–50 are more elaborate in B:

> Now God that is of mythes most,
> Fader and Sone and Holy Gost,
>   Of owre sowles be fayne.
>
> All that hath herd this talkyng,
> Lytill, moche, old and yyng,
>   Y-blyssyd mote they be;
> God yeve hem grace whan they shal ende,
> To hevyn blys here sowles wend,
>   With angelys bryght of ble.

SIR AMADACE

1 The loss of almost exactly the same number of lines at the beginning of the Auchinleck text suggests that both descend from a common original that was already defective. This view is borne out by a number of common readings that are defective in rhyme (as at 183, where A, too, has *styd* instead of the *stede that is required) or metre (as at 247, where A's '*Yee*,' *seyd tho marchand*, '*God gyff hym yll grace*' is, like the reading of I, hypermetric).

71 The replacement in A of *stinke* by *saver*, here and at 91 and 125, may imply a more 'polite' approach on the part of the redactor of that text: see also the note to 769–71.

85–7 and *93–5* are omitted in A.

97–8 are distinctly less awkward in A:

> Then commandyt syr Amadas
> Hys sqwyar to loke what ther was.

108 The meaning here is, presumably, that although—as the next stanza proves—the squire is able to give more information about the widow than the boy could, he could not bear to wait long enough to hear all the facts of the case. It is curious that A should here read *Ye mey wytte for me*, since it omits the whole of 109–20, in which the squire makes his report to the hero.

113 *kyng* is followed by the beginning of the abbreviation for *-es/-is*; if this had been completed, the rhyme would have been improved, but at the cost of shifting the genitive flexion to the wrong word.

160–2 The reading of A is more individual:

> Ther myght no mon is bred sowe,
> Nor no drapur is clothe drawe:
> His meyt was redy to ylka a wyghth.

The general drift of this is plain (Amadace, like Timon, was accustomed to feast men of all professions), but the phrase *bred sowe* is unusual.

168 The sequence of tail-rhymes is broken in the same way in A (*What gud that we ther aght*), further proof of a defective common source. At 279 I again spoils the rhyme-sequence with *aghte*, but A has the correct *hyght* this time.

199 Here A is much more succinct: '*Dame, what is tho marchandus name?*'

205–40 While making very much the same statements as in I, these three stanzas read very differently in A:

> Syr Amadas toke his palfrey than;
> He was a full sory man,
> His deydus he hym forthoght:

'This mon [and] Y myght wele be sybbe,   *(closely) related*
That here apon tho bere thus lygkus,   *lies*
   For as sche says thus have Y wroghtt.'   *done*
He cald apon his sompter mon;
'At tho marchandus hows owre yn thou takon;
   On hym is all my thoghtt.
Loke thou dyght owre soper be tyme   *get ready*
Of delycyus meytus gud and fyne,
   And that thou spare ryght noght.'

Tho mon dyd as tho lord hym bad;
A reydé wey to tho town he had,
   He spyrd to tho marchandis yn.   *asked the way*
And when he to his yn come,
His lordis soper he dyght full sone,
   Of gud meytus and fyne.
Be that tho soper was dyght,
Syr Amadas was com and don lyght,
   And hit was soper tyme,
He commandyd a sqwyar to goo
To byd tho marchande and is wyfe also
   That nyght to sope with hym.

Tho sqwyar dyd as tho lord command;
Tho marchande in his halle he fand,
   And prayd hym as he con.   *was best able to do*
Tho marchand seyd full redy sone,
'Thi lordus wylle schall be downe;
   Y wyll com to that mon.'
Tho bord was seyt, tho clothe was layd,
Tho soper was all redy greythyd: *prepared*
   Tho marchandis wyfe began.
Syr Amadas made bot lytyll chere;
Bot on tho deyd cors on tho bere,
   Full mykull his thoght was than.

301-12 This stanza is omitted in A, and two subsequent lines are altered to agree with the resulting change of the speaker from the merchant to Amadace: *Hyt is in tho deyd name that Y speyke* (313) and *All thei dyd as syr Amadas bad* (316).

372 is followed in A by an additional stanza:

Syr Amadas seyd in that stonde,   *time*
'Tho warst hors is worthe ten pownde,   *least valuable*
   Of hom all that here gon;

Sqwyar, yomon and knave,
Ylke mon his owne schall have
   That he syttus apon:
Sadyll, brydyll and odur geyre,
Fowre so gud thoffe hit were,   *four times, even if*
   Y woch hit save, be sen Jon.   *grant*
God mey make yo full gud men,
Cryst of hevon Y yo beken:'   *commend to*
   Thei wepud and partyd ylke on.

385–420 In A the third of these three stanzas is reduced to six lines and is placed before the second; there are also many differences of detail:

'Now am [Y] he that noght hase
As of a mon that sumtyme was   *once*
   Full mykyll seyt by;   *esteemed*
Ther Y had an hondorthe marke of rent
Y spentte hit all in lyghtte atent: *frivolously*
   Of suche forlok was Y;
Ay whylyst Y howsewold helde,
For a greytte lorde was Y tyld
   And mykull Y was seytte by.
Now mey whyse men dwell at home
And folus be full whyse of won:
   God wotte, so am Y.

Alas, for wantyng of wytte,
As a foule Y am forflytte: *cast out*
   Of my frendys have made my fous;
And all for my gud wyll,
Y am in poynt forto spyll:'
   Thus chydus syr Amadas.

Now God, that dyed on rode,
And boght me with his precyos blode
   (Me and all myne),
[So] lette me never com in ther syght   *of them*
That hase me kent a gentyll knyght: *known as*
   That thei me never kenne.
And gyffe me grace noght to come tho,
At my londis that ar wonde me fro,   *passed away*
   Bot Y myght helpe my men;
Or els, Jesu, Y aske the reyd,
Astely that Y wer deyd: *soon*
   Therto God helpe me then.

It will be noted that the layout here is not only more economical, but also slightly more logical, than that of I, and that the redactor avoids the clumsy repetition of 397 at 415. This type of phrase, indeed, is a distinct favourite in I: it also occurs in this text (but not in A) at 445, 730 and 736.

429   As suggested in the gloss, *conciens* may here stand for some form of *conissaunce* ('emblem', 'device'); it may owe its unusual spelling to the blending of this notion in the scribe's mind with that of 'was aware of a knight'. There is no such ambiguity in A where we have simply: *He was areyd lyke a knyght*.

436–8   A clumsy passage that is not found in A: perhaps the common source was here, as in this text, of nine lines only, and the three extra lines in I a late attempt to patch things up.

463–5   would make better sense if they followed 466–8; the same unsatisfactory arrangement is also present in A, and presumably derives from their common original.

472–4   are in A, more sensibly, placed after 475–8.

487–9   make better sense in A:

> Sython schall Y cum to the   *later*
> In what place so-ever thou be,
>   Among thi frenchyppus in that steyd.   *friends*

494   That the White Knight is an agent of God's providence is suggested even more strongly at this point in A: *Yf ye be comun thro Goddus grace*.

523–8   make clearer sense in A:

> This betyd besyde a towre;
> Aftur befell hym greyt honour,   *came to*
>   Besyde that feyr ceté.
> The kyng hymselfe saw hym with syght,
> And his doghttur feyr and bryght,
>   The turnament that for schuld bee.

542   A has simply: *And toke the knyght be the hond*; a *quite honde* (which is also ascribed to the hero in I 614) is in any case more usually a feminine than a masculine attribute in the romances.

553–64   are omitted in A, which makes the king's subsequent familiarity with the hero's circumstances in 583–5 rather unexpected.

601–12   read very differently in A:

> To tho kyngus palys then con thei fare;
> Thedur thei went and wold not spare,   *delay*
>   Allso fast as thei myght dryfe.   *go*

Tho kyng made hym full nobull chere,
And seyd, 'Welcum, my frynde so dere:'
　　To tho chambur yede thei swyght.   *at once*
Hee sent aftur his doghtur gent;   *noble*
In hast thei wesche and to meyt went:
　　Ylke mon glad and blythe.
Then mey ye wytte, withowtyn wene,   *doubt*
When eydur of them had odur sene,
　　Ther luffe began to kyghthe.   *show itself*

624 is followed by an extra stanza in A:

'Gramarcy,' seyd syr Amadas,
And thonkyd tho kyng of that grace,   *favour*
　　Of his gyfftus gudde.
Sone aftur, as Y yow sey,
To tho kyrke yode thei,   *church*
　　To wedde that frely fode.   *noble creature*
Ther was gold gyffon in that stonde
And plenty of sylver, mony a ponde,
　　Be the way as thei yode;
And aftur in hall thei satte all,
Tho lordus and tho ladis small
　　That comon wer of gentyll [blode].   [ ] *for* kyn

The omission of these lines has been made less obvious in I by the fact that
the wedding ceremony is mentioned in the stanza which follows (in 628–9).
The corresponding lines in A refer only to the actual festivities:

Tho revell last a full synyght,
With meyttis and drynkus wyll dyght.

625–6 These lines misleadingly suggest that the happy ending has now
been reached; in fact, the most painful tribulation of all is still to come.
Compare *Isumbras* 718–20, which, while sounding equally decisive, are also
followed by fresh dangers for the hero and heroine.

718–20 A has an interesting variant here:

'Syr,' he seyd, 'be sent Albon,
Odur gud wyll Y non,
　　Bot tho chylde then parte thou bode.'

The third line is puzzling as it stands, but could be a corruption of earlier
*Bot the parte (*that*) *thou bode* ('promised'); such a reading would be pre-
ferable to its counterpart in I, which simply repeats 711.

769–71 These, the most sadistic of the lines ascribed to the White Knight
in I (they are even worse than 754–6) are avoided in A, which reads:

> All that wer abowte hyr ryght
> Wer full sory of that syght,
>   And fast to hur con pres.   *push forward*

808–10 An odd shift of tone that in its much less sophisticated way recalls the realistic footnote which Chaucer's Clerk adds to his story of the ideally subservient Griselda (*Canterbury Tales*, E 1163–9).

817–40 are omitted in A; the redactor of that text may have considered them expendable because the story had reached its natural ending in the preceding stanza (which does, after all, take the hero and heroine to the end of their lives, and ends with a pious generalization).

DATE DUE